TAKE YOUR RV TO EUROPE

The Low-Cost Route to Long-Term Touring

Adelle and Ron Milavsky

Take Your RV to Europe
The Low-Cost Route to Long-Term Touring
By Adelle and Ron Milavsky

Published by:
The Intrepid Traveler
P.O. Box 531
Branford, CT 06405
http://www.IntrepidTraveler.com

Copyright ©2005 by Adelle Milavsky and J. Ronald Milavsky
First Edition
Cover design by Foster & Foster
Interior design by Celine Allen
Interior photos by Adelle and Ronald Milavsky
Maps by Evora Taylor

ISBN: 1-887140-54-9

LCCN: 2004113895

9 8 7 6 5 4 3 2 1

Printed in the United States of America

DEDICATION

Our thanks to all those people who answered our many questions, especially Mike Donald and Myra Sims.

And we need to say thank you to the other Americans we met in campgrounds in Europe. The fact that we met Bob, and then Jack and April, who also loved this way of traveling gave us the confidence to think that more people would be interested in knowing about it.

In addition, we'd like to dedicate this book to:

Our family and friends whose enthusiasm for the letters we wrote while on our RV trips led us to thinking we could and should write this book;

Our friends Cees and Maartje in the Netherlands who helped us when we first landed on their shores as well as all those friends in Great Britain who made our stay so memorable;

Our publishers, Sally and Kelly, whose questions helped us focus and whose knowledge and experience so improved everything we wrote.

Contents

Appendices

Western Europe

INTRODUCTION

Our first RV trip, in May 2001, was an 11,000-mile trek across the United States in both directions. In 72 days, we went from Florida across the southern U.S. to the Four Corners area, where Utah, New Mexico, Colorado, and Arizona meet and some of the most beautiful scenery in the West can be found. Then we visited Las Vegas and San Diego, continuing up the California, Oregon, and Washington coast to Vancouver. Finally, we drove west to east across the northern U.S., heading for our home in northeastern Connecticut. Traveling in our other comfortable home—on wheels—allowed us easily to visit places we had heard of all our lives, but had not yet actually seen. It was a great experience and made us want to take another long trip via RV.

Where should we go next? Our first impulse was to make another U.S. trip, going to places we had skipped the first time around. But way in the back of our minds another idea was beginning to form. There were so many places in Europe we had heard about but never visited. Would it be feasible to make the same kind of trip, but travel around Europe rather than America?

We had been to Europe before, but always on "vacation trips"— two or three weeks at a time. Wouldn't it be great to be able to meander around Europe over a longer period? We didn't happen to know anyone who had ever done that. There were a lot of questions. Could we afford such a trip? Should we rent a rig in Europe, or should we take our RV there? How would we get it to Europe if we wanted to do that? Are there good camping facilities in Europe? At first it seemed way beyond what is possible. But the more we thought about it, the more the idea of combining the ease, comfort, and freedom of an RV trip with a European tour sounded attractive.

We began to look into the feasibility of taking such a trip. The more information we gathered, the more it seemed not only a possibility, but also the least expensive way to spend a long time overseas.

We told people that we were thinking about shipping our 21.5-foot motor home to Europe in the spring of 2002 in order to travel around for an extended period of time. Everyone looked at us as if we were crazy. Then they were likely to ask the same questions we had asked ourselves. Why didn't we just rent a rig there? Or buy one in Europe and resell it at the end of the trip? Of course, those were and are valid questions. We decided to look into all the alternatives before we even started to discuss shipping our own rig.

On the Internet, we found a list of firms that rent RVs in Europe. (See Appendix G at the end of this book.) One was a major auto rental company that also rents RVs in Europe. Since they had an 800 number, we phoned them. When we called in November 2001, we found that the company already had reservations for every unit that they could rent for the entire upcoming summer season. But we still needed the information, so we asked the agent the obvious question: "Can you just give us a ballpark price so we can see if this way of traveling will fit our budget?" No, he could not. In fact, he could not even tell us how much a week's rental would be!

Fortunately, a Canadian firm—Owasco Camper Rentals—was one of the companies listed. We called them. Their agent was able to give us a price for renting an RV in Europe. The $800 to $900 a week was a lot more money than seemed sensible to us, given our plans for such a long trip. We were thinking that we would spend at least three months touring Europe, so we used the figures supplied by the Canadian firm as the "going rate" for purposes of comparison.

Then we started looking into shipping our own rig. We weren't sure how to go about this, but we did understand that we had to start with a freight forwarder. (A freight forwarder is like a travel agent for freight.) Since we don't live in a port city, the local telephone directory had few forwarders listed, and none were much help. So it was off to the library to look up the New York Yellow Pages and get some telephone numbers for the firms listed. (We have since checked the Internet. There are a great many firms listed there now.) After many calls, we came up with three firms that had experience in shipping RVs to Europe and were willing to handle a one-time job for an individual. They answered our questions, and the prices they quoted seemed reasonable, especially compared to renting an RV in Europe.

Then we began to look at the things you really need to know in advance of making such a commitment of time and money.

We worked out the estimated costs and discovered that it would be far less expensive to ship our own unit than it would be to rent one for three months! Furthermore, once the rig was in Europe, we thought that we might have the option of storing it there over the next year and making another trip the following year, cutting our costs even more. And that's exactly what we did. Our first trip in 2002 was to continental Europe. We stored the RV over the next year near Amsterdam, and then took it via ferry to England in 2003 for our second trip.

In late March 2002, we began our nearly three months in Holland, Belgium, and France, with a very short trip up the Rhine Valley in Germany. Our original intention had been much more ambitious, but we decided for several reasons to keep to this part of northern Europe for our first trip. There was a distance factor, of course. Although both Spain and Italy would have been very interesting, they would have required a lot more driving. We had been to both Spain and Italy on other, more traditional trips, and had loved them both, but for this first RV trip, we decided that we would not go farther than southern France.

We visited the cultural, artistic, and historic attractions of Europe both on the Continent and, on our second trip, in the United Kingdom (UK). During our combined six months on European roads we enjoyed spectacular scenery while driving through beautiful farmland and along famous shorelines. We drove through mountains, moors, and dales, visited lakes, and saw seacoasts from the Cote d'Azur in France to those in Scotland, Wales, and England.

On both trips, we saw wonderful sights. We enjoyed quiet, secluded campsites with views of streams, lakes, and mountains. We camped in city parks and at the edge of the ocean. In fact, driving through both continental Europe and the United Kingdom is often nicer than driving through the United States. For one thing, the distances between stops are usually shorter, because Europe is considerably smaller than the United States. For another, the roadsides do not usually have billboards cluttering up the vistas. As a result, there are unobstructed views. The sight of agricultural fields filled with livestock, cultivated areas of rapeseed (which is a beautiful yellow), vineyards, olive groves, and fields of flowers in a great assortment of wildly vivid colors added to the natural beauty of rolling hills, mountains, rivers, and streams. Often there were distant vistas of the ocean.

Further, the fact that these countries are relatively compact means that the traveler is treated to an ever-changing countryside.

Even the architecture can change within the course of a very short drive. One never has to drive through vast territories like Iowa and Texas where the scenery seems to stay the same for days.

On our first trip through the western U.S., we often stopped to take photographs of the vistas, and the same was true on our trips to Europe. There is a great deal of natural beauty to be seen, and anyone wishing to concentrate on the splendors of nature will find camping in Europe just as rewarding as camping in the midst of America's natural wonders.

When we traveled across our own continent, our main goal had been to visit America's fabled natural wonders. Most of our destinations were beautiful national parks, monuments, and other scenic areas. We did visit some cities—including San Diego, San Francisco, Portland, and Seattle—but spending time in cities was not a priority for us on that trip.

In Europe, our intentions were quite the opposite. We wanted to focus on Europe's cities and on its historic and cultural sites. Our plan was to use our RV as our home as well as our transportation, and to park it in or near the big cities so that we could explore as many of them as we could. And this is in fact what we did. In perfect comfort and for very little money, we visited the cultural and artistic attractions of Europe, both on the Continent and in the United Kingdom. We were able to see many places where history had been made. There is no way we could have traveled so extensively without the convenience of the RV.

On drives between cities, we stopped to view the beautiful scenery and often spent the night in campgrounds in scenic areas rather than cities. We chose to use local roads as often as we could so that we could get an idea of what these countries really looked like. Overall, we struck a nice balance between country and city camping.

We saw beautiful cities that were of great historical interest, and others that were mostly big, modern, and industrial. There were cities that, though in the same country, had an entirely different architecture, history, and sometimes even language from each other.

Because we used the camper as both hotel and car, we could afford to stay for a long time, so our trips from city to city allowed us to see more of Europe than most tourists normally have time for. Visiting cities when traveling by RV is easier in Europe than it is in the United States. There are campgrounds within the city limits or at the outskirts of even the largest cities. Moreover, there is always good and affordable public transit to take you anywhere you want to go within the city. This applies even to the biggest and most desirable cities—those that most tourists want to see. There is a campground in London (on the grounds of the Crystal Palace), there is one in Paris (in the Bois de Boulogne), and in Amsterdam there are five! These particular cities are the stars of tourism, and they are easily accessible to the RVer. Can you imagine staying in Paris for the equivalent of $25.00 per night for two people? You can stay as long as you like. We stayed in two separate campgrounds in Amsterdam over a period of several weeks. The daily charge was under $20.00.

In all the time we spent in these countries, we never felt any twinge of unease. We were very comfortable and very well treated. Our fellow campers were from all over Europe, including the British Isles, and many spoke English. We even met some Americans doing exactly what we were doing. In fact, we met an American who has stored his RV in Europe for the past six years. He returns twice a year to travel for six weeks at a time.

On the Continent, the people in the campgrounds, the markets, and the tourist attractions always knew enough English to answer questions. Everyone was always quite welcoming and the entire experience was exhilarating and memorable.

It is worth noting that the language barrier was much less important than we had anticipated. Almost everyone in Holland and a large number of people in Belgium knew enough English to talk to us. We even found people who spoke English in places where there is very little tourism, such as the small city of Freiberg in Germany, where we wandered through an indoor flea market. While it is true that the French do not always speak English, we found that people in the tourist areas and the open-air markets spoke enough languages other than their own to conduct their business. One reason why so many can handle English is that a great many Britons vacation on the Continent. English is also recognized as the international language of business and is taught in most schools. We always walked around with a pad so that people could write down the prices for us—and we never had to use it. As soon as vendors heard us speak English, they quoted the price in our language, not theirs. But if we had needed the pad, it was available.

When—during our nearly six months on the road—we met other American RVers, we exchanged information and each of us learned a bit from the other. Along the way we learned many things that can make planning such a trip much easier—from information on shipping to finding a covered storage place to leave the RV until the next trip. We returned home full of information gleaned the hard way—through experience.

This book has been written for people who own a motor home.

There are about eight million RVs of all types in the United States. That's a lot of people who are accustomed to the idea of camping. We think that many of you will be intrigued by the idea of traveling in your own motor home through Europe. And many of you will have the two or more months available to travel this way. We are sure that you will agree with us that driving an RV is not only the least expensive way to see a foreign country but also has its own advantages. Those who are still tied to a two-week schedule may want to read some of the details and then consider renting an RV in Europe.

Our intention in writing this book is to provide you with everything you need to know to decide whether such a trip is right for you and, if so, whether you are going to ship your own RV and stay a long time or just rent one for a short vacation. And, if you decide to take such a trip, we believe that we can help you be so well prepared that you will enjoy every minute of it.

We have tried to put together all the information that you will need. Here is how the book is organized:

Chapter 1: "New Uses for Your Old RV"
provides a general overview of what traveling through Europe in an RV is like.

Chapter 2: "Strangers RVing in a Strange Land"
uses the experiences we had on our trips to give you an idea of what you can expect if you decide to travel this way.

Chapter 3: "Figuring Out the Costs"
gives you tools for estimating and comparing three kinds of RV travel: renting an RV in Europe, buying an RV in Europe, or shipping your own.

Chapter 4: "Preparing the RV for Europe"
discusses the steps you'll need to take to prepare your RV for shipping to Europe and using it there.

Chapter 5: "Getting Ready for the Trip"
deals with the preparations you'd need to make for any trip—things like money, insurance, required paperwork—and preparations required for this particular type of trip—things like getting an International Camping Card, an International Driver's Permit, and guidebooks for European campgrounds.

Chapter 6: "The Shipping Process"
tells you all you need to know to actually ship your RV to Europe—everything from the names of some of the companies that do the paperwork (freight forwarders) to what's involved in getting the vehicle off the dock in Europe.

Chapter 7: "On the Road"
goes into detail about driving in Europe, describing the way the highway systems are designed and work and explaining the road signs you'll see.

Chapter 8: "The Campground Scene"
gives you a good idea of what to expect when you pull into a campground in Europe.

Chapter 9: "Staying in Touch"
goes into detail on the various options you'll have for communicating with your family and friends back home via phone and email.

Chapter 10: "Shopping & Eating Your Way through Europe"
highlights what is probably the chief advantage of this kind of trip—the fact that, because you have a kitchen, you can prepare, taste, and enjoy all the foods available in the local markets.

Chapter 11: "European Horizons Unlimited"
contains an overview of various European countries, providing an introduction to each country and information on its camping facilities. Reading this chapter could help you decide where you'd like to go on your trip.

Chapter 12: "To Be Continued..."
gives you information about storing an RV in Europe and invites you to learn more about our travels and begin planning your own.

To give you a better feel for what traveling through Europe in an RV is really like, we've added two appendices that contain excerpts from the letters we wrote home while on our trips. The letters provide "on the scene reports" of the delights we experienced as well as the problems we encountered and how we solved them.

Appendix A: "Letters from the Road: The Continent"
contains excerpts from the letters we sent home during our first trip to Europe in 2002.

Appendix B: "Letters from the Road: The United Kingdom" contains excerpts from the letters we sent home from the United Kingdom in 2003.

Finally, to make the information you might need easier to find, we've added five other appendices:

Appendix C: "Useful Things to Know About..." has "fact sheets" for many of the countries in Europe. These fact sheets contain essential information, such as emergency phone numbers, locations of Tourist Offices, names of camping organizations, highway information, explanations of road signs and special rules of the road, and information on camping and security.

Appendix D: "Ports in America and Europe" lists ports both in the U.S. and in Europe that are easily accessible if you want to ship your RV. There is also information about campgrounds close to ports.

Appendix E: "Suppliers" provides contact information for suppliers of services and other things you may need on your trip. It includes a list of some firms that handle the paperwork for shipping (freight forwarders) and information on insurance companies that can insure vehicles in Europe. It also has a list of service providers, such as telephone companies, as well as a list of places where you might consider storing a vehicle in Europe. We have included a special section with names of UK RV dealers who specialize in American-made RVs. They can be useful in a crisis since they can answer questions about American rigs. Another excellent source of information is the British magazine, ARVM, and its related club, ARVE. Its members are Brits who own or are interested in owning American RVs.

Appendix F: "Useful Internet Sites" lists a number of Internet sites that may prove useful when planning a trip. At these sites you can find information on such things as European campgrounds, hotels in Europe, and currency conversion.

Appendix G: "Dealers Who Rent & Sell RVs in Europe" has a list of dealers who supply RVs in Europe.

The book concludes with a glossary of terms, a bibliography listing books that you might find helpful, and an index.

1

New Uses for Your Old RV

Why Europe?

The reasons for going to Europe are pretty much the same whether you are living and driving in a motor home or going the more traditional route, i.e., renting a car, staying in hotels, and eating in restaurants. Europe is a fascinating place. Its history is long. Every modern European country is made up of regions that had their own culture and customs (and even language) for hundreds of years before they became part of a larger entity. As a result, there are big differences in culture, architecture, and traditional foods from one city to another.

Western culture was born here—and there are numerous artifacts attesting to its birth and development. There are ruins dating back to the Roman Empire, medieval walled cities and castles, palaces and citadels, chateaux and cathedrals. Driving around France, we were made aware that the Romans had a lot of outposts in Gaul (the Roman name for what is now France). And there are Roman ruins all over Great Britain, not only Hadrian's Wall, but buildings of all sorts. In Plymouth we revisited the age of exploration, and we stood on the dock where the *Mayflower* left England for the New World.

We saw places whose names are familiar from two World Wars. We visited the battlefields of World War I, as well as the place where the armistice was signed that ended that war. We toured the beaches of Normandy, the Belgian city of Bastogne (made famous during the

Battle of the Bulge in World War II), the extensive Duxford Air Museum in England, and Bletchley Park near London where the Nazis' Enigma code was broken. Even after spending nearly six months on the road, we know there are still plenty of interesting places to visit on future trips.

Museums are everywhere and many have been around a long time. Their collections are extensive and unique. There are museums of Roman antiquities, art museums, folkways museums, history and house museums, as well as war museums and monuments. Every big city has its great museums, but in Europe even small cities are likely to have something very special to see or experience. We spent longer in Paris, in Amsterdam, and in London than we did in smaller places, but only because there were more things to be found in the big cities so it took longer to see the sights. Paris has a number of famous art museums, including the Louvre and the Musée d'Orsay, but there is so much more. You can visit places that figured in history and in literature, places that are famous or infamous.

Visiting Europe allows you to visit history. For example, if you're able to wander freely, you'll find signs throughout France alerting you to tourist attractions. In one town you may be able to see a thirteenth-century abbey and in another a battlefield from World War I (or II). A castle may be in ruins, or it may be part of a huge complex that still remains intact, like Carcassonne. Smaller cities, like Antwerp in Belgium, have their museums, but they also have many remnants of the past—like the beautiful home and studio of the artist Peter Paul Rubens. You can visit Claude Monet's home in Giverny outside of Paris and wander through his house and the magnificent garden that he considered his "greatest masterpiece." Amsterdam has the impressive Rijksmuseum, and museums devoted to Van Gogh, Rembrandt, and others, but it also has other monuments—like the house where Anne Frank was hidden and the seventeenth-century home of Rembrandt.

The same is true for Great Britain. London has the British Museum, and many, many other museums. The Museum of the City of London, for example, chronicles two thousand years of history, displaying artifacts unearthed when construction companies dug down into the earth. You can visit the Houses of Parliament, Westminster Abbey, St. Paul's Cathedral, or the Tower of London. You can put your feet in places you've always heard about—like Hyde Park or Downing Street (though you're not allowed to get too close to Number 10!). As you walk through city neighborhoods, you'll see plaques on buildings relating to various historical events or figures. One of Ron's favorites is the plaque that marks the home of Captain Bligh of the HMS *Bounty*. But Britain is so much more than London!

Every American tourist knows about Shakespeare and Stratford-upon-Avon, but these are only a tiny part of what the country has to offer. The harbors at Plymouth, from which the Pilgrims embarked, and of Portsmouth, where the D-Day invasion was launched, are places whose names are as well known in America as in Britain. Winston Churchill was born at Blenheim Palace and lived at Chartwell, both of which can be visited. Even though your ancestors may not have come from the Highlands of Scotland or the Yorkshire moors or the mountains of Wales or ever have "taken the waters" at Bath, these are all places that are probably familiar to you from literature.

The myth is that Robin Hood lived in Sherwood Forest (near Nottingham Castle), that King Arthur and Queen Guinevere had a castle at Tintagel in Cornwall. A museum in the Yorkshire town of Thirsk will bring you into the life of the veterinarian known as James Herriot. If you are a fan of Brother Caedfael (created by Ellis Peters), you can visit the beautiful town of Shrewsbury. Fans of Jane Austen can visit Bath, tour the Assembly Rooms featured in *Persuasion*, or even go to the home where Miss Austen lived. There are castles and cathedrals too numerous to list.

The harbor at Plymouth, from which the Pilgrims embarked for the New World.

We found it particularly exciting to be in the place where the Industrial Revolution began—a Shropshire town called Ironbridge. After going through the museums there, we had to admit that everyone in the modern world owes a debt to Abraham Darby, the Englishman who invented an inexpensive way of smelting iron. Where would we be without iron?

Equally interesting was the Greenwich Observatory, where a tourist can view the actual timepieces made by the Yorkshire carpenter named John Harrison. His invention revolutionized travel by allowing sailors to figure out for the first time in history exactly where they were in terms of both latitude and longitude.

A lot of American history begins in Europe, not only because so many Americans are descended from Europeans, but because we have been involved in two World Wars. In the beautiful cathedral at Durham in northern England we looked at a display of the coat of arms of the Washington family, as well as a plaque mentioning that among their descendants was a colonial named George Washington.

If you plan to stay in Europe for only two weeks or a month, you may want to go the hotel and restaurant route or to rent a motor home in Europe. But if you have more time to travel, doing so in your own motor home will provide you with an experience of foreign travel that is totally different from anything you may be familiar with. In fact, the RV experience is unique.

The RV Advantage

It was not until we returned home that we realized how much richer an experience traveling in an RV can be. For an extended stay, nothing beats traveling in your own motor home. Your motor home is your car, getting you from place to place. But it is also your hotel. It always has a clean bathroom and a comfortable bed. More than that, it is your own home, no matter where you are traveling or in what strange place you are parked. You rarely need reservations and you can make or change your own schedule on the spur of the moment. Food can be purchased in the usual way and prepared accordingly, or you can eat meals out. A suitcase is unpacked when you arrive and repacked only when you fly home.

You can see some of Europe in a two-week or even a one-month long vacation. But of course you can see much more if you stay longer. Once you ship your RV to Europe, you'll want to stay as long as you can, just to justify the costs. But the big difference between a traditional hotel-and-restaurant trip and a trip in an RV is not just the time you are able to spend in Europe.

In an RV, you are free to follow your own inclinations. You don't need to get from one place to another quickly—so if you see something interesting on the way, you can stop, find a campground, and stay until you've explored the area as thoroughly as you want. You can go out to a restaurant for dinner, or you can have dinner in your own home and then go into town for a cup of coffee and a long look at the local nightlife. You can change your mind about which direction to follow according to a whim or the weather. There is so much to see. On a very long trip, you can elect to see more of the place you are in—or go on to other equally interesting places.

While we were our way to Paris, for example, we saw a sign for an "Historial" about the Great War (World War I). Had we been driving a rental car toward a hotel reservation, we might have made a note to see that town on our next trip. Instead, we made an on-the-spot decision to stay. We found a campsite within walking distance of the town center of Péronne. This small city is in the Somme, that part of France where World War I was fought. In fact, there are World War I trenches to explore nearby. We spent a very interesting couple of days exploring the town's Historial, which turned out to be a kind of museum, as well as the historical sights. You wouldn't find this town in most guidebooks, since it's small and guidebooks generally concentrate on the big cities.

There are no time constraints to this kind of travel. You don't need reservations most of the time. We did find that very popular campgrounds in parts of the United Kingdom (like the Cotswolds, Bath, and Edinburgh) were totally booked during the height of the season, but we discovered other places nearby. As long as you arrange to get to your new campground in the afternoon, there is little chance of being turned away. Most campgrounds, even if they are crowded, can still make room on the grass for another camper. In the few instances when they really couldn't fit us in, they had suggestions to help us find a place close by. And the fact that this is considerably less expensive than other forms of travel means that you can stay for the extended period that allows you to explore Europe in depth.

Some of the main advantages of RVing in Europe:
- *you are free to follow your own inclinations*
- *there are no time constraints*
- *it's considerably less expensive than other forms of travel*
- *you can stay for the extended period that allows you to explore Europe*

The People You'll Meet, the Places You'll Stay

If you travel in the "normal" way in a foreign country, you meet local people who work in the tourist industry—hotel, restaurant, museum, and other tourist-attraction personnel. If you are gregarious, you might meet other travelers. It is even possible to meet other "kinds" of people by staying in bed-and-breakfast establishments. But you cannot replicate the RV experience. Since you and everyone else in a campground have a common bond in your choice of camping as a way to travel, you get to meet people from many walks of life in spite of differences in language. Even the "wardens" in campgrounds are more likely to be interested in you than the personnel in large hotels would be. After all, they don't often have American guests!

We have met people in ways very different from those open to travelers who stay in hotels, even if they rent a car and drive around. Touring with an RV requires you to do the same "chores" that everyone else does. This means that you will meet the local residents in the supermarket, in the laundromat, or waiting for the bus. We've met some very nice people at bus stations or on the bus ride itself. Even when there was a language barrier, people would ask where we came from and offer suggestions on where else we should go, or would share details about life in their country.

Often we would find ourselves setting out from the campground with others who were obviously going to the bus stop for a ride into town, allowing us to meet campers from all over. Once, when we needed change for a clothes dryer that took many more coins than we had in our possession, we had to ask around the campground. We met an English lady who invited us to join her and her elderly mother in the screened-in awning off their caravan (trailer) to have a glass of wine and we spent a lovely evening sipping wine and talking about our lives.

Since we went into markets and supermarkets for groceries, we spoke to people waiting on line and to cashiers. One day, in a market in Blackpool, we met a couple from Liverpool who not only wanted to show us the town but insisted on giving us several small gifts to remember them by. Sitting on a bench in the same city, we talked for a long time with a couple of "OAPs"—old age pensioners—who told us a lot about the British retirement and health systems.

The campground warden in one of our stops in France had a beautiful Doberman pinscher whom we loved. The dog loved us in return, though that didn't mean anything. She loved everyone. But her attention brought us attention from her owner, who went out of her way to help us. This lady made sure that when we set off to buy some Beaujolais we got what she considered the best wine produced locally.

Often our new acquaintances spoke English, but we sometimes got along in a primitive French. One of our most memorable encounters was with a Tunisian farmer in southern France who did

The garden-like setting of our campsite in Glasgow.

not speak English. Somehow we managed to have a very long conversation about America while waiting for a bus to our campground and on the bus as we rode along. We can't speak any German, but we met several people who spoke our language, including one member of a large party of Austrians in the Paris campground who came over to "meet the Americans," and a Good Samaritan who spoke not a word of English. (The details of this encounter are described in the next chapter.)

In the campgrounds on the Continent, we met fellow Americans as well as people who saw our license plate and wondered about us. Many of these folks were memorable. We were invited to "have a drink" by English and Dutch travelers who were camping in Holland, and in England, we were invited for a drink by a couple returning home from Holland on the ferry to Harwich. A young man in a pup tent staying in the Antwerp campground in Belgium came to tea and told us about his life. And during our stay in one Amsterdam campground, we met a Scottish couple who have since become very good friends (see our letters in Appendix B).

Europeans get much longer vacations than Americans normally do. Having four weeks off in the summer is not unusual. Camping is a common way of spending those long vacations. This means that there are campgrounds everywhere. According to one source, there are 10,000 licensed facilities in France alone. They range in size and location from huge city campgrounds with spaces for hundreds of camping units to wilderness camps way out in rural areas. There are vacation resorts with pools and facilities for other activities and there are also "pitches" on farms. (A pitch is the equivalent of a site in the U.S., that is, an individual campsite in a campground.)

In many villages, municipal campgrounds are within easy walking distance of the town center. If there are no campgrounds within the city limits, most cities have one or two facilities either on the outskirts of town or in suburban towns near the city, with easy access to the city via public transit.

Because fuel is very expensive in Europe, there are efficient public transit systems nearly everywhere. We suspect there is an efficient public transit system in absolutely every city. However, since we haven't been "everywhere" yet, we can't say that with certainty. But during our first trip of 83 days on the Continent, we never had a problem finding public transit in any city. Although the public transit service in England is not quite as good as it seems to be on the Continent, we still found adequate public transit everywhere. This means two things. First, it is never necessary to tow a smaller vehicle as is common in the U.S. (Indeed, that would be a very expensive proposition!) Second, it means that you can drive to a city, find the campground, park your RV there, and then take public transportation into the city. Rarely do you have to drive through the narrow lanes and heavy traffic that every city seems to have. But if it is necessary to go through the city center in your vehicle, just remember that big trucks do it every day.

As you drive on the roads, you will see many signs with the international symbol for campgrounds (a tent and a stylized caravan). Most large cities have one or more campgrounds. The campgrounds in the mountains or at the seashore are more popular with European campers who wish to stay away from cities on their vacation. That translates into empty spaces in urban campgrounds even in high season (July and August). This is good news for those who wish to visit cities in the summer in an RV.

Because there are so many tourists in every interesting European city, there is an efficient system of government Tourist Offices. As you drive into a city, you'll usually see a sign for the Tourist Office. Often such signs have a large "i" on them, since the word "information" appears in some form in many different languages. Sometimes this "i" stands for very specific information. For example, it may indicate that this corner has a large map of the area, or it may

Because there are campgrounds all over Europe, and because public transportation is so good,

- *you never need to tow a smaller vehicle (as is the case in the U.S.), and*
- *you rarely have to drive through the narrow lanes and heavy traffic that every city seems to have*

mean that you can get information about trains in a train station. In France, the sign for the Tourist Office may read "Syndicat d'Initiative" or "Office du Tourisme." In very small towns, which don't generally have extensive operations, the office of the mayor ("Office du Maire" in France) is open to help tourists. In Holland the standard sign for the Tourist Office is three inverted "V"s arranged in a circle. If you don't see any signs for tourist information, there is always a sign that leads you to the center of the city (Centre Ville, Centrum, Centro, Zentrum, or something similar). There is always a Tourist Office in "Centre Ville." The employees in these offices are very helpful and generally speak more than one language. (English apparently is one of the prerequisites for working in such offices, perhaps because of all the British tourists.) When we weren't able to find a campground by consulting our guidebooks, we often drove into the center of the city, found the Tourist Office, and got a list of nearby campgrounds. Even when we managed to find the campground on our own, we always stopped to talk to the people in the Tourist Office because they are the best source of local information.

While it is true that there are frequent language changes within short distances, it is equally true that Europeans frequently speak English as well as their native language. People in the campgrounds always are able to speak at least a little of a variety of languages, and they will gladly advise you on where to get public transit, give you bus and metro schedules, and help you out in general. (In one Amsterdam campground, we spoke to the young lady who was helping the campers register. We asked how many languages she spoke. She replied that she was fluent in Dutch, French, German, and English, but she regretted that her Italian and Spanish were only passable!)

Problems

Traveling by motor home has disadvantages, as well as advantages. Since you already own a rig, you know all about them. But taking an American "camping car" to Europe does present the traveler with a new set of potential problems.

When we first seriously considered the possibility of taking the RV to Europe, we saw all kinds of "problems" immediately.

The first problem we thought about was size Was our rig too big for European roads? This turned out to be a non-problem. In fact, most of the camping cars we saw in Europe were Class A rigs of about 24 to 25 feet. A high percentage of them had diesel engines, which is an advantage in Europe where diesel is about 30 percent

---

How big a rig can you take to Europe?

We looked up the maximum size each country allows and found that the regulations are fairly uniform. The RV may not exceed:

- *4 meters high*
- *2.55 meters wide*
- *12 meters long.*

That's approximately
- *13.12 feet high*
- *8.37 feet wide*
- *39.37 feet long*

less expensive than benzine or petrol (gasoline). Almost none of them had air conditioning units on top, which kept them slightly under the height of 9 feet (or about 2.7 meters). But there are some very large (30 feet and over) American-made RVs there, owned by Europeans who are very comfortable using them. We saw many caravans but almost no SUVs and only one pick-up truck in all the time that we were traveling on the Continent, although Great Britain is loaded with home-grown SUVs—that is, Land Rovers.

The height of our unit did turn out to be a difficulty, but only because we hadn't thought about using meters instead of feet when judging height. Europe uses the metric system for measuring length and volume. So, before you go under any European overpasses, be sure that you know the height of your rig in meters. That way, you can avoid low overpasses and other kinds of obstructions. In fact, you can save yourself a lot of grief by figuring out how many meters high your rig is and posting the figure on your dashboard. You may need that information in a situation where you are faced with an immediate decision about whether or not you can go under an overpass.

Before we got to Europe, we worried a lot about the cost of fuel. We knew that gasoline is very expensive there. In March 2002, it averaged $4 per gallon. By 2003, it was even more expensive, and it went up again in 2004, when it ranged between $4.50 and $5.50 a gallon. But you won't travel as far between stops in Europe as you do in the U.S. For example, you can go from Brugge in Belgium to Amsterdam in Holland in just a few hours. Paris is only 314 miles from Amsterdam. Furthermore, if you stay in a city for two or three days, the daily cost of fuel will not amount to a significant expense.

To give you a perspective on the "problem" of fuel, let's use our three RV trips. Our RV gets between 10 and 13 miles per gallon. In the U.S., distances are very long. On our 72-day trip here, we drove 11,400 miles and our fuel costs were about $1,200. In Europe, we drove 4,500 miles in 83 days, and our fuel costs were about $1,400! In the United Kingdom, we traveled only 3,200 miles on our 77-day trip, and the fuel cost was $1,056. Each of these trips was equally pleasurable, and the fuel costs were not very different.

But, now that we have made all these trips, we'd have to say that our trips in Europe were much nicer in at least one way than our trip in the U.S. Because the distances are so small, we spent considerably less time driving.

So, the "problem" of expensive fuel turned out to be no real problem at all. We figure that we averaged between $13 and $17 per day in fuel. Add that amount to the price of a campground. Most ranged from $15 to $25, no matter how large the vehicle. That means that

---

Converting feet to meters is not hard to do, but you'll need a formula as well as a calculator.

Here's the formula:
- *height in inches*
- *times .3048*
- *divided by 12.*

In other words, if your rig is 108 inches high, multiply this number by .3048 and divide the result by 12. Thus:

$$108''$$
$$x \quad .3048$$
$$= 32.9184''$$

When you divide 32.9184 by 12, you get 2.74. So your rig is 2.74 meters high.

To be safe, you might want to round it up to 3 meters.

our "hotel," "rental car," and fuel costs were only $30 to $40 per day—not counting the original investment in shipping.

We wondered about the differences in roads between America and Europe. As it turned out, while the road system in Europe has certain distinct differences that should be reckoned with (see chapter 7), we quickly learned to handle those differences. Trickiest for Americans are the narrow streets in cities and in some rural areas, as well as a few overpasses (usually in small cities) under 3 meters (9.8 feet) high. However, you will see extremely large tractor-trailer semis in Europe, many with six rear wheels. They snake through the narrowest of streets with seemingly little difficulty. And watching the large numbers of buses traveling along the roads makes you realize that size doesn't matter very much.

Before we got to Europe, we were concerned about the language "problem." We do not speak other languages. Our French is limited to the vocabulary and grammar of a two-year-old. Our German does not exist. But we spent 83 days on our first trip happily speaking mostly English, pointing a lot, and using single words to indicate things. We had a little electronic gadget that could translate a single word into another language if necessary. There really was no problem. In the United Kingdom, far from being a problem, our accents were enough to attract all kinds of interest and attention from all kinds of people.

We also worried about shipping. But getting the RV to Europe is really not a problem if you know how to go about it—and you will after reading this book. The first questions are: where and how? There are ports all along the coasts. Obviously, it is much more expensive to ship from the coast of California or even from ports on the Gulf Coast than from ports on the East Coast. But it is not a difficult process to ship via what is called "RO-RO." This stands for Roll On–Roll Off, which is how vehicles get on board and leave the ship. We shipped our rig via an RO-RO ship and were very pleased. A full description of the process can be found in chapter 6.

The differences between European and American electrical systems was a concern. We have often seen the little adapters that are sold in luggage stores, but we had an entire 110 volt electric system to run. Europe runs on 220 and 240 volt systems. The transition obviously couldn't be done with one little adapter. But this problem, too, disappeared quickly and easily. There's more about the solution to the electricity problem in chapter 4, "Preparing the RV for Europe."

The one problem that we did not anticipate turned out to be the only real "problem" we had to deal with! That was the problem of the difference in propane systems between the U.S. and Europe. Even this, however, was only an annoyance. (But it won't be for you after you've read the complete discussion of the propane situation in chapter 8.)

Speaking with the advantage of hindsight, all the anticipated problems turned out to be easily solved and each one of our European tours could be termed "the trip of a lifetime."

2

STRANGERS RVING IN A STRANGE LAND

Year 2002—On the Continent

No matter how experienced a traveler you may be and no matter how many times you have been to Europe, there is no way that you can ever know enough in advance to plan out every moment of an RV trip that will take you through the many places worth visiting. But that is an opportunity, not a disadvantage. Europe is very compact compared to the United States and it is very rich in great places to visit. Most are relatively unknown to travelers from the U.S. So if the phrase "Go with the flow" means anything at all, it is apt for driving an RV through Europe. Because you do not need reservations and do not have a schedule to keep, you are able to take advantage of new knowledge and serendipitous recommendations as they inevitably come up.

We began our first European journey in late March and we did have a few "must-sees." Because we had shipped the RV to Zeebrugge in Belgium, we were certain to visit Brugge, which is the closest real town and has the campground closest to the docks. We wanted to visit Amsterdam and Paris again, and we thought that we would visit the Normandy invasion beaches and after that head for Brittany (particularly the beautiful walled city of St. Malo). Then we would head south where it would be warmer. We knew that we should avoid mountains whenever possible, since our underpowered four-cylinder Toyota engine is very slow in the mountains. This would mean driving south through France via river valleys, particularly the Loire Valley. That's really as far as we had thought about the prospective trip.

Most of what we saw was unplanned. For example, we were in an Internet café in Brussels, sending a letter home, when we struck up a conversation with the manager. He spoke English and asked if we came from the UK. We explained who we were and where we were staying, and he told us that he hoped we would stop in Antwerp (where he lives) because it is an interesting city. We'd never thought about Antwerp one way or another, but it seemed as good a way to go as any other, so we went to Antwerp and found a campground. We ended up staying there four days.

Antwerp is a beautiful city, the "diamond capital" of Europe, with a brand new Diamond Museum, an art museum, and a great zoo right in the middle of the city. The artist Peter Paul Rubens lived there and his beautiful home is open to the public. On Sunday there was a huge open-air market, which was a joy. The campground was very nice and extraordinarily inexpensive, and public transportation was good. Adding to the charms of this lovely city for us was an enormous book fair being held within walking distance of our campground. We were able to replenish our supply of books (in English) at very inexpensive prices.

This is exactly what makes traveling by RV so special. On the spur of the moment we made a decision to visit a place that we had no prior information about, found a comfortable place to stay, and were able to remain as long as we wanted. We enjoyed Antwerp so much that we're planning a return visit.

In Belgium, we visited the city of Liège. This is not a city high on any tourist list, but we enjoyed it. We toured the old parts of the city, had crisp, tasty *Vlaamse frites* (known to Americans as French fries), and visited both an interesting flea market and a spectacular open-air market that has run continuously for hundreds of years and sells, among other things, small livestock to local farmers. A European acquaintance couldn't believe we had gone to Liège. According to him, no one goes to Liège! That may be true, but we went and stayed several days quite happily.

On another occasion, an employee in a campground in Arles, which is in Provence, told us about a nearby town in the mountains. He said that it had been designated the most beautiful town in France for 2002 and would be the most beautiful town in the world in 2003! That certainly piqued our interest. So we made a small side trip to an exquisite place we'd never heard of—and probably would not have heard of—called Les Baux, high in the Alpilles Mountains. This little town was truly spectacular and we might never have seen it. The remains of a Roman fort that had been constructed on the solid rock at the very top of the mountain were impressive—like Hadrian's Wall, a testament to the technical skill of the ancient Romans. The beautiful village had been built in medieval times just under the Roman fort. The narrow streets were crowded with little shops, restaurants, and cafés—it was all very magical. It was also puzzling. It was easy to understand why the Romans had settled there. You could see in all directions from the top of the mountain and this was therefore a perfect place to head off any attacks. But although the village has been continuously occupied, it must have been very difficult to make a living in this rocky soil in the days of medieval farming. We managed to ask some local people about this, and it became clear that the residents in the Middle Ages were mostly thieves and bandits, not farmers. In more recent history, the discovery of bauxite (the ore that becomes aluminum) kept the city alive, but did not modernize it! To get into the village, we had to park our RV on the road and walk up to the very top of the mountain. It was well worth the effort.

Actually, the entire area of France called Provence and Languedoc was magical. The countryside of vineyards and farms, hills and valleys was uniformly beautiful, and the cities were fascinating. For example, we stayed in a campground *sous le pont* (under the bridge) of Avignon, and walked across a new bridge into the walled city and the Palace of the Popes. It is called this because in the twelfth and thirteenth centuries the heads of the Roman Catholic Church were

A section of Hadrian's Wall in northern England.

unable to live in Rome for political reasons, so they took up residence in this city under the protection of the French Catholic king. Following the signs for the daily market, we discovered a sixteenth-century Jewish synagogue in the shadow of the Popes' palace. Intrigued, we walked over to look at the front of the synagogue. The rabbi happened to come out. He noticed that we were interested and invited us in for a tour, telling us about the history of the Jewish community known as "the Pope's Jews" in Avignon. The rabbi told us that the Roman government had exiled the Jews from Jerusalem after an anti-Roman revolt in the first century. They had been sent to live in Gaul in a Roman city now known as Avignon. When the first Pope moved to this city more than a thousand years later, he was told about the Jewish settlement and he declared that these people had been there longer than the Popes had and so were under his protection. That's when they became known as the Pope's Jews.

Our English neighbors in this campground suggested that we make a point of seeing the Pont du Gard. A piece of this huge, ancient Roman aqueduct is still standing, and seeing it became one of the high points of our trip. We saw very few Americans and heard very little English spoken, but there were lots and lots of tourists speaking Italian, French, and German.

In the beautiful town of Arles, which has the finest collection of Roman antiquities we have ever seen, there are many Roman ruins, including an an outdoor concert hall, a bath, an arena, and a race track. Perhaps the most remarkable part of some of these was the fact that they are still in use. The outdoor concert hall has a new stage, modern sound equipment, and even some new seats, but we were able to sit on seats that had been used by Roman citizens in the first century AD when they attended performances of drama or music. We had no desire to see a modern bullfight in the Roman arena, but we understand that such fights take place at regular intervals in this first-century venue. (Perhaps if we'd realized that the French bullfight is quite different from the Spanish and that they do not hurt the bull, we'd have gone in.)

The medieval part of the city is beautiful, and within walking distance of the more ancient area. In the nineteenth century the city was home to many artists, notably Vincent Van Gogh and Paul Gaugin. The city Tourist Office sold us an inexpensive map with a walking tour of the city center. It gave directions to reach the places made famous by Van Gogh paintings—the Café Étoile (Star Café), the outside of the arena, the famous little drawbridge which once stood within the city but has now been moved away from city traffic—and many others.

Another place that simply "blew us away" was the southern French walled city of Carcassonne, in the region of Languedoc. After consulting our guidebooks, we had decided that this would be our next stop, since there was at least one campground in the city. Driving along a winding country road, we suddenly were confronted by a scene from Camelot. The view of this medieval walled city complete with many conical turrets was so striking that we both exclaimed out loud at the sight. We found that there was parking especially set aside for *les camping cars* in the area just outside the walls of the city, so we drove from the campground to the walled city. Then we walked the narrow streets within the walls, watched the local children dancing in a square, toured the ramparts, and learned a little about the local culture and the Cathar heresy which had been ruthlessly extinguished by the medieval Church in the thirteenth century. After spending a lovely couple of days in Carcassonne, we moved on. (Incidentally, if you've ever seen the movie *Robin Hood, Prince of Thieves,* you've seen the walled city of Carcassonne. No one could design a more beautiful castle than this one, so the film company used the walled city as a prop.)

Equally magical were other areas in southern France. In the Camargue, white horses, black bulls, and pink flamingos roam freely in the marshes and can be seen from the road. In the distance we could see the walls of the medieval city of Aigues Mortes. We decided to skip this oddly named city (the name means something like "nasty death"). Later we learned that the city had gotten its strange name because it had been a port for ships leaving for the Crusades many centuries ago and that there are fourteen campgrounds in Aigues Mortes. Although we bypassed this town, we ended up in an equally interesting place.

That is the major problem on an RV trip. There is too much to see. You can't see it all, and you have to make choices. Reading guidebooks was some help, but since we were not tied to schedules, reservations, or big cities, such publications did not really help us very much. They tend to concentrate on big cities and tourist destinations that appeal to Americans traveling city-to-city in Europe. We were able to visit many places where European tourists go, places too small to get into American guidebooks.

Obviously, serendipity played a big part in our trip. For example, we drove through the French city of Périgueux. We were on our way to the caves of Lascaux, where Stone Age artists had painted on the walls. In the beautiful center of the city, we followed people with empty baskets in their hands and found out that a big open-air market was being held that day. The city also boasts the ruins of a

> *"We were able to visit many places where European tourists go, places too small to get into American guidebooks."*

Roman cella (the most sacred part of a Roman temple), a huge Roman mansion that was in the process of being excavated, and an incredible walled medieval city. We loved it, but we certainly didn't find much about it in guidebooks. The caves at Lascaux, on the other hand, were written up in all the guidebooks—and they lived up to expectations. The original caves are no longer open, but the French government has exactly duplicated them and their ancient paintings so tourists can feel that they have visited the place where art was created twenty thousand years ago!

Equally felicitous was our "discovery" of Pérrone in the area of France known as Le Somme. We were both fascinated and moved by the various unexpected sights of World War I that still remain.

We also visited a number of World War II areas—not only Normandy but also Bastogne, in Belgium on the edge of Luxembourg, where a group of Americans stood fast against the Nazis during the Battle of the Bulge. While we knew about Bastogne, we hadn't planned on visiting it. It was only when we checked our map that we saw that the city was on our route. In the main square sat a World War II American tank with several holes in it.

The center of the city is named McAuliffe Square after the American general who defended the city against the Nazis. He is remembered for his terse response to a German demand that he surrender—"Nuts!" A privately owned museum in a storefront boasts thousands of artifacts from the battle, all dug up from local yards and farms over the years. Just outside the city is a monument to the men who died in that battle and a museum that explains it. The Battle of the Bulge cost more American lives than any other single battle in World War II. In fact, we had a friend who had been taken prisoner in that battle. Just being in the actual location was a very moving experience.

Perhaps most amazing to us was something we saw on our way out. As we drove past the houses on the main street, we noticed that one house had a truly unusual lawn ornament—the turret from a Sherman tank, complete with the artillery piece. For all these reasons, Bastogne proved to be one of the most memorable stops on our trip. It was one place where we saw other American tourists.

Our stop in the French town called Martel was short, but the town itself was charming. It has an additional attraction for the British and for Americans interested in history. One of its many medieval buildings has a sign that notes that in the twelfth century, Henri Court-Mantel (Henry Short Coat) died in this building. Since Henry was the oldest child of King Henry II of England and his queen, Eleanor of Aquitaine, and the older brother of both King

Richard the Lion-hearted and King John (of Magna Carta fame), we found this to be an interesting spot.

We didn't stop in every place that we would have liked to explore. There were towns along our route that were very old and looked charming, but we just could not see everything. We passed through towns that looked as they had hundreds of years ago, towns that had highway signs for thirteenth-century monasteries and all kinds of other interesting places. We still regret not staying longer in Besançon (a citadel city), and we really would have liked to explore the little medieval town called Baum des Dames, for example. But if we'd stopped at every town that looked intriguing, we'd never have gotten very far. In the most mundane places, there was always something interesting to see.

Later in our travels we learned about some places that we should have visited but didn't know about. An Englishman in Paris told us about the remains of an entire town named Oradour-sur-Glane wiped out by the Nazis in 1944 in retaliation against the French Resistance. He said that visiting the remains of this village had been one of the most moving experiences of his life. After the war, General de Gaulle ordered the French government to leave everything just as it had been on the day of the massacre, so the town was never rebuilt. Someday we plan to return, and we have marked this site on our map so we will not miss it again.

Seeing the beaches and the monuments of Normandy was an emotional experience, of course, but so was visiting a little mountain town called Le Chambon-sur-Lignon, where the Huguenot (French Protestant) population had hidden Jews from the Nazis during the war. This behavior was so unusual that the town is the subject of a book (Philip Hallie's *Lest Innocent Blood be Shed*) and a documentary film. This is one of the few areas in Catholic France where the population is mostly Huguenot. A blue and white sign shaped like a cross is posted at the side of the highway as you drive into town, announcing that this town is the home of a "Protestant Cult"! That got our attention!

Driving through France, one is constantly reminded of history by the signs that announce military cemeteries: Cimètiere Américain or Nederlander or Belgique or Angleterre. We didn't stop to visit these cemeteries, but their presence kept reminding us of the history we were driving through. And we immediately changed course when we came upon the sign for the Clairière de l'Armistice, the clearing where the armistice ending World War I was signed in a railroad car. Hitler forced the French to surrender in that same railroad car at the beginning of World War II. The nearby museum boasts a replica of the car, but it happened to be closed that day. So we spent hours exploring the outside exhibits, which included the two separate sets of railroad tracks on which the adversaries traveled to the site. Marshall Foch's tomb lies between the two rails on which the allied car stood.

There was no place in our travels that did not offer something interesting. Some of the places were so beautiful that they simply took our breath away. A city like Toulouse, on the other hand, is a big, modern industrial city where few tourists would go. We spent a day there. It had, among other things, an art museum with a very extensive collection of masterpieces by famous artists. Everywhere we went, it seemed, there were 700-year-old buildings and majestically beautiful cathedrals.

Oh, the cathedrals! Most towns seemed to have at least one. Many are ancient. Some date back to well before the eleventh century. Every one was worth a visit. There are usually no entrance fees for these cathedrals, unless there is a special exhibit inside.

We visited St. Bavo's in Ghent (Belgium), which houses the famous Van Eyck altarpiece "The Adoration of the Lamb" as well as at least two huge paintings by Rubens. The cathedral in Haarlem contains a beautiful old pipe organ that both Handel and Mozart played, as well as the tomb of the Dutch artist, Frans Hals. The enormous cathedral in Antwerp is perhaps the biggest one we saw, with seven naves (long corridors between columns running from the front of the cathedral to the back). The cathedral in Lyons is built atop a cliff, high above the city. Although it is "new," having been built in the nineteenth century, it had the most ornate interior we had seen. And, of course, Paris has Notre Dame, Sacre Coeur, and Sainte-Chapelle. All of them are extraordinarily beautiful.

In our drive through the Loire Valley, we passed many chateaux, but we didn't stop to visit them all. That would have taken days (and would have cost a lot in entrance fees). We are familiar with old building-museums, and we didn't feel that we needed to visit another sixteenth- or seventeenth-century building with antique furniture. After reading the information given to us in the Tourist Office near our municipal campground in Azay-le-Rideau, just below Tours, we picked just one chateau to visit—an early building in a nearby town called Loches. This chateau boasts of being the site of a visit to the Dauphin (eldest son of the king of France) by Joan of Arc. She persuaded him to be sworn in as King Charles VII of France, defying the English. This particular chateau was an older one, a stone building with very few amenities. The only warmth and comfort came from tapestries hung on the wall and huge fireplaces. The next day, we visited the chateau that was next door to our campground in town, just because it was there. It was an elegant eighteenth-century building with beautiful furniture. There really are an incredible number of beautiful and very old chateaux open to the public in the Loire Valley. Just driving along the road is an experience.

The fact that even those most visited tourist cities of Paris and Amsterdam had campgrounds within the city limits made staying for long periods of time easy and inexpensive for us. It's probably impossible to get a hotel room in Paris for $25—but that's what our campsite cost us. We spent more than a week of our tour in Paris, doing all the tourist things. Our campsite in the Bois de Boulogne was a bus and metro ride away from the center of the city. We were able to visit the Louvre Museum for three days in a row so we got to see a little of its collection. We also saw the newer Musée d'Orsay, which houses a huge collection of Impressionist paintings, and the beautiful Jacquemart-André museum, willed to the city by its original owners together with the mansion in which they had lived. (Here, again, there is a Hollywood connection. In the musical film *Gigi*, this mansion was used as the setting of the home of the immensely rich hero, Gaston.)

Leaving Paris we decided we would spend a day in a small town not too far away where the artist Claude Monet had lived. Giverny is now a huge tourist attraction, with Monet's house and garden open to the public. Walking through the furnished house with its yellow and blue interior and especially touring the exquisite gardens was a memorable experience.

Our extended stay in Amsterdam made us feel almost like natives. We bought our food at the Albert Cuypstraat daily market, visited lots of tourist sights and a few of the myriad museums, learned a lot about the public transit system, and kept fresh-cut flowers in our home! We went to Haarlem, Delft, and Naarden, and visited the once-every-10-years floral event called Floriade. Because we were in Holland, looking at flowers was very important. That included Floriade with its acres of exhibits and a 100-meter high hill that was the pride of the Dutch planners. Since we come from a place where 100-meter high hills are the norm, we weren't as impressed with this as we should have been! (Remember, much of Holland lies below sea level.) There were walks in Keukenhof near Amsterdam, where the nation's tulip growers plant new and different—but always absolutely beautiful—exhibits every year using millions of flowering bulbs. In Amsterdam there is a flower district where you can walk around and buy inexpensive flowers. You can

"It's probably impossible to get a hotel room in Paris for $25— but that's what our campsite cost us."

A street in Amsterdam.

also visit the daily wholesale flower auction that takes place in the suburb of Amstelveen, very close to one of the campgrounds we especially liked. In fact, on our next trip we visited the market and were overwhelmed with its immensity, the pace of the action throughout the huge building, and the beauty and variety of the flowers.

Holland has many interesting museums besides the incredible art institutions. There is a war museum at Overloon, on the site where a huge battle was waged during World War II. In Amsterdam there are museums devoted to history, World War II Resistance, the house where Anne Frank hid before her family was discovered, a secret church meeting room, and all kinds of antique homes. At Arnhem, near the site of another World War II battle, is a huge collection of all kinds of buildings from different areas and different eras of Dutch history. None of these places is very far from Amsterdam, because the entire country is so small. Kinderdijk boasts many beautiful old windmills. We visited Delft to see the Nieuwe (New) Cathedral (built in the fifteenth century) and the Oulde (Old) Cathedral (built in the thirteenth century). We walked in the main square and watched a wedding party leave the seventeenth century city hall in a horse and buggy. In Naarden, we toured the pride of the town, a huge fortification in the shape of a star that is separated from a second, larger star-shaped fortification by a defensive moat. (The double barrier didn't stop any attackers, as far as we learned.)

Incidentally, we were startled when touring Naarden to find an empty storefront with black-bordered pictures of four young men and women in the window. They had Dutch names and the captions said they had died on September 11, 2001, in Tower Two. Truly, we are all connected.

Walking in the Amsterdam flower market and other places, we marveled at the number of tourists in the city. It is easy to see why Holland—and particularly Amsterdam—is such a favorite tourist destination, especially for Americans. Most of the Dutch speak English, and the country has great works of art and interesting architecture as well as a long history and a distinctive culture. Our favorite Internet café was inexpensive and served great coffee.

One day we happened upon the giant clear plastic tubes in City Hall which measure sea level at several points along the seacoast. Water levels in all the tubes were over our heads. The realization that we were beneath sea level at all times while in Holland was both scary and exhilarating. The Dutch have a saying: "God made the world, but the Dutch made Holland." It is certainly not an empty boast.

In the course of our long stay, we were able to see more than most tourists, but there are plenty of things we haven't seen yet. We made the conscious decision to spend a lot of time in this city rather than go dashing off to other places because we felt so at home here, and because the other places we might go would be as interesting but not more so. There are still many trips to Amsterdam left in our future, and we'll see other equally interesting places then!

Colmar in Alsace was an interesting combination of French and German culture, with architecture to match. Unfortunately, the rains came while we were in Colmar, making it impossible for us to stay as long as we would have liked. We enjoyed the day we were able to spend there—even though the rain made sightseeing nearly impossible and there was a lot that we could not see. In fact, half of the lovely riverside campground where we were staying in the city was unusable by the morning after our arrival. There were swans swimming in the spaces usually reserved for campers!

These rains were the reason we spent very little time in Germany. Extremely heavy rain makes touring very difficult, and the rain dogged us through Freiberg, Karlsruhe, Mainz, and Aachen, so we returned to the minor rains in Holland rather than going through Cologne and touring other parts of Germany. It is worth saying, however, that the campgrounds in Germany were lovely, with good electric service and hot water.

Mainz, Germany, was the home of Johannes Gutenberg, who invented the printing press. There is a museum in the city devoted to describing this effort. Also, we were both surprised and delighted to see that Mainz has a Wal-Mart Supercenter! A clerk told us that Wal-Mart has 150 stores in Germany. We've spent nights dry camping in Wal-Mart parking lots all over the United States, as many of you may also have done. We don't know whether the German Wal-Mart would permit such camping, but we did make it a point to visit the store so we could compare it to those at home. The German store certainly sold more beer and wine than any store in the U.S. Generally speaking, the products were different, and the store itself was not as large as those we are used to. The food section favored the deli department. It was huge and it featured an enormous selection of wurst and lunch meat. It was also the only place where we were able to buy onion powder to add to our selection of spices on the RV.

In Aachen, we encountered a Good Samaritan who proved the point that you don't need to speak the language. We had arrived with kind of loose instructions about the municipal campground in this German city on the edge of Holland. We had a lot of trouble finding the campground and were reduced to asking for directions in small retail establishments staffed by people who spoke no English. We got some directions by showing them the book of campground listings with its address. After two people pointed us in the same direction, we turned and headed the way our informants had indicated. Shortly thereafter, we found ourselves in front of a police station. By now, it was 5:30, and the sign outside the door seemed to indicate that the station was closed after 5 PM, but it also indicated you should ring for service after regular hours.

So we rang. A very nice policeman who spoke English was found to help us and, with the aid of a huge city map, he explained how to get to the municipal campground we were looking for. Off we went, and soon we were right there at the park where we were supposed to be. The street was quite narrow and we could not find an entrance. We pulled over as much as we could and stopped, so that we could ask in the adjoining stores about the entrance. There was honking behind us as I climbed down onto the street with the guidebook in my hand, and then several cars pulled out and went around us. But the RV behind us didn't pull out. He stopped his engine, got out of his rig, and spoke to me in incomprehensible (to me) German. I showed him the campground book and pointed to the park. More German, and this time I caught one unpleasant word. *Kaput!* (Gone! Dead!) That explained why there was no entrance. After trying, in vain, to give me directions, he motioned that we should follow him, and we did. He drove out of his way to take us to a parking area where truckers and a few other campers were dry camping for the night, made some recognizable hand signs that indicated "sleep here," and said *Gute Nacht.* A Good Samaritan indeed.

Year 2003—The United Kingdom

On our second trip, we concentrated on touring the United Kingdom (UK). We tried to get to as many different places as we could, but had to leave equally interesting sites for some other trip.

Our experiences on this second trip were quite different. There are the obvious differences, of course. We do, after all, speak nearly the same language as the British. As an added bonus, this meant we could read local newspapers and listen to local radio. That ability added a dimension to the trip that had been missing (though we hadn't realized it at the time) from the trip to the Continent.

Of course, the traffic moves on the left instead of the right, but that turned out to be no problem at all. Our experience has been that staying on the "wrong" side of the road isn't difficult. What had been difficult on other trips when we were driving in rented English cars was driving from the "wrong" side of the car. In English cars, the driver's seat is the right-hand seat instead of the left-hand seat, which means that for Americans, who are used to having the car end at the driver's left elbow, it is very hard to judge where the left side of the car ends.

We were now driving a much wider vehicle than a car. Because we could afford to stay for a really long period of time, we were able to go to a lot of places that were off the large highways. The narrow, winding lanes meant that the slightest misjudgment of the width of the vehicle could have resulted in an accidental side-swiping. Since the driver knew where his vehicle ended on the left, we had no problem. However, a trip without even a minor accident would have been difficult to achieve if we had had to deal with a rented British vehicle. That reason alone would be enough to warrant taking your own RV to England!

As we mentioned earlier, we found that the fact that we were obviously strangers who spoke the same language—but with an accent—got us a lot of attention. Strangers on the street or at bus stops were anxious to talk to us, to find out a little bit about us, and to help us find our way.

Although the United Kingdom is now a part of the European Common Market, there are enough differences between the UK and the Continent to warrant a special section on camping and driving through England, Scotland, and Wales (see chapter 7).

Traveling in England (and the rest of the British Isles) does present a special case. There are lots of pluses. The biggest ones are the shared language, the friendliness, the short distances between stops, and the interesting weight of history that most locations have. English history and English literature are an integral part of American culture. The names of the cities are familiar. Wherever you go, you find sights whose names you know.

The story that everyone tells is that if you go to an English pub, you'll make friends. That is probably quite true, but it does not tell the whole story. The English are just plain nice. If you are standing on a corner looking confusedly at a map, people will stop and ask you if they can help. If you say "Good morning," they will not only respond to your greeting but also talk to you. Our experience was that the first question that was asked after people heard our accents was "Where are you from?" and the second was "How long are you going to be here?" It is easy to talk to people, whether in a campground setting or on the street. More important, people will go out of their way for you. Two stories illustrate this.

First, we want to point out that English campgrounds are quite well protected. They always have barriers. Usually, these barriers are hung so that vehicles higher than an SUV cannot drive through unless the "wardens" raise the barrier. Since this seemed odd to us, we asked about it. It turned out that campgrounds wish to keep out unwanted caravans, i.e., those owned by English Gypsies, known as "travellers." If no barrier were present, "travellers" might pull into the campsite and stay for a long period of time without paying for the privilege. It seems that the United Kingdom has very liberal squatter laws. Once you are parked in a lot, no matter who owns it, you are entitled to stay for 60 days if you insist on doing so.

We've also seen barriers placed so that no motor van or caravan can get into a parking lot. While this seemed a bit strange, we didn't give it much thought. One morning we drove from our campground near Cambridge to a "Park & Ride." There seem to be such facilities in every good-sized English town. You park your car in the lot and pay a minimal round-trip fee to take a bus that runs every 10 minutes or so into the center of the city. This keeps down the amount of traffic in town.

There was a barrier hung in the parking lot of this Park & Ride. The sign said the barriers were at 2.7 meters, and we thought we could get away with that. We were wrong. Even without our air conditioning unit, we're higher than that. We didn't get into any real trouble—we just knocked off the lens of one of our top lights. The attendant helped us turn around by directing traffic. He explained that there was a Park & Ride not too far away that could accommodate a camper, and he gave us complete but very confusing instructions on how to get there. As we were pulling out of the facility onto the road, a man who had been standing on the sidewalk approached us. He had overheard the conversation with the attendant. He said, "I know this area like the back of my hand. I'll take you there." We weren't quite sure where "there" was, but we decided to follow him. He got into his car and pulled out in front of us. Then he led us for miles down several roads to the Park & Ride that accepted vans. As an added plus, it was on the same road as our campground. Another Good Samaritan. And not the last one we encountered.

At a supermarket parking lot in Cambridge, Ron took a map over to the driver of an empty tour bus that was parked nearby. He asked for directions to the highway. He got the directions and came back but, before we could leave, the bus driver climbed down from the bus and walked over to us. He told us that he had to leave in a minute anyway. He usually went another way, but he volunteered to go our way so that we wouldn't get lost! We followed him through many turns for 15 minutes until we reached the highway. We can't imagine such a thing happening in the U.S.

It is rumored that the British speak nearly the same language as we do. Of course, you may dispute that when the sign in the supermarket advertises "courgettes" (zucchini) or "marrows" (squash), or you see a sign that advertises a "boot sale" (similar to a flea market). There are certainly language differences, but it is easy to talk to people. We found that we understood nearly everything—we didn't have a problem with finding a "lift" (elevator) in a shopping mall, for example, or knowing we could put our vehicle into a "car park" (parking lot)—but we did need an explanation now and then.

The British are friendly and helpful; the campgrounds are well run, beautifully clean, and well equipped (see photo below). The highway signs are somewhat easier to read than those on the Continent. They provide the names of the towns, clearly specify route numbers, and often include an indication of direction (though not always, as we will explain in chapter 7 where driving in Europe is covered). However, both here and on the Continent, you will need to know what towns lie ahead in order to navigate successfully.

There was plenty of public transit in the UK. Although it could not always be characterized by the words "efficient," most of the time it was fine. We realized soon after we began to be familiar with the bus system that the buses belong to large companies that run fleets all over Europe. Our experience, sadly, is that the branches of those companies in Britain are noticeably less dependable than their continental counterparts. The system often breaks down, and we believe that this is a frequent occurrence because transportation inefficiency was a frequent topic of comment on the BBC radio programs we heard and it figured prominently in the newspapers.

Petrol (gasoline) is much more expensive in Great Britain than it is anywhere else in Europe except Scandinavia. (As noted earlier, however, driving distances are short, so it's possible to keep costs well within planned expenditures.) Actually, we found most prices in Great Britain to be generally higher than they had been on the Continent. This was not immediately evident, because the British use similar language for quoting prices. A cup of coffee may be "one pound and twenty pence" which is written and spoken of as 1.20. At first glance, this seems to be $1.20. However, since a pound was

A typical campground office (on the right) and warden's quarters (on the left) in the UK, complete with ubiquitous flower arrangements.

worth $1.60 or more in 2003, the coffee was really $1.92. Our camp-sites usually cost us 14 pounds. That sounds like a bargain, until you realize that it means we were spending $22.40 per night—about $2.50 more than similar campsites the year before on the Continent. While some of the increase may have been due to changes in the value of European currencies between 2002 and 2003, there is no doubt that many things in the UK are more expensive than they are on the Continent. Nevertheless, there are no hotel rooms to be found in the London area for $22.40 a night and that's what the campground at the Crystal Palace Park cost! So, for two whole weeks, we stayed in London. We had to agree with Dr. Samuel Johnson, who said that "when a man is tired of London, he is tired of life."

Incidentally, there are several other campsites close to London. Since they are in the surrounding towns, they require the use of train service into London. Train service is more expensive than bus service and seems (from what we read in the paper) to be less reliable. A more experienced camper said he preferred the Crystal Palace campground to all the others because it was the only one where you could get to town for just one quid (one pound).

The camp wardens told us that, for a very modest price, we could buy a bus pass that would allow us to take as many buses as we needed for an entire day. They directed us to a local shop—it was only a 10-minute walk away—that sold passes. Every day of our two-week stay we used passes to get all over London.

Few tourists are able to enjoy as many cities as we were able to visit. Our more than 3,000 miles and nine weeks on the road in the UK allowed us to visit castles in Colchester, Conwy, Caernarfon, Edinburgh, and Dover. There were many more castles, including at least two we really had planned to see but simply could not fit in. We saw the great cathedrals—St. Paul's in London and those at Cambridge University, York, Durham, and Canterbury—but missed Salisbury's great cathedral because we couldn't find a parking space. Sadly, time constraints made us drive past the little town of Welles and its beautiful cathedral. We visited Stonehenge and a tiny Bronze Age burial site in a small town in Scotland, as well as Hadrian's Wall and other Roman ruins.

We stayed a full two weeks in London because there were so many things we wanted to see in that great international city. The campground was convenient and we were able to go anywhere we wanted with our bus passes. Museums, cathedrals, famous Christopher Wren churches, art galleries, government buildings, different neighborhoods, and the suburbs were all open to us via public transit, and we took advantage of it. Even so, we missed a lot.

In Scotland we visited Edinburgh (beautiful, full of tourists, and very hilly), Braemar (a lovely village in the Scottish Highlands near the Royal Palace at Balmoral), Oban (a resort town on the western coast), and Glasgow (very much like an American city, but with a couple of particularly good museums). We did see a bit of modern Aberdeen, but were camped near the city in a rural area outside a tiny village. We visited Exmoor, the Yorkshire Dales, and the Scottish Highlands. We took a cog railway ride up to the top of Mount Snowdon in Wales and then drove through the Welsh mountains to return to England. We toured the cliffs on the seacoast of Cornwall, visited the seacoast cities of Plymouth, Portsmouth, and Dover, and saw the beach resort cities of Blackpool and Brighton.

One of the more interesting things about the cities in the United Kingdom is how different each is from the others. We mentioned Edinburgh and Glasgow—which are quite different—but the same is true of all the cities we saw. The English have a fondness for tradition, so each city has apparently worked to preserve as much as possible of its former self. That translates into very interesting cities and towns. No matter where we stopped, we found something that was worth seeing.

Our trip took us through the beautiful walled city of Chester, full of half-timbered buildings. In the thirteenth century, the residents of Chester built covered walkways on the second floors of commercial buildings. These "rows" allowed customers to walk from store to store without going back down into the street. (Why this brilliant idea didn't catch on in other places is not obvious!)

In Nottingham, only parts of the sheriff's castle survive. Down the road from the castle, we stopped at a pub that advertises itself as the oldest in England—although that claim may be false. Close by, in a series of connected old buildings, was a museum devoted to depicting the way people used to live—and included was a tour of the caves under the town. Caves were never mentioned in the Robin Hood legends! Speaking of Robin Hood, he didn't appear, even when we stopped in Sherwood Forest, although we did join a large number of English visitors in viewing a huge 800-year-old oak tree that may well have sheltered Robin Hood's merry men.

When we toured the ancient cities of Shrewsbury and York and visited some of the scenes of William Shakespeare's life in Stratford-upon-Avon, we saw half-timbered buildings, ancient pubs, and fifteenth-century farmhouses. We stopped at the Assembly Rooms in Bath (which figure prominently in Jane Austen's books) and enjoyed seeing the city's beautiful eighteenth-century architecture

Half-timbered building in Chester complete with covered walkways (called rows) to adjoining buildings.

as well as its Roman bath and Victorian flower gardens.

We saw very little that was old in Bristol or Liverpool. They are big, modern cities that have been rebuilt in a very modern fashion since World War II. Bristol's Maritime Heritage Centre had several interesting ships on display, including a replica of John Cabot's fifteenth-century ship. Both cities had museums that were interesting, and some architectural gems. We never did look for the parts of the city of Liverpool that are associated with the Beatles. But we loved the Merseyside Maritime Museum on the Albert Dock in Liverpool. There wasn't time to see everything in its collection, but we were able to learn something of the history of this maritime nation. We stayed on a farm across the channel from Liverpool, where our closest neighbor was a beautiful brown Welsh Cob—an enormous draft horse.

Between stops in cities, we drove through villages that still looked as they must have in the days of the great English writers like Anthony Trollope and Thomas Hardy. We stopped to see Duxford, one of the largest World War II airfields, which now has two Air Force museums—one maintained by the Royal Air Force and the other by the American Air Force. We spent hours one day touring Bletchley

Park, where World War II code-breaking operations were centered.

When we got to Yorkshire, we stayed in the market town of Thirsk, made famous as Darrowby in the books of Alf Wight—also known as James Herriot. One afternoon we drove through a part of the Yorkshire Dales, and the next day we took a series of buses designed to let tourists see the Dales without having to drive the narrow roads that cut through. We camped for a night in one of the most beautiful campsites we've ever seen—on the waterfront (though very high off the sea) in Cornwall, in a village named Tintagel, where King Arthur and Queen Guinevere were supposed to have lived. We also drove through a number of Cornish towns with names that Americans know as cities on Cape Cod—like Truro and Falmouth. In fact, we noted that these towns in Cornwall were as crowded, busy, and heavily congested as their namesakes on the Cape.

In Scotland, we visited places where people come to "shoot" during grouse and pheasant season, just as they do in the English books we've read. One night we went to a party where we were the only ones who were not (1) Scottish and (2) associated with pipers and pipe bands. We enjoyed ourselves hugely—and learned a lot about how important pipers are to the Scottish tradition. We ate at an excellent restaurant where there were over 90 different single malt scotches on the drinks menu!

One sunny day we drove through the beautiful Scottish Highlands to get to the western shore of Scotland and the resort city of Oban. There were miles and miles of small mountains, very few visible farms, and lots of sheep and cattle. But it was not at all like the sparsely settled far western U.S., which is mostly dry. These were beautiful green mountains, fed by near-constant rain and, where the slopes weren't green, they were purple with heather. We took the local ferry from Oban to the Isle of Mull and visited an oceanside village named Tobermory that is the setting for a very popular children's TV show in England.

The year 2003 was an unusual one in the annals of Scotland and England. The weather was unseasonably warm and the precipitation level low. In Aberdeen, the salmon trying to get up the Dee River to spawn died by the hundreds because there was so little water that they got stuck in small depressions, which are usually not seen because they are under lots of water. Bad for the fish, but particularly good for us! Although we were well prepared for a lot of rain, we didn't need our raincoats very much at all.

On our travels we saw some English towns with funny names—like Unthank in Northumberland and Pity Me in Durham—and drove through Welsh towns with names that we could not even begin to pronounce. In Wales, the first language on all signs was not English but Welsh. Driving back to England after visiting Mt. Snowdon and taking the cog railway to the top, we passed through miles of mountains with very few people. It was like Scotland, only more wild and wooly!

We even stayed in a real English village where all the four hundred or so inhabitants know each other; the church was built in the fourteenth century; and houses nearly as old are still in use. One weekend we drove with a friend in his car along roads with a 25 percent (!) grade and then hiked along cliffs lining the Bristol Channel on a route that had long ago been a railway line used to bring ore out of a mine.

In Holland in 2002 we had seen a lot of people on bikes. In the United Kingdom in 2003 we saw a lot of people wearing hiking boots and carrying walking sticks. Everyone in the UK seemed to be walking somewhere!

We stuck to highways most of the time we were in England, Scotland, and Wales—and there were lots of modern six-lane highways—but to get to various sights we sometimes had to drive on narrow, windy roads with lots of blind curves. Cornwall, other seacoast areas including Kent, and the area around Loch Ness in Scotland were particularly hard. Although we were tense while driving under these conditions, we had no real problems. We found that the English are much more polite than their continental counterparts, and this made driving on less-than-perfect roads possible.

We have talked at length about the differences between the two trips, but we were never really able to decide if one was in any way better than the other. Certainly there were differences. For example, most campers in England use "caravans," the British word for trailers, although motor homes are becoming increasingly popular there. In continental Europe, the mix of vehicles seemed to include more RVs (or "camping cars") and vans than caravans.

In general, driving an RV through either the Continent or the United Kingdom is a wonderful experience. The UK's biggest pluses are the language, a stronger connection through shared history, and the sense of belonging that comes with speaking the language. France, on the other hand, proved to be true to its reputation as a country full of food "to die for" and offered astounding differences from city to city. The old cultures of its various regions have stayed somewhat intact within the modern state, making the entire country an absolutely fascinating place in which to travel.

The Netherlands and Belgium are less closely connected to our past history, but they share a great deal of modern history with America, and the fact that they are compact and have a lot of people who speak English make them great destinations. We're going to have to travel more in Germany and Eastern Europe, Spain, Italy, and Scandinavia before we can try to put them into the equation.

We've been asked many times to sum up our experiences RVing in Europe. It seems an impossible task. There is no other touring experience quite like it. You could rent a car and drive exactly the same route. However, the expense of renting the car, staying in hotels, and eating in restaurants would make it prohibitive. Actually, not eating in restaurants is one of the things that make this kind of trip interesting.

On a hotel-based trip, you must eat in restaurants. You won't be doing much food shopping, and food shopping was one of the best parts of our trip. It was as fascinating to wander through the typical little stores, the open-air markets, and the wonderful supermarkets as it was to visit the architectural and cultural sights of Europe. And, to be honest, being able to buy and use the foods that caught our fancy from time to time turned out to be one of the high points of our travels.

3
FIGURING OUT THE COSTS

We began this book by saying that taking an RV to Europe makes economic sense only for relatively long trips—two to three months at a minimum. For trips that length it is more affordable than any other form of traveling.

In this chapter, we will look carefully at the approximate costs of a three-month trip in Europe for each of the alternate kinds of traveling. Keep in mind that the numbers that we are using may not be current. Our first trip to Europe was in 2002 and the trip to the UK was in 2003. We have updated the costs to 2004—but there is no way to know as we write what prices, or the value of European currencies, will be in the future. Be sure to check for their current values. And bear in mind that whatever the values may be, the cost relationships of traveling in these different ways will remain the same. Traveling in your own RV is the only way to stay a long time at considerably less cost.

We have tried to make it easy for you to figure out the additional costs for each of the ways that you can travel. You can rent an RV, purchase an RV with a buy-back agreement that guarantees that you can sell it back to the dealer, or go the hotel/restaurant/rental car route. You can even join a guided group of Rvers. Or, you can ship your own RV to Europe.

Before discussing more specific information, however, one point needs to be clearly made. In some of our calculations, we did not count the cost of food or the cost of insurance on your vehicle. These two items do cost money, but they do not cost more than what you would pay for them if you stayed at home. Here's what we mean:

First, let's take the cost of food. We found that the cost of buying food at supermarkets and open-air markets was just about the same when we were in Europe as it is when we are home. Since everyone has to eat no matter where they are, we did not add this in as an additional "cost." We did not add in restaurant charges either, since this is a cost that is entirely up to you.

Next, let's look at the cost of insurance. Since all motor vehicles require insurance wherever they are, the cost of the insurance for European travel is not an additional cost; it is a transfer of costs to a different company while you suspend your RV insurance in the U.S. Insurance costs differ even at home in terms of different insurers, areas of the country, types of coverage, and unit value. The insurance that can be purchased for European travel may therefore cost somewhat more than your "normal" insurance—or it may cost somewhat less. Here again, we left this cost out of our calculations.

Renting an RV

It is not difficult to rent an RV in Europe. All countries have dealers who will either rent you a vehicle for a specified length of time or sell you an RV with a buy-back agreement, which guarantees that you can sell it back to the dealer at the end of your trip. (See the list of dealers in Appendix G.)

Let's take the straight rental first. Prices from these dealers are quoted in euros or in English pounds. Both currencies fluctuate in value against the U.S. dollar. There is an Internet site listed in Appendix F that makes it simple to find out the current value of the euro and the English pound. If you don't have access to the Internet, just look in the business section of a newspaper for this information.

When you do rent (or buy) in Europe, you can get insurance from the dealer, but it is extra. Should you decide to ship your own RV, you'll find only a few companies willing to insure an American unit in Europe, but the cost is much the same as insurance would be at home.

In order to see if shipping your own rig is the way for you to go, you will need firm price information. For the purposes of discussion, we are reprinting some information from the brochure of a Dutch company, Braitman & Woudenberg, one of the largest of the Dutch rental companies (see Appendix G for contact information). According to its web site, the charges shown were accurate for 2004. The prices vary by: the time of year, whether or not you require automatic transmission, and the length of time for which you plan to rent the unit. These figures are for a 21-foot motor home, which may be smaller than what you are used to, but which does have advantages. This type of unit is set up to accommodate four or more travelers. The appliances are appropriate for Europe, and the engines on rental units are as fuel efficient as the Europeans can make them. Insurance charges will, of course, be extra, but this firm does not charge extra for mileage. A 19 percent value added tax (VAT) will be added to the rental charges! This is a kind of sales tax that is used throughout the Common Market. If you buy something that you then take out of the country, such as clothing, gifts, or tourist souvenirs, you can sometimes arrange with the vendor for a rebate of the VAT. But no rebate is possible if you use or consume the item within the country.

Rates for Renting an RV—Braitman & Woudenberg, Holland			
	*Low Season**	*Mid-Season***	*High Season****
Cost of rental per week	€650.00	€700.00	€800.00
Premium for automatic transmission	70.00	70.00	70.00
Discount for long-term rental (4 weeks or more)	-45.00	-45.00	-45.00
VAT (use or sales tax) of 19%	128.25	137.75	156.75
Total for long-term rental per week	€803.25	€862.75	€981.75

*   Low season = January 1–April 30, October 1–December 31
** Mid season = May 1–31, September 1–30
*** High season = June 1–August 31

Note that you can rent a camper for two or three months during the winter at a special bargain rate of between 2,650 and 3,600 euros if you spend part of your time in Italy or sunny Spain. That is the equivalent of $3,180 to $4,320 when the euro is worth $1.20. Even so, it opens up the possibility of spending the winter in Spain or Italy!

To really see what these prices mean, you must look up the current value of the euro in comparison with the U.S. dollar.

It is obvious that renting a unit for any length of time longer than a few weeks would be very expensive. Our plans in 2002 were to spend 12 weeks in Europe, beginning March 24 and ending June 24. Our ballpark costs for a rental unit for that time would be figured as follows:

March 24–April 30 (Low season)	€803.25 x 5 weeks	€4,016.25
May 1–May 31 (Mid season)	€862.75 x 4 weeks	€3,451.00
June 1–June 24 (High season)	€981.75 x 3 weeks	€2,945.25

The total cost for renting an RV for this length of time would be €10,412.50 for a 21-foot motor home (or a bit more, since our calculations round to full weeks), and at the time, the euro was roughly equivalent to $1.00. This was considerably more than the $4,100 it would cost to ship our own 21.5-foot rig both ways.

Obviously, renting is an option more suitable for a shorter trip. The figures should give those of our readers with less leisure time a good idea of how much it will cost if you should decide to take an RV trip in Europe utilizing a rented motor home.

In our case, we realized that the $4,100 that it would cost to ship our RV round-trip would be the equivalent of only five weeks of rental during the low season. We decided to go the "ship our own" route unless we could purchase an RV with a buy-back guarantee for less than it would cost to ship our RV.

Purchasing an RV with a Buy-Back Guarantee

We felt that we should at least consider buying a vehicle in Europe with a guarantee of a buy-back at the end of the trip, an arrangement that many dealers offer. In fact, we did meet people on our travels who had done just this. They had bought a used Volkswagen camper van. This seemed quite small, even smaller than an American full-size van. We noticed the size mostly because we saw that the couple who had the van had to sit in either the driver's seat or the passenger seat in order to read a book! But they found the van quite comfortable. They liked to camp in Europe, and they had done this before.

At the end of their trip, this couple was planning to sell the unit back to the dealer. They had purchased it second-hand for the equivalent of $5,000 (plus 19% VAT), and planned to return it to the dealer when they left Europe. They would get back $2,500 of their original $5,950. This seems quite reasonable, but you must be willing to put up with the small size.

We had never considered buying such a unit because it was too small and uncomfortable. We did, however, consider buying a 19- or 20-foot camper more similar to the 21.5-footer that we own.

However, we soon eliminated this option because it was too

costly if the unit was purchased new and we felt that it would be too chancy to go for a used unit.

We are very comfortable in our 21.5-foot unit, but we would probably be okay with a European unit that was just a little smaller. Once you get into Class C vehicles instead of vans, however, you find a different cost structure. Even if you were to find an RV for €30,000, the true selling price would be €35,700 because of the 19 percent VAT. Dealers say that they will buy the unit back within the year for between 50 and 70 percent of the original purchase price. If you get back 50 percent of the purchase price without the tax, or €15,000, the unit will actually have cost €20,700. That works out to be over $26,000 at the rate of exchange as we go to press.

When we asked about the VAT, we were told that on returning the unit we would not be entitled to a refund of this tax. However, if we could allow the dealer another year to resell the camper, we would get back that portion of the VAT that the new owners had to pay. Sounded a little iffy to us.

There is always the possibility of buying a second-hand unit, of course. We tried to figure out how much that might cost by reading the ads in our monthly magazine from the English Caravan Club. The average price seemed to be about 12,000 pounds, or over $22,000 as of this writing. A 19 percent VAT on this amount would amount to nearly $4,200.

We checked our numbers by going online to see exactly what these dealers were offering. The assumption is that you'll be able to find such a vehicle and that it will be in perfect shape. Our experience with dealers in second-hand RVs in the U.S. has convinced us that there are a lot of things that could be wrong with a used unit, and that getting a used RV means taking a chance—and in a foreign country at that.

Of course, anything that needs to be repaired in a used unit can be fixed. But that could be a time-consuming and costly process. We have done this at home with our used unit and found that repairs were indeed difficult, costly, and time consuming, even though we knew good mechanics and could speak to them in our own language. We had no desire to have to do this in a foreign country while anxious to begin a trip or continue on our travels.

Another consideration is the driver's seat. If you buy or rent from a dealer on the Continent, the unit will normally be similar to American-style units with the driver's seat on the left side. But in England, virtually all vehicles will have the seat on the right side. As we've said before, this makes it difficult to judge exactly where the vehicle's sides are, and on some narrow roads this ability is critical.

However, if you wish to drive around England, it is possible to find some vehicles that have left-hand drivers' seats, since there are dealers who specialize in American vehicles.

There are inventories of used units available on the web sites of the various dealers if you wish to look into it further. See the list of dealers in the Appendix G.

An Interesting Alternative — Guided RV Tours

There is another alternative that deserves a mention. You can go on a guided tour in Europe with an organized group traveling in rented motor homes. This is considerably less expensive than going the traditional route of staying in hotels. Included in the price are campground fees, basic insurance, transportation for events, and entrance fees for tourist sites. Such tours also offer special group activities. Tours are mostly one month long and the price is about $5,500–$6,000 per person, double occupancy.

We never considered going on such a tour because we would find it too confining. Someone else would be making arrangements, picking places, and dictating schedules. But it might be right for you. We have included in our list of useful Internet sites a web address for information on guided RV tours in Europe (see Appendix F).

Going the Traditional Route

Most of the time, when Americans travel in foreign countries, they stay at hotels, eat all their meals in restaurants, and either rent a car or take trains or planes to travel from one city to another. Although such a way of traveling is truly not comparable to traveling in an RV, it certainly deserves to be considered as an alternative.

The reason why it is not precisely comparable is that reservations are required and therefore the trip is more likely to be on a set schedule going from big city to big city, rather than being a more leisurely trip where you can decide where to go as you travel. It is also obviously the most expensive route to take.

Just to be sure that all the bases are covered, we have provided a way to estimate costs of traveling the "standard" way. Another way to estimate these costs is to call a travel agent. Travel agents are experts in this type of travel and can probably give you a very good idea of approximately what such a trip would cost. But if you want to try it on your own, here are our numbers—in dollars.

We figured the cost by assuming the euro's value to be $1.20— which was correct when we did the calculations for the tables that follow. Thus, if a 3-star hotel in continental Europe was listed on the Internet as charging 90 euros, we figured the dollar cost at $108.

Since the figures in Part A must include a cost for food, we have

---

A. Costs associated with "standard" travel for 90 days and 4,500 miles using 2004 prices

Charges	Daily	Total Cost
Food for two in restaurants	$ 100	$ 9,000
3-star hotel	120	10,800*
Rental of economy car	43	3,600**
Fuel (18 mpg)	15	1,350***
Costs for all expenses	$278	$24,750

*   The range of prices on 3-star hotels is wide. The charge depends not only on the hotel, but also the country. The range we found went from $115 to $180. We simply created a mythical average.

** The range of prices for a compact car was also wide, from $357 to $567 per week depending on model, features, and country of rental. Monthly rental was less expensive—approximately $1,200 per month, the figure we've used.

*** We obtained this cost using the price of $5 per U.S. gallon, which is roughly €1.20 per liter when the euro is valued at $1.20.

---

added an estimate for food to Part B below, which shows comparable figures for traveling in a rented RV. Note that we estimate fuel costs for a rented car at 18 miles per gallon, but use 12 miles per gallon as the figure for a rented RV. These amounts would obviously vary with the size of the unit and the type of engine.

B. Costs associated with a rented RV for 90 days and 4,500 miles using 2004 prices

Charges	Daily	Total Cost
RV rental	$150	$13,500
Fuel (12 mpg)	21	1,890*
Food for two in RV	25	2,250
Camping fees	20	1,800
Total costs including RV rental	$216	$19,440

*We obtained this cost using the price of $5 per U.S. gallon, which is roughly €1.20 per liter when the euro is valued at $1.20.

In working these figures out, we used our own experience in 2002 and 2003 for approximating the cost of food. We found that our cost for food in Europe closely matched what we spend at home. Obviously, it would cost more if two people ate in restaurants all the time, but if they shop in supermarkets and open-air markets for food to bring home to the RV, these figures are reasonably accurate.

To use the numbers successfully to calculate costs for your own trip, you will have to get more current information. But even if they underestimate the costs, the numbers above should be helpful in comparing travel costs for a "standard" European vacation with the costs of renting an RV or shipping your own rig (see below).

Shipping Your Own RV

Now for the third alternative, traveling in your own RV in Europe. The major (and unique) cost here is shipping. The cost of shipping includes shipping charges (price is based on cubic meters—height times width times length of RV in feet converted to meters), plus bunker (fuel) charges, plus fixed charges (terminal costs, freight forwarding fee, and insurance cost on the voyage).

Shipping via RO-RO (Roll On–Roll Off) in March 2002 cost approximately $2,000 for our 21.5-foot RV. This amount included the freight forwarder's charges and dock fees in the U.S., as well as special insurance for the sea voyage. (Although the shipping company carries some insurance, it would not be sufficient to replace the rig if there were an accident at sea.) By fall 2004, the cost had gone up slightly, and we've used the 2004 prices in the worksheets below.

The worksheet on page 52 shows what the cost would have been for shipping our 21.5-foot unit at the September 2004 rate. On page 53 there is a worksheet that you can use to figure out how much your particular rig will cost to ship. To find out, you have to measure its height, width, and length, and then change these figures to a metric measure. The height measurement must be to the top of any permanent fixtures on the roof. Measure the width from the farthest permanent points. Assume that you will be taking your side-view mirrors off before you ship. (We explain the reasons for this below.)

Once you have this information, you can use the instructions that follow to figure out the cost, or you can get a ballpark figure from a freight forwarder. (For a list of forwarders, see Appendix E.) It is worth noting that prices may vary slightly depending on which shipping line you use, which port you ship out of, and so on. The shipping company will measure everything carefully before giving you a firm price.

Side-view mirrors pose an interesting problem. Because they stick out about six inches beyond the sides of the vehicle, they can end up making the RV much more expensive to ship. When we got to the dock, the shipping company suggested that we take them off to save money. Remember that those two mirrors, if not unbolted, are figured in our 21.5-foot rig at the rate of 0.5' x 21.5' x 9.5" x 2 sides! This works out to be 204.25 cubic feet, or 5.78 cubic meters. Leaving the side-view mirrors on our unit would have cost an extra $267.04. So there was a considerable saving in shipping costs if we simply removed them and put them inside the RV.

There is another cost that is worth mentioning, and that is port charges. For example, when we came to the shipping office in Belgium, we had to pay €85 in port charges. No checks, no credit cards. Be sure to have euros with you.

Also, you cannot drive away from the dock area in any European port without at least a "green card." No, this is not a permit to work in Europe, but a piece of green paper certifying that you have liability insurance, also called "third party insurance." Since the rules for insuring RVs in Europe and in the U.S. are different, you might qualify only for this liability coverage and not for full insurance coverage. (As we mentioned earlier, the cost of insurance is not an "extra," since it replaces your current insurance.) Also required at the dock are the customs forms and other paperwork provided by the freight forwarder in the U.S.

Once you have found a probable price for shipping your own RV by estimating the dates of your projected trip and by using the worksheet on page 53, you can figure out when it becomes cost effective to ship your own RV.

If you do decide to ship your rig, your first step really should be to check with some of the insurance firms listed in Appendix E. Although everyone can get some kind of insurance, it is wise to be sure that your particular rig will qualify for the coverage you want. Then you will have to decide when you want to leave.

The freight forwarder will be able to give you information on possible shipping dates. Forwarders have access to all the information needed and know all the ropes involved in shipping—including how to fill out customs forms, which they do for you. The forwarder will figure out which shipping company has a vessel that will get your rig to the desired port city in Europe at the right time. The forwarder may even arrange to have the rig driven from its office or some central point to the dock, a service that may save you time. (You'll find a more complete discussion of the kinds of arrangements that need to be made in the next chapter.)

> **TIP**
>
> *When you pick up your RV in Europe, you'll have to pay port charges at the shipping office. No checks, no credit cards. Be sure to have euros with you.*

Figuring the Cost* of Shipping Our RV

1. • First, measure the length, width, and height of the rig.

   Cubic feet = length x width x height:

Length in feet	21.5 feet	times
Width in feet	7.0 feet	times
Height in feet	9.5 feet	equals

   Cubic Feet = 21.5 x 7 x 9.5 = 1,429.75

   • Change the cubic feet to cubic meters by multiplying this answer by .028316847.

   1,429.75 x .028316847 = 40.49 cubic meters

   • Figure *Shipping Charges* by multiplying cubic meters by $38.50 per cubic meter

   40.49 cubic meters x $38.50 = $1,558.87

2. Get *Bunker (fuel) Charges* by multiplying Shipping Charges by 20%.

   $1,558.87 x 20% = $311.77

3. Subtotal: Shipping Charges plus Bunker Charges

   $1,558.87 + $311.77 = $1,870.64

4. *Fixed Charges:* Add Terminal Costs, Freight Forwarder Fee, and Insurance Cost

Subtotal	$1,870.64
Terminal Costs	65.00
Freight Forwarder Fee	135.00
Insurance Cost	125.00**

5. *TOTAL SHIPPING (2004)* $2,195.64

* *Costs based on Fall 2004 prices.*

** *Our unit has a book value of only $8,000, so our costs for insurance coverage against loss or damage at sea may be lower than costs for a more expensive rig.*

Figuring the Cost* of Shipping Your RV

1. • First, measure the length, width, and height of the rig.

   Cubic feet = length x width x height:

Length in feet	(a)_____	times
Width in feet	(b)_____	times
Height in feet	(c)_____	equals

   Cubic Feet = (a)_____ x (b)_____ x (c)_____ = (d)_____

   • Change the cubic feet to cubic meters by multiplying this
   answer by .028316847.

   (d)_____ x .028316847 = (e)_____ cubic meters

   • Figure *Shipping Charges* by multiplying cubic meters by
   $38.50 per cubic meter

   (e)_____ cubic meters x $38.50 = (f) $_____

2. Get *Bunker (fuel) Charges* by multiplying Shipping Charges
   by 20%.

   (f)_____ x 20% = (g) $_____

3. Subtotal: Shipping Charges plus Bunker Charges

   (f) $_____ + (g) $_____ = $_____

4. *Fixed Charges:* Add Terminal Costs, Freight Forwarder Fee,
   and Insurance Cost

Subtotal	$_____
Terminal Costs	65.00
Freight Forwarder Fee	135.00
Insurance Cost	145.00**

5. **TOTAL SHIPPING** $_____

* *Costs based on Fall 2004 prices.*

**We are assuming a higher insurance rate because most motor homes have a higher
value than our 1986 unit.*

What Will It All Cost?

If you do decide to ship your own RV, you can figure out approximately how much the whole trip will cost. There are certain costs that are basic, though others depend on where you go, how long you stay, how far you drive, how many tourist attractions you decide to pay for, and so on. Obviously, there is no one-size-fits-all cost to such a trip. But there are factors that you can consider. The basic costs are:

- the amount that it will cost to ship your rig

- campground fees, which average of $20 to $25 per day

- your transportation to and from Europe (and, by the way, if you're wondering if you can sail with your rig on a different kind of ship, for example a freighter, the answer seems to be no—largely because of security concerns since 9/11)

- costs of a hotel room on arrival and departure, which will be $115 to $180 per night at a 3-star hotel

- cost of fuel for your trip (you can get an approximation of this cost by using the table on page 56)

The cost of insurance on the vehicle while it is in Europe is not included in our calculations here because it will be close to the amount that you save by suspending the regular motor home insurance you carry on your vehicle. No normal U.S. insurance will cover any mishaps in Europe. You will have to arrange separately for insurance that will cover you there. You'll find more information about it in chapter 5.

We also did not include the cost of food on this list. As we said before, the cost of eating in the RV is approximately the same as the cost of eating at home in the U.S. However, you may wish to add an estimate for food costs if you plan to eat mostly in restaurants.

There may be other expenses. After you have been in Europe for a while, you could find that you need to change your propane system or want to change the oil in the vehicle. You should be aware that these are sometimes more expensive procedures in Europe than in the U.S. We changed our oil twice in our first three-month journey. In France, it cost us $30. In Holland, it was about $50. When we changed the oil again in 2003, it cost us $46. Keep in mind that Europe uses imported oil for almost everything. In fact, the oil that the Dutch mechanic used for our RV came from the U.S.! Since fuel costs are very volatile and the cost of fuel is a big factor in any decision to use an RV in Europe, we've worked out some figures for you.

Figuring the Cost of Fuel

The chart on the next page makes it easy to approximate the cost of fuel for your prospective trip. Before using it, you'll need to:

- estimate the length of time you will be in Europe

- decide where you will start and what cities you *must* visit

- use a map of Europe to estimate trip distances

Remember that you will not want to be moving every day. You will want to spend several days in most cities, and even more in others. Figure that you will be driving an average of 50 miles a day. You may drive a little more between stops in continental Europe, Scotland, or Wales or a little less in southern England.

If you travel an average of 50 miles a day, which is about what we averaged, in 90 days you will cover a maximum of 4,500 miles. In England we averaged only 41 miles per day. The Cost of Fuel chart below covers trips of 1,500 miles to 5,000 miles. The table assumes a fuel price of €1.20 per liter, or about $4.54 per U.S. gallon when the euro is worth $1.00. Once you find the current value of the euro, simply multiply these numbers by the new value. That will give you a very good idea of the price of fuel. If your rig has a diesel engine, you will be pleased to know that diesel fuel is considerably less expensive than gasoline. Our experience is that it is often 25 to 30 percent less expensive, depending on what country you are in.

Incidentally, fuel in Great Britain is more expensive. Even in 2003, the actual price in U.S. dollars was from $1.23 per liter ($4.66 per U.S. gallon) to $1.46 per liter ($5.53 per U.S. gallon). Still, it did not amount to a lot of money. On our 77-day trip, we drove only 3,200 miles. Certainly the price per gallon is high, but the distance between stops is low, and you won't be driving every day.

To figure out how much fuel will cost for your RV, find the column that corresponds to the number of miles per gallon your RV uses. Then look at the row that shows your estimate of the number of miles you intend to travel.

For example, this table shows that a trip of 1,500 miles can range in cost from €379 to €1,363, depending on the fuel consumption of your vehicle. In our RV, which gets 12 to 13 miles per gallon, on a trip of 4,500 miles, our fuel costs at €1.20 per liter when the euro was worth $1.00 were about €1,575. The same trip in mid 2004 when the euro was equivalent to $1.20 would have cost just $1,890.

To adjust the following for changes in the value of the euro, multiply the number given by the current value of the euro. For example, if a euro is worth $1.20 when you read this, multiply by 1.20 to see what you'll spend in dollars.

COST OF FUEL
Price per liter: €1.20
(Multiply the price per liter by 3.7854 to get the price per U.S. gallon)

LENGTH OF TRIP   VEHICLE FUEL EFFICIENCY

Miles	Kilometers	5mpg	8mpg	10mpg	12mpg	14mpg	16mpg	18mpg
1,500	2,414	€1,363	€ 852	€ 681	€ 568	€ 487	€ 426	€ 379
2,000	3,219	1,817	1,136	908	757	649	568	505
2,500	4,023	2,271	1,420	1,136	946	811	710	631
3,000	4,828	2,725	1,703	1,363	1,136	973	852	757
3,500	5,633	3,180	1,987	1,590	1,325	1,136	994	883
4,000	6,437	3,634	2,271	1,817	1,514	1,298	1,136	1,009
4,500	7,242	4,088	2,555	2,044	1,703	1,460	1,278	1,136
5,000	8,046	4,542	2,839	2,271	1,893	1,622	1,420	1,262

So how much might it cost to drive an American RV that gets 12 miles per gallon of fuel on a 4,500 mile trip through Europe? An estimate follows. Then, on page 58, there is a blank worksheet so that you can use your own numbers to estimate the cost of your trip. To do this, add the shipping expenses you worked out on page 53 to your fuel costs adjusted for the current value of the euro.

To get our estimate, we used our actual mileage, but figured the costs not on what we actually paid back in 2002 but on the the current price of fuel in Europe as we write in 2004. You can check the current value of the euro and the English pound as well as the cost of fuel in Europe on the Internet. (See Appendix F for web sites with up-to-date fuel costs.) Be sure to change euros and pounds into dollars and liters into gallons. If you don't have Internet access, ask your reference librarian to help you get the information.

Cost Estimate Worksheet
RVing in Europe for 90 Days and Traveling 4,500 Miles

	Our Estimates	
	Daily Costs	*Total Cost for Trip*
Cost of shipping RV round-trip*	$ 50	$ 4,500
Dock fees (both directions)		170
Average campground fees	20	1,800
Cost of fuel (€1.20 per liter, 12mpg)**	21	1,890
Total	$ 91	$8,360

* We didn't ship both ways, but we doubled our one-way charge to get a round-trip cost. Note that the actual shipping cost for our 21.5-foot rig would have been about $4,300 in 2002, or about $4,500 in 2004 due to increased shipping costs.
** Our costs in 2002 were lower because the value of the euro was lower.

When we originally worked out this table, we used our actual 2002 costs. The total was $8,226. The table above represents what we would have spent if we'd taken our trip in 2004. As you can see, the costs are higher, but only by $134.

We've tried to give you an idea of how much a three-month stay in Europe will end up costing by providing you with a way to compare the different kinds of travel. Our estimates on page 49 for traveling the traditional hotel/restaurant/rental car way and in a rented RV foth include a cost for food. So, even though food prepared in an RV does not cost any more than what it normally costs at home, we must add it to the $8,360 cost of bringing our own RV. That will make the numbers for all three ways of traveling comparable. At $25 per day for two people (our average cost for food eaten at home), food will cost $2,250 over a 90-day stay. If you add that amount to the $8,360 it costs to pay the shipping charges, dock fees, campground charges, and fuel usage, shipping and using your own RV will cost approximately $10,610. Now you can compare that to the

$24,750 it would cost to use hotels or to the $19,440 that an RV trip would cost if you rented an RV. Obviously, shipping your own is the least expensive alternative. The $8,830 you would save by shipping your own RV rather than renting one is more than enough to ship your rig back and forth for another trip! Remember, these costs include some normal living costs (like food and entertainment), so the actual extra expenditure is considerably less than this.

To get a true estimate of what your own situation might be, you have to get correct figures. First, find the current value of the euro. If it is more or less than $1.00, you will have to adjust prices by the percentage above or below $1.00. Next, take the shipping price of your own unit from the worksheet on page 53. Then, check out the current price of fuel in Europe (see Appendix F for fuel price web sites) and convert the price per liter to the price per gallon by multiplying by 3.7854. With these figures, you can get a pretty good estimate of what your trip will cost you.

Your Cost Estimate Worksheet

	Daily Costs	Total Cost for Trip
Cost of shipping RV round-trip	$_____	$_____
Dock fees (both directions)		170
Average campground fees	20	1,800
Cost of fuel (€_____ per liter, ___ mpg, _____ miles)	_____	_____
Total	$_____	$_____

Finally, we offer our own actual experience as a kind of reality check. In 2002, we ended up spending only 83 days in Europe, rather than the original 90 we had planned. At the end of our trip, we ran into a problem that required us to change our departure day. We had decided to store the RV in Holland and we needed to be available to leave the RV at the storage facility on a weekday when the storage area was open. We called the airline, trying to change our reservation from a weekend day, which is what we had, to a weekday. But, at the time, we could change our tickets only if we shortened the trip by one week. We opted to do this.

We know exactly how much we spent because when we left the U.S., we had no euros. When we began our European stay, we got euros out of an ATM in the Brussels airport. At the end of our trip, we were able to see what we had spent by simply adding all the European charges. They appeared either in our checking account as ATM withdrawals or on our Visa bill.

There were some savings on normal expenses because we didn't need some services that we use when we are in the U.S. For example, we put our telephone, newspaper, and cable service "on vacation" and we changed the insurance on our cars to the bare bones policy required by law, since they never left the driveway. We haven't included these savings in our analysis.

So, what did we spend? Exactly $6,360, and this included the cost of food. We *must* include food because we cannot extrapolate the cost of food from our ATM and Visa charges. Our RV insurance cost in Europe was essentially the same as that of our normal policy in the U.S., so we did not add it in. However, this $6,360 includes charges for hotels at the beginning and end of the trip, all museums and other attractions, gifts, food (including meals in restaurants), campgrounds, and fuel. It does not include the $75 we paid for telephone service (see chapter 9), because we saved more than that by putting our telephones on temporary suspension. If we add the $2,000 it cost us to ship the unit to Europe to the $6,360 expenses, our total outlay was $8,360. That means that two people spent 83 days in Europe traveling 4,500 miles for a total of just over $100 per day—$50 per person. (Note: If we had shipped our RV home at the end of the trip instead of storing it in Europe, we would have spent an additional $2,000, increasing our total daily cost to $125, or $62.50 per person.)

There are some expenses that are not included in these calculations. We did not include the cost of the voltage converter ($125) or the miscellaneous charges for locking nuts and other upgrades made to the RV prior to leaving home. An example of another expense not included was the installation of a security system. Different RVs would require different systems, but, in general, a system should be available from any retail outlet for between $300 and $500.

Another upgrade you might want to consider has to do with the radio in your RV. We had decided to buy a new radio for our RV, and we wanted it to work without our having to turn on the ignition so that we could use the radio in the evenings at the campgrounds. When we discussed this with a young man who installs radios in cars, he noted that there are normally two wires going to the radio. One goes directly to the battery. It keeps electricity flowing to such functions as the time shown on the display and the favorite stations you store. The other wire connects to the ignition. He suggested that we attach both the wires directly to the battery, bypassing the need to turn the ignition key when we wanted to use the radio. The rewiring cost us nothing, since we were putting in a new radio. However, if you should want to rewire an existing radio, the charges could range from $25 to $50.

The last uncounted expenditure is somewhat more difficult to determine. Although we have carefully reported what we spent, we have not mentioned the cost of airfare to get to Europe. It's not that we are unaware of it. Rather, our omission stems from the fact that there are so many different ways of (and so many different prices for) getting across the Atlantic that covering them all would be impossible. Besides, if you are going to travel in Europe, you must include the cost of getting there, no matter how you decide to travel once you're there.

In figuring your costs, bear in mind that since you'll be going for a long stay, the chances are that you'll begin your flight in what the tourist industry calls "the shoulder season"—that is, the time period before most travelers begin their trips. That will certainly mean that there will be deals out there—directly from the airlines, from travel agents, or via the Internet.

It is also worth mentioning that it is often possible to book airline tickets that let you fly into one airport and out of another if that arrangement suits your plans. This would be especially useful if you should decide to leave your RV in storage in Europe and therefore need to leave for home from a different airport. Of course, you would have to have this information before you booked your tickets. Ask your ticket agent about "open jaw" tickets.

Even when we add these expenses to the $6,350 we mentioned above, the total expenses figure is not quite correct. Over such a long period of time, we would have spent money even if we had been at home. Since we were figuring all of this out, we went back and estimated our normal expenses. We did this by adding cash withdrawals from our checking account to checks and credit card charges for a three-month period. We found that for this period of time we would normally have spent nearly $5,000. This amount does not include monthly expenses that do not change, that is, costs like mortgage, rent, insurance other than auto, taxes, and other expenses that must be paid whether or not you are away. It does include food, entertainment, and discretionary spending.

That amount is a very conservative figure. On our first trip in 2002, our extra outlay was only about $3,350, or approximately $40 a day over what we would have spent at home—truly a bargain.

Our second trip to Europe in 2003 was equally parsimonious. Our total outlay was $8,060. Included in this amount were two large charges peculiar to this trip. We spent more than $500 to take the ferry from Holland to England and back. We also paid $500 to store the RV in an Amstelveen greenhouse from July 2003 to July 2004. That brings the real cost down to $7,060. Our normal living expenses in 2003 averaged $1,400 per month, or $350 per week. This 10-week period would have cost us a minimum of $3,500 had we remained at home. So the total extra outlay was $3,560 for 10 weeks of traveling for two people. This trip was more expensive than our first trip, since prices in the UK are higher than those on the Continent, but the total cost of the trip amounted to only $50 per day over normal costs at home. Remember that this covered, among other things, "hotel," fuel, "car rental," food, entrance fees to museums and other attractions, restaurant charges, and gifts.

4

PREPARING THE RV FOR EUROPE

It may be even more important to get your vehicle into good mechanical condition prior to a trip to Europe than it is when you are preparing for a lengthy trip in the U.S. Obviously you should check and service the power train, the suspension system, and the tires as well as the brakes and cooling system on your vehicle prior to shipping. You may want to make changes to increase security, such as putting in an alarm system, installing locking nuts on tires, and providing good locked storage.

You can minimize future problems by stockpiling extra parts, such as fan belts, light bulbs, oil filters, an air filter, and possibly fuel and water pumps and an alternator. (Note, however, that car batteries are readily available in Europe and are too heavy to bring!) Although all major auto companies have dealers in Europe, they do not necessarily handle every model the companies manufacture.

It might be worth your while to check whether the model of your engine is available in Europe. You can do that on the Internet. All car manufacturers whose engines are used in RVs have dealers in all the Western European countries as well as web pages, and they are good about answering questions put to them via e-mail. You might also check to see if tires of the right size for your rig are available in Europe. We had trouble finding an oil filter because the particular Toyota engine that powers our motor home was never used in Europe, although Toyota sells millions of cars in Europe. We were glad that we had brought extra filters with us.

Once the RV is in perfect shape, you can feel pretty confident that you won't have to face any mechanical problems in Europe. If an emergency arises, there are competent mechanics in Europe. Of course, in some places language may be a problem. We had no problems with the mechanical systems on our rig, but we did have the oil changed in the south of France. Luckily, we had no language problem there. The Dutch who did the other oil changes all spoke English. Since every Dutch child studies English in school, nearly everyone can manage to speak some English, and most Dutch people are fluent in more than two languages!

You may not even need to change the oil if you bring your RV home after three months or so. Remember that the distances between cities are short and the roads in most of Europe are very good to excellent. In three months of travel you are not likely to exceed the recommended mileage between oil changes.

Getting Street Legal

Check for all equipment required on a motor home in the various countries. (Appendix C lists the requirements for Western European countries.) You should have a first aid-kit, a red reflective emergency triangle to put in back of the unit if you are in trouble on a highway, an extra light bulb, and an international European-style decal indicating the country in which the vehicle is licensed. (Information on how to get a decal can be found on page 72.) These are required in nearly every country in Western Europe.

Many countries require two license plates. If your home state issues only one license plate, you can do what we did. Make a black and white copy of it. (Color copies are likely to be illegal in most places.) We taped such a copy to the inside of our front window, and we taped the real license plate to the inside of the back window. We decided to keep both "plates" inside the vehicle because a lost plate could not be easily or quickly replaced while we were in Europe. In our travels, however, we met a fellow American who leaves his license plate in the normal place and says he has had no difficulty.

TVs and Radios

Consider leaving your TV at home. An American TV won't pick up over-the-air signals in Europe and, even if it could, there is very little English-language programming on the Continent, although you could certainly understand the local service in England. We discovered that there is a difference between English and continental TV sets as well. There is a kind of TV set sold in England that can be

> **TIP**
>
> *Before you leave, check the web site of the manufacturer of the engine in your RV. You'll find a list of dealers in Europe who carry those engines. If you have such a list with you, unexpected problems with the engine can be dealt with easily.*

used for either the European system of broadcasting or the English system. If you are on the Continent, a satellite dish would probably get you some service. Keep in mind that you will spend most of your days being a tourist. That translates into lots of walking and not much lounging around a campsite! We found that we were so tired that we were happy with a book and bed after a long day's walk.

As we mentioned at the end of the last chapter, we modified our automotive radio, wiring it to stay on even when the engine was off, so that we wouldn't have to turn the ignition key to "accessory" in order to hear the radio in the evening. Although this, combined with our portable CD player, was enough to provide music in the evenings during our first trip to Europe, we were unhappy with our inability to hear even the big news stories. We felt out of touch. So, on our second trip, we took a small short-wave radio with us. This radio served us perfectly, since it allowed us to get the BBC World News in English every day, even on the Continent. BBC programs were on the medium-wave band.

Preparing the RV for the Ship

Some things you can store in a locked RV compartment:
- *tools*
- *electricity converter*
- *spare parts*
- *short-wave radio*
- *warning triangle*
- *copies of important papers*

Both the freight forwarder and the shipping companies insist that the RV be "empty" for shipment. Pilferage on the docks is possible. In fact, we were specifically told not to ship our clothes in the RV and were advised to remove our license plate from the vehicle and carry it with us on the trip overseas in our luggage. U.S. license plates make great souvenirs that might prove tempting.

Everything valuable needs to be stowed in compartments. We had to ship such things as our sleeping bags, dishes, and utensils in the rig, but we put them away or made them as unobtrusive as possible, and we had no problems. We also stowed coffee and a few staples for our breakfast. We did leave our folding chairs at home, because they are easy to steal and nice to use. We normally store them in the shower while we are under way. In fact, we replaced them while on the trip with two identical chairs for exactly what we had paid for the same chairs in America.

There are some things that are just too heavy to bring onto an airplane, but too valuable to be left loose in the RV. For these items—things like tools, spare parts, and electricity converters—we secured an outside compartment so that it would be very difficult to open.

Obviously, this special compartment would be different on every rig. The first thing we did was to walk around the RV, trying to look at it in a different light! The big question was which of the several outside compartments could be used to make a safe place to ship this kind of gear. On our rig, there was a small outside storage compartment with a fold-up door that looked promising. Ordinarily, we used this for carrying outside gear like hoses. Now we would prepare to lock it up, tight.

We bought a length of one-inch angle iron and cut it into three pieces, two about six inches long and one equal to the width of the door. The two short ones were installed on the inside of the compartment with the upright side positioned to just touch the door when it was closed. Each was attached firmly to the bottom floor of the compartment with lag bolts (see photo on left, below). One hole was drilled into the upright side of the angle iron to accept a standard automotive wheel lug. These kinds of lugs are the same as those in brake drums on cars, and can be obtained in any auto parts store. Nuts screw onto the end of these to hold wheels in place. Then holes were drilled in the compartment door through which the brake lugs could protrude (see photos in center and on right below). We used tire lugs because we planned to secure them with the kind of locking nuts that are used to lock tire wheels onto the housing on an automobile's brake. (The tire lugs and a tire lock set can be bought in any auto parts store.) Two holes were drilled in the longer length of angle iron so that the tire lugs would also stick through that piece of angle iron on the outside of the compartment door. Then two of the locking nuts were screwed onto the tire lugs using the key that came with the set, thereby locking the door onto the inside angle irons. The only way the locking nuts could be removed was with the same key. We stored the locking nut key on a short piece of monofilament fishing line and stuck it behind the settee (see photo on left).

This view shows both short angle-iron pieces in the compartment.

Top view showing the three lag bolts which anchor the angle iron to the floor of the compartment. The stud, shown at the bottom of the picture, will protrude through the hole drilled in the door.

This view shows the closed door of the outside compartment, with the long angle-iron bolted to the studs with wheel nuts.

The wrench-nut that must be used to turn wheel nuts. This piece was stored behind the settee in the RV. The monofilament line attached to the wrench aided in retrieving it.

Our microwave is not built in, so we simply removed the door and put the door into the locked compartment. We figured that no one would want to take a portable appliance without a door and no one did.

Adjusting the Electrical System

Every appliance in an American-made RV runs on 110-115 volts, but all of Europe uses only 220 (or, in England, 240) volts. Obviously you cannot adapt the entire RV by using the little individual appliance adapters that are sold in luggage stores. Instead, you will need to buy a converter.

A converter does just what its name implies. It converts the 220 (and/or 240) volt current available at the campsite to 110 volts. You can usually find these converters in tool catalogs and at electrical supply houses. Full information about the dealer who sold us the 3,000 watt converter that we bought in 2002 can be found in Appendix E. It cost us $119, including shipping.

When we bought the current converter, we thought that we could simply plug the electric cord of the RV into it and then plug the converter into the campground socket. Actually, it was a bit more complicated than that.

The output side of the converter (into which you plug the electric cord that controls the entire 110 volt system in your RV) has two sockets. One is a standard 110 volt 15 amp female socket of the type used in the U.S. The other is a 220 volt socket of a type used in Europe. The RV's electrical system gets plugged into the 110 volt 15 amp socket. Since the RV wire comes with a 30 amp male plug, you must use a pigtail adapter. Most RVs will already be equipped with a pigtail adapter that goes from 30 amp to 15 amp. You simply plug the RV's electric cord with the 30 amp male plug into the female 30 amp socket at one end of the pigtail. Then you plug the 15 amp male plug that is on the other end of the pigtail into the 15 amp female socket on the converter.

The other side of the converter, the input side, has a wire that needs to get plugged into the campsite's 220 volt source. The wire comes with a standard 110 male plug, but this plug will not fit into the European socket, so you will need to use another adapter. Information on European fittings and the adapters you will need can be found in chapter 8, in the section on electric service.

We found during our travels that electric outlets were often clustered around a central pole every four to six "pitches" ("pitch" is the word commonly used in Europe to indicate each individual campsite), forcing all the campers to use long cords. We eventually bought a long extension cord with European plugs on both ends. This made the hook-up even easier, because we were able to keep the converter inside the RV rather than placing it near the campground socket. Before we bought the long extension cord, we simply explained that we needed a pitch close to the electricity. Occasionally there wasn't such a space left, and the campground loaned us a long cord.

The voltage converter also has a 220 volt outlet. We used that to plug in a little 220 volt electric heater, purchased in Europe, which took the place of our propane furnace. A full discussion on propane can be found in chapter 8.

Security

While traveling with the RV in the U.S., we had never had a problem with security and we had never had an alarm system, but now that we were going to be away from our home turf, we decided that it would be a good idea to have such a system installed as a protective measure. We did not think that the usual car alarm system was a good idea, because such alarms too often go off when triggered by motion. After all, we would be away for hours at a time, and the people in the campground would be very unhappy if a car alarm started screaming while we were gone.

We explained our problem to a young man who puts in alarm systems. He suggested that we install a system that was more like a house alarm. The doors and hatches would be wired so that only forcing them open would trigger the alarm. Microphones would be installed so that if anyone tried to break any of the windows, the high-pitched sound of breaking glass would also set off the alarm. An alarm system like this—with installation—cost us $250. However, this amount is probably a bit low. If your RV does not have an alarm system already and you go to a store that installs alarms, you will probably find that your cost for an alarm is somewhat higher than that.

Once we were in Europe, we took care to park in parking lots and/or at campgrounds, and we never left the vehicle in places where we felt we were vulnerable. When we left the RV on the outskirts of a city while going into town, we would set the alarm when we left and disarm it upon our return. It never went off. The RV was never broken into, but knowing that we had the alarm system certainly increased our peace of mind.

5

GETTING READY FOR THE TRIP

Currency

Much of Western Europe (excepting the United Kingdom, Switzerland, and much of Scandinavia) now has one currency, the euro. For a traveler, this is a great boon. You no longer have to change money when you reach a border. You can use the same bills and coins in Austria, Belgium, Finland, France, Germany, Greece, Ireland, Italy, Luxembourg, the Netherlands, and Portugal. And it is easy to figure out what things cost, since you have to calculate only the euro/dollar relationship. If you are traveling in the United Kingdom (including Northern Ireland), you will have to learn to translate the signs that say an item costs 1.20 to its real value (to you) in dollars! It took a while before we made such conversions automatically.

To get either euros or pounds, simply do what most of us do all the time at home. Use your ATM card and get money "out of the wall." Just be sure before you leave home that your ATM card belongs to one of the large networks that allow you to get money when you're away from home. The names of the networks are listed on the ATMs.

The only problem we ever heard of using this approach happened to an American who had a pin number with too many digits. The networks all require a four-digit pin. So, if your pin has four digits, you should have no problem.

The bank will dispense the money in euros or in pounds, and the withdrawal will appear on your bank statement in U.S. dollars. The best part of this approach is that it is likely to give you the most favorable exchange rate at the time you withdraw the money. If you are carrying either U.S. currency or travelers checks, you will need to go into an office or a bank that changes money and you will be charged what looks like a small percentage for the exchange. This small percentage mounts up. If you simply take the money out of your account, your costs may be lower, depending on your bank's policies. Some banks charge their customers a fee for withdrawals made in Europe. Check with your bank before you leave. Also ask if the bank will charge a currency exchange fee. Both fees will raise your costs slightly.

It is a good idea for each of you to carry an ATM card for the same account so either can withdraw money from it. This is not only convenient, but also gives you a backup if anything happens to one of the cards. Once in a while, there are problems with ATM machines, and since you are in a foreign country, the loss of access to your account could considerably complicate your life. If you both have a card and one card is damaged or pulled into the machine, you can always use the second.

Although we never needed a backup card during our first trip, we did need one in England. Ron inadvertently put a card into a broken ATM unit in England. The ATM unit pulled in the card and the bank kept it. They said that they would return it to the bank in the U.S. that had issued the card, which they did. We have known other people whose card did not return from the slot in the wall for some reason, impairing their ability to get money out of their account. Since we still had my card for this account, it was not a problem. However, as a matter of security, we also used our inexpensive international telephone card to call our bank and cancel Ron's card. A new card was waiting for him when we returned home.

It is worth noting that credit cards are not accepted everywhere. Since merchants who accept these cards have to pay a surcharge on each transaction, many places refuse to honor credit cards. We found that many campgrounds and some supermarkets would not allow us to use our credit cards. Other merchants, restaurants, and tourist attractions did accept them, however.

Insurance for the RV

U.S. insurance policies for motor homes cover the vehicle only on the American continent—principally the U.S. and generally also Canada and Mexico. But you cannot drive around Europe without some insurance. You may be able to obtain exactly the same insurance (including collision) that you have in the U.S., but, if not, the law requires proof of liability insurance, also called "third-party

> *TIP*
>
> *It's a good idea to have two ATM cards with you, so if one of your cards is damaged or pulled into a machine, you'll still have access to your funds.*

insurance." You must show proof that you have insurance before you are allowed to drive your RV off the dock, so you'll need to have this proof (the "green card" mentioned earlier) with you on your trip over. One thing is important to keep in mind. The charges for such insurance will be on a par with the insurance that you carry on your rig in the U.S. That means that these charges are not really extras, since there would be no point in keeping your American insurance coverage while the vehicle is in Europe. The American insurance company will suspend coverage for the duration of the trip if instructed to do so.

After checking the Internet and making a lot of telephone calls, we were able to find only a few insurance representatives selling insurance for an American RV in Europe. In fact, as far as we can determine, there are very few American companies underwriting such insurance, although more than one brokerage agency is equipped to issue their policies.

This type of insurance is available only if the following conditions are met:

- You must be a U.S. (or Canadian) citizen; you cannot be a citizen of the country where you will be traveling.

- You must own the vehicle.

- You must be between 25 and 75 years of age.

- You must keep a U.S. license plate on the vehicle.

Our direct experience is with the Long Island firm of Michael I. Mandell, an brokerage specializing in insuring motorcycles that are being taken overseas. This company will also insure RVs, but there are differences in coverage depending on such factors as the age of the vehicle and its size. Another brokerage, the Thum Insurance Agency L.L.C., has a complete overseas service for RVs, including freight forwarding and marine insurance. In fact, it has a special unit devoted to insuring only RVs.

Other agents may represent American International Underwriters (AIU) North America, which underwrites this kind of policy, although they don't advertise the fact. By the time you read this, more companies may offer this service.

It is easier to get coverage on units of 25 feet or less, but larger units are considered on a case-by-case basis. In point of fact, we know of at least one 30-foot American RV with American plates that is covered, although we do not know which company agreed to write the policy. No coverage is available until you submit informa-

> Insurance underwriters will want to know about the driver, possible motor vehicle accidents, safety deficiencies, length of time the driver has been licensed, and RV value. They will also want to know whether the RV is rented or borrowed. And they will want to confirm that the vehicle does not have more than 200 horsepower.

tion about the age, size, and value of your vehicle, as well as your driver's license and driving record. The underwriters use all the information submitted to them to determine eligibility and cost. Newer vehicles can qualify for liability plus collision coverage. Vehicles fifteen to nineteen years old may qualify only for liability coverage. At twenty years old or older, a vehicle does not qualify even for liability insurance. Our 21.5-foot RV is over fifteen years old, so we could buy only liability insurance.

AIU offers two options:

• Option 1 is Liability Only Coverage (or "Third Party Insurance"). This policy offers $500,000 "Combined Single Limit," which includes $2,000 Medical Payments Coverage. The cost for one month's coverage in 2004 was $186 (plus an additional $15 per month for insuring an RV, not a car). That was the "minimum earned premium" in 2004. Coverage for three months cost $304 (plus the additional $45 for an RV). The underwriters need completed applications before they will provide a quote.

• Option 2, which is for newer vehicles, is Liability Coverage plus coverage for fire, theft, vandalism, and collision. This policy has a $250 deductible for fire, theft, and vandalism, and $500 for collision. Prices ranged from $386 for one month to cover a vehicle valued between $5,000 and $10,000 to nearly $4,000 for a year's coverage on a vehicle valued between $45,000 and $50,000.

You can buy the insurance either from brokers like Mandell and Thum or directly from AIU North America (see Appendix E for contact information).

On our travels, we met another American who kept his RV in Europe. He told us about a German company that insures RVs. When we contacted his agent in Germany, we learned that company's business is mostly with RVers going the other way—from Europe to the U.S. As of this writing, they apparently no longer insure Americans going to Europe.

We needed liability insurance in 2002 and 2003. We checked around each time to see if there were other insurance plans out there, but found none. Prior to our first trip, we arranged for the insurance coverage before we made the final arrangements to ship the RV, since we knew that a "green card" (proof of liability insurance) was a necessity. After our first trip, we simply downloaded the insurance application form from the Internet several weeks before we embarked and sent the form and the premium to the Michael Mandell Company. Our "green card" arrived in the mail in plenty of time for our trip.

If you are planning to visit Spain, there is one very important

GETTING READY FOR THE TRIP

insurance detail that must be addressed. Apparently, if foreigners have an accident of any kind in Spain, the police have the authority to detain them and impound their vehicles until the circumstances surrounding the accident have been clearly determined. Since you need your vehicle to live in, it is wise to have special insurance that guarantees bail when in Spain.

U.S.A. Decal

Once you are in Europe, you will notice that every European car has a decal on the rear with one or two letters on it. These are the so-called nationality plates. If you are French, your nationality plate will be an "F." If you are German, your plate will be a "D" for Deutschland (the German way to say Germany). Another one that took us a while to decipher was "E" for España, or Spain. It's always fun to see where everyone else comes from!

U.S.A. decals are available here at all auto parts stores for about $3 each. Some countries in Europe require such a decal. If you decide to put one on, it should be placed on the bumper of the vehicle as near to the license plate holder as possible.

International Camping Card

Every campground reception desk in Europe asks you for both personal ID and your license plate number. Personal ID may be either a passport or the International Camping Card, or sometimes both. The card is easy to obtain. Just write to Family Campers and RVers at the address under International Camping Card in Appendix E. Note that you'll need your passport number when you fill out the application for the card.

There are some campgrounds in Europe that will not accept you without this card, but they are relatively rare. However, the card is very useful even if it is not required. For one thing, it will often get you a discount at the campground. For another, it is a valid form of ID as far as the campgrounds are concerned. Since many continental campgrounds prefer to have you pay at the end of your stay, they require you to leave your identification with them until you leave. If you have an International Camping Card, you can leave it with the campground and keep your passport on your person, just as the guidebooks advise. Should you then run into some problem that requires showing your passport to the authorities, you will have it with you.

International Driver's Permit

This document translates your driver's license into several languages, and may be of some use in certain countries, principally Italy and Spain, but also several of the less traveled areas of Europe where the authorities prefer to see your license in their language (or at least one that they understand). Such a permit is not absolutely necessary, but is easy to obtain. The AAA (Automobile Association of America) issues International Driver's Permits (also called International Driver's Licenses) even for non-members. You just go to any AAA office with two original passport-size photos and your valid driver's license, and pay $10. You will leave with an international permit.

While you are at the AAA office, ask for their booklet called "Offices to Serve You Abroad." This handy pamphlet will give you phone numbers you may need in case of a breakdown. Also, you should at least look at the latest edition of the *Europe TravelBook* which the AAA publishes. While this is not a free publication, it could be very useful.

If you plan to drive a rig owned by someone who is not making the trip with you, be sure to carry a signed letter from the owner giving you permission to drive the RV in Europe.

Health Insurance

Regular health insurance is likely to cover you for emergency care no matter where you are. If you are on Medicare, however, you should be aware that Medicare does not pay any overseas bills. Fortunately, your secondary insurance usually has a clause that will allow you to seek emergency care abroad. You probably will have to pay the costs up front and then try to collect whatever the insurance company will allow once you are home. You can also purchase temporary insurance from AAA and from various travel insurance companies. These policies tend to be quite expensive because they are designed to pay for guaranteed travel and hotel arrangements that must be cancelled because of illness. They are not really suitable for RV travelers who plan to be away for longer than the standard two weeks to a month that the policies normally cover. AAA has a variety of medical insurance offerings for longer-term travelers, but again, they cost a lot. If you are concerned about the possibility of being hospitalized far from home, Medjet Assistance (see Appendix E) has a medical evacuation policy that covers travelers under age 75 for an annual cost of $295 per family. Should you be hospitalized more than 150 miles from home, it will fly you to the hospital of your choice at no additional charge in a medically equipped and staffed aircraft.

Guidebooks for Campgrounds

We were already in Europe, struggling to find good campgrounds, when we finally realized that there were three good sources of information: tourist offices, books, and best of all, the directories published by two British camping clubs, which are similar to the Good Sam Club here in the U.S. The best general information available on European campgrounds can be had by joining one of these clubs. One is called the Caravan Club, the other the Camping and Caravanning Club.

Both publish extensive listings of campgrounds in the UK, of course, but they also publish the best available listings of campgrounds on the Continent. Their continental directories are compilations of sites that members of the respective clubs have identified as worthy of inclusion. Each site directory includes a form on which members are asked to list and evaluate the campgrounds they visit. It was described to us as "camper helping camper," and it's like having 800,000 investigators checking up on campsites for you!

The Caravan Club has an additional publication that might interest you. If you ask for its brochure listing selected sites, you will get a more comprehensive description of a few sites each Fall. The Club itself does the investigating for these listings.

Note that the directories put out by the British camping clubs are specific in describing facilities. For example, if showers are not listed, they are not available.

When you join either of these clubs, you get the club's UK directory listing large numbers of campgrounds that the club runs in Great Britain, along with an even larger number of Certified Locations (or CLs, see below) and selected "commercial sites." You will also be offered the chance to buy the club's continental guide. (See Appendix E for contact information.)

CLs merit special mention. They are not campgrounds per se, but rather sites equipped to handle five or six campers with a varying mix of facilities. We found them to be very inexpensive and very intimate, since they are typically owner occupied and have so few campers. You do have to learn to read the information printed in the guides about this kind of facility, though. There are a lot of abbreviations. To use the Caravan Club listings as an example, at a minimum, we wanted to be sure that the CL we chose would have a "wc" (toilet facility), (!) showers, "el pts" (electricity), and "PTA" (public transit available). Note that the guidebook descriptions are very specific. For example, if showers are not listed, they are not available.

Our second trip (to the UK) was in the summer, and we found that at the height of the season it was frequently necessary to call ahead for a reservation. We also found that it was preferable to have membership in both organizations if traveling in Great Britain in the summer, simply in order to have a more complete listing of sites available. If you are planning a camping trip to the Continent, one set of books about camping in Europe put out by either of these organizations, combined with the signs that are posted in the towns you drive through, would probably be sufficient.

Incidentally, don't expect the Camping Guides to be Tourist Guides. You should have at least one comprehensive guidebook for each country you plan to visit so that you can see what things are worth visiting and get an idea of when the attractions you are interested in seeing are open.

Other information on campsites is available from the books listed in the bibliography and also from Tourist Offices, which also have listings of local tourist sites. Such offices are usually in the center of the tourist area. Since we tried to avoid going into the center of the city in most places until we were able to use mass transit, our goal was to go directly to a campground. Therefore, when we decided on a city, we would consult our guide sources to see if a campground was listed. It didn't matter where the campground was. Frequently we found that, as we drove in toward the city, we would see a sign for a different campground. Then we might just follow that sign and forget about the original site.

The advantage of this was that it allowed us to go where we wanted on the spur of the moment. When we consulted a map and found that there was a town coming up that looked interesting, we would consult our collection of books to see what interesting attractions were in that town. Then we would look to see if we could find a campground (or, in Great Britain, a CL). Frequently we would just take a chance on finding something when we drove in!

Before leaving the subject, let us explain why the CL can be such a different experience. As an example, let's look at one that we loved. It was near Glasgow. We wanted to visit this city, but there really are no campgrounds there. In this and in many other ways, Glasgow is apparently more like an American city than other cities in Scotland. However, we did find a CL in our book. It was listed under Glasgow but located in a suburb of the city. Since a CL needs to have space for only five or six vehicles, we called ahead and found that the proprietor did have room and that there was convenient bus service into the city. We had some difficulty with the directions to the CL (entirely our own fault!), but we finally got to what was a farmhouse on a large estate in a town in the Campsie Mountains. Our landlady had room for a few campers. The bathroom was in a separate part of her cottage, and the electricity was simply an extension cord plugged into her cottage's electricity. Nothing fancy, but

View from our CL site on a farmhouse near Glasgow in Scotland's Campsie Mountains.

the facilities were adequate and the bus service to town convenient.

Meeting this lady was one of the high points of our trip! She described herself as "gentry." Her family, we were told, had been in Great Britain since 1068 and had lived on this estate since sometime in 1508. One of the Stuart kings had granted an ancestor the title of baronet, but the title had passed to an American descendant of the male line quite recently. The estate, however, remained with her elder son. We found her charming and interesting and thoroughly enjoyed our conversations with her.

This experience highlights again one of the most important benefits of traveling in an RV. It is only because of the freedom and flexibility we had that we were able to meet this woman and so many other memorable people in our travels.

Maps

Before we left for Europe, we had purchased a book of maps, drawn to a scale of 1 to 1,000,000. We used it very successfully as a planning tool. In fact, we used it extensively on our trip. But a map of this scale cannot include all the small towns one drives through, so it was not a truly useful local map. If you drive on the secondary roads, as we did when on the Continent, you'll need a more detailed map for two reasons. First, it will show you the names of all the towns in the area. You need to be able to find the names of the villages that are coming up in order to read the map and pick the right road. Second, it's better to have a map that shows the little towns that you are passing through, just so that you can tell that you are on the right road. All of this will be explained in chapter 7, "On the Road."

What is really required is a map drawn to a scale of 1 to 250,000 (more detailed is even better). These take the form of large, detailed, fold-out maps of individual countries or books of maps. Each has a downside. While a single country map is huge and hard to handle, a book of maps has pages that seem to end in the middle of nowhere! You have to turn the pages back and forth to see where the road leads, so that you know what towns are coming up, while still keeping on eye on where you are now.

When we finally did buy a really good Michelin map of just one country, we found that a very good, detailed map had an additional advantage; it showed campgrounds, using the universal sign of a tent to indicate which towns had them. Although we did not have written directions, a campground's position on the map made it relatively easy to find by just following the roads on the map.

Staying in Touch

Since you are going to be away from home for a long time, it is wise to make arrangements in advance of the trip so that you can call home on a regular basis. A discussion of differences between European and American telephone services, ways to control your phone costs, and renting or buying a European cell phone can be found in chapter 9, "Staying in Touch," along with notes on public Internet facilities in Europe.

Preparations on the Home Front

There are always problems caused by long absences from home, but when you are traveling in your home country, they do not seem too large. When you are traveling in another country where your current location is five or six hours ahead of the time at home, however, they loom a lot larger; so you will want to prevent as many potential problems as possible.

Obviously, the first challenge is getting money into your checking account. This is easily solved if you arrange to have all income automatically deposited electronically to your checking account. It is also wise to leave extra money in that checking account for unexpected charges. Just in case something unanticipated does happen that requires additional money, you'll be able to handle it without

Some of the things you'll want to pack in your luggage:
- *passports and drivers' licenses*
- *title to your RV*
- *proof of liability insurance*
- *license plate(s)*
- *documents, such as customs forms, supplied by your freight forwarder*
- *International Camping Card*
- *cell phone*

having to request help from someone at home.

Paying bills as they come due can also be a problem. However, there are two easy ways to deal with that. A few telephone calls will allow you to find out what kinds of arrangements you can make with utilities, mortgage companies, and service providers that bill monthly. Most, if not all, will be glad to arrange either to charge your credit card or deduct payment from your checking account electronically.

You can consolidate your credit cards and use only one or two for everything. The credit card companies will be delighted to arrange to deduct your monthly bill from your checking account. You can tell them to deduct any amount from the minimum to full payment. Most insurance bills can be paid either electronically or by charging them to your credit card. So, in preparation for your trip, you simply pay off everything except those bills that will be paid automatically out of your checking account. Check with your credit card company to see how many months you have after the billing date to remedy any mistakes that you might find. When you explain the situation to them, they can probably arrange your account so that if there are problems, you can fix them when you return home.

The money you'll save on utilities that you won't be using is money you can use on the trip! Don't forget that:

- You can put all cable accounts "on vacation."

- You can put all telephone accounts "on vacation."

- Your cars need to be insured only for the absolute minimum because they will not be used.

- You won't need RV insurance in the U.S. during your stay in Europe.

The only expense that you should *not* arrange to put "on vacation" is your Internet account, if you have one. But do check with your service provider to make sure that they have a web site through which you can access your e-mail account from a foreign country. If they do not offer this service, consider signing up for an Internet provider that allows you to get your e-mail from anywhere. While you are in Europe, you can go into any Internet café and use its system to go to your e-mail provider's web site. Once you are on the site, you can get your e-mail by using your password. Then you can read any e-mail messages that have been sent to you in your absence and send any that you want. Since this can be done on European time, it is less complicated than phoning home. Friends and family will be able to contact you easily.

One difficulty that you do not face in the U.S. even while traveling for long periods of time is being unable to obtain prescription medicine. An American doctor's written prescription is of no use to you in Europe, because no drugstore would be allowed to fill it. You will need to fill all your medication prescriptions in advance and take them with you, preferably packed in the original bottles that they came in. Should there be an unexpected problem, you will need to use some kind of pre-arranged delivery system. For example, you might arrange that, in an emergency, drugs can be picked up by a family member at home and sent via FedEx to you in Europe. You'd have to make such arrangements prior to the trip, and then you'd need to ask at your campground of the moment if they will accept delivery of the package for you.

You should join AAA before you leave. Although there are always charges for emergency breakdowns, the European equivalents of the American Automobile Association do have reciprocal agreements with AAA and they will come to your aid at a special rate should that become necessary.

Breakdown insurance is available, but only for citizens of European countries, so far as we have been able to ascertain.

Planning the Details

Once you've made the decision to ship, you can start the process of planning the trip more carefully. You will have to begin at whatever port you have chosen to land your RV, so start by getting hold of any map of Europe that will give the names of cities in the vicinity of the port. You will need to find the airport closest to the port where your rig will be unloaded and locate a campground in the vicinity for your first night on the road. You can safely assume that there are campgrounds in most cities or in nearby towns. Sometimes there will be indications of a facility in the map or book of maps. Look for the triangle that indicates a campground.

For example, if you arranged for shipment to Zeebrugge in Belgium (where there are no tourist facilities), the closest tourist destination is either the beach town of Knokke-Heist or the medieval city of Brugge. You'll want to begin your trip as close as possible to the point of disembarkation, and these two are within an hour's drive of the dock. (Appendix D lists a number of campgrounds near disembarkation ports.)

There are a number of shipping companies that offer RO-RO (Roll On–Roll Off) service between the U.S. and Europe. Some units may be able to fit into a container, but RO–RO is the least expensive and easiest way of shipping an RV. Appendix E contains a list of shipping companies. Some ship only to northern European ports, others ship to Mediterranean ports as well. The latter will be most convenient if you are interested in Spain, Italy, or Greece.

Most of the companies use the same ports. However, Wallenius Wilhelmsen, which is a Belgian firm, ships to Zeebrugge in Belgium and not to Amsterdam or Rotterdam in Holland. Since we used Wallenius Wilhelmsen, we shipped our RV to Belgium. We had no problem finding a campground for our first night. The campground in Brugge was listed in the admittedly very incomplete information that we had available on our first day. We did not book the space in advance, but since we were going to be arriving at the site early in the day and also early in the season, we were sure there would be no problem, and indeed, there wasn't.

In July and August during the "high season," however, many campgrounds are full up. Therefore, we were worried when we left the ferry dock in Harwich, England at 6 PM to begin our 2003 trip that the campground in Colchester about a half-hour away would be either full or closed. That turned out to be a non-problem. But, since this is the hottest time of the year and also the time when Europeans take vacations, everything was and is very crowded. That does not mean that you cannot get into a campground without reservations in the high season; there is usually space on the grass. But we were unable to get into some campgrounds even with a day's notice. Still, we always found alternative sites.

Even in a huge campground like Blaarmeersen in Ghent, Belgium, with literally hundreds of pitches, space is tight when there are a lot of campers in high season. When our daughter and son-in-law pulled into Blaarmeersen at 1 o'clock on a July afternoon, they were asked to wait in the parking lot until 6 PM when all the reserved pitches would be allotted. Anyone going to Europe in an RV would be better off arriving at a less crowded time. We found that May 1 was a good time to begin. Almost all campgrounds are open by then, and the weather is good.

No matter what time of year you choose to arrive, it is always best to get to your destination early in the day. Many places on the Continent, including campgrounds, close for long lunch hours (12 to 2) and few are open past 7 or 8 PM. Moreover, if you turn up early in the day, you are more likely to find a space. Arriving early will also give you a chance to get acquainted with the city. However, early does not mean early morning. Even in Britain, most places will not accept you until 11 AM, after yesterday's transients have left their campsites.

TIP

If you're planning to travel through Europe in an RV, you'll find that campgrounds are less crowded in the "shoulder" seasons.

If you ever do have to arrive at a campground after it has closed for the night, there often are spaces just outside the barrier at the entrance where you can spend the night. Often these spaces are even equipped with electric outlets.

The best source of information about any town, once you are there, is the Tourist Office. In Western Europe, the standard sign for information is a large "i" or, in Holland, three inverted "V"s in the shape of a circle. If you have no other information on the location of campgrounds, the Tourist Office will be able to give you a list. They also will have information on public transit, museums, points of interest, and so forth.

Since Tourist Offices are usually in the center of tourist areas, it may be difficult to drive there in your RV. Indeed, there are places, like the center of Brugge, where "camping cars" are not allowed because of the narrow streets and crowded conditions. But Tourist Offices are usually found near public transportation.

We offer just one small warning about such offices on the Continent. Very often these offices are closed for lunch between 12 and 2 PM. Europeans take lunch seriously. Try to avoid these hours. In the United Kingdom, however, you will not have difficulty with extended lunch hours. Business hours in the UK are just like business hours in the U.S. Even on the most heavily booked weekend of the summer, the August Bank Holiday, we had no problem with closed facilities.

As you drive into any city, look for signs that indicate a campground. Many cities have municipal facilities right in the heart of town. They often do not open until May 1, but there may be privately run places that are open all year or by April 15. Cities put up signs for all campgrounds, including privately owned facilities. They use the stylized tent and/or caravan on all such signs. Just follow them to find a campground.

Eastern Europe does not yet have an extensive system of Tourist Information offices. However, every city has its own system. In Poland, for example, the sign "TI" is the equivalent of the information "i" in Western Europe. If you plan to travel in any Eastern European country, you will need to check with the government for details about its system.

> ## TIP
> *While some campgrounds are open all year, many open in May and stay open only until October. Be sure to check this detail when you pick out campgrounds, especially when you pick one for your first night on the road.*

6

THE SHIPPING PROCESS

There are a number of shipping companies that run RO-RO (Roll On-Roll Off) service to Europe. As of this writing, Wallenius Wilhelmsen, HUAL North America, and K-Line all offer this service. Each leaves from more than one port on the East Coast of the U.S. and each ships to a selection of different ports. The telephone numbers and Internet addresses of these companies can be found in Appendix E under "Shipping Companies." Appendix D lists ports in America where there is RO-RO service, the name of at least one campground that is within an hour of each port, European disembarkation ports on the Atlantic and the Mediterranean, and campgrounds convenient to these disembarkation ports.

The rig must be delivered to the dock at the port of departure. Arrangements for shipping are made by professional shipping agents, called freight forwarders, who handle all the paperwork on this side of the Atlantic, including dealing with the shipping company, arranging marine insurance for the voyage, and preparing customs documents. Not all forwarders are accustomed to shipping RVs and a great number of the ones we called said that they could not do it. But there were a number who do this on a regular basis, and they were able to give us good information about the names of the shipping companies, how the costs are computed, and how long everything would take.

Appendix E includes a list of freight forwarders willing to handle the shipment of a RV. Although they may not be anywhere near you, all routinely use fax machines and e-mail to handle arrangements for shipping freight from all over the country. Any of them can handle shipment from whatever port is convenient for you.

In preparation for our trip and as we wrote this book, we called a great many of the thousands of freight forwarders we found listed in various places; we found very few who were accustomed to shipping individual lots or to shipping via RO-RO service. We have listed only those forwarders known to do such shipping. Some we identified personally, others were recommended by the various shipping companies. There are certainly many more that we did not happen across. You can check for more on the Internet, in your local phone book, or by going to the library where they may have phone books from New York, Baltimore, or other port cities where such companies may be based.

When we shipped our unit to Europe, we were in Florida. We arranged the shipment with Sims, Waters & Associates, a freight forwarder in Jacksonville, about a three-hour drive from our home in Tampa. The morning we were to take the unit in, we left in two vehicles. Ron drove the RV, while Adelle followed in the car. We found Sims, Waters' Jacksonville office and spent some time there getting the paperwork started. They gave us instructions about what we should do next.

Since the vehicle had to be on the docks that day, we drove it to the docks in Jacksonville Harbor. Having shown the guards at the gates our paperwork, we were directed to U.S. Customs. We drove there, still in our two vehicles, and filled out the remaining customs forms. Then we drove to the office of Wallenius Wilhelmsen, the shipping company, which was also in the dock area.

They inspected our RV (to assess the condition of the vehicle and make sure it was not damaged) and then measured it carefully. They made two suggestions: first, to remove the license plate and carry it to Europe in our hand luggage; and second, to remove both our side-view mirrors in order to minimize shipping charges. (See explanation on page 51.) In fact, they loaned us the tools to do both. Then they filled out more paperwork, took our keys, and we said *au revoir* to our RV.

It takes more than two weeks for a ship to get to Europe from any of the East Coast ports of the U.S. and be unloaded. Your vehicle must be on the U.S. dock a number of days prior to sailing. So, after your trip to the dock, you have time to get yourself ready. We were told we should arrange to arrive in the European port between three days and a week *after* the estimated time of arrival, in case the ship was delayed for any reason. If the ship should arrive earlier than scheduled, you get one week's free parking on the dock before a very modest daily fee is imposed. Using this information, we made arrangements to get to Europe via airplane three days after the RV's proposed landing date.

Be sure to make the airplane reservations late in the process. We found that the shipping company can change its proposed sailing date with very little notice. When we first called the freight forwarder, shipping was scheduled for February 20. The shipping company cancelled that sailing and substituted one two weeks later. This would have been a problem if we had been committed to fly to Brussels on a particular date, since we might have had to pay the airline to change the date of our flight.

On our first trip, when we shipped our RV from Jacksonville, Florida, to Zeebrugge, Belgium, we flew into Brussels. The Belgian rail system has a stop at the airport. From there, you can go into Brussels, change trains, and travel on to Brugge or to Zeebrugge. We arrived at the airport early in the morning, but we did not attempt to pick up the RV from the dock that day. Fortunately, we had decided ahead of time to use that day to orient ourselves, get European money, and rest up from the trans-Atlantic trip. So, we took the train from the airport to Brussels, then another train to Brugge, and then a taxi to the hotel where we had booked a room (using the Internet), and rested a bit. Then we spent the rest of the day sightseeing in Brugge, a lovely medieval city. We used an ATM at a bank to get enough euros so we could pay the €85 dock charges and other costs at the docks in the morning. We had been warned that no checks or credit cards would be accepted. Cash only.

In the afternoon, we tried to check by phone from the hotel to make sure that the ship had docked as scheduled. Even this telephone call was a problem. There are differences between telephone service in the U.S. and service in Europe. The European area code system is different and an English-speaking person is at a disadvantage when an error triggers a recorded message. The hotel manager was kind enough to help us get through to the shipping company after we had dialed the wrong way five or six times. (See chapter 9 for a discussion of how to navigate European phone systems.)

Finally, after the hotel manager dialed the call, we were able to speak to someone at the shipping company and found that the ship had indeed docked. (Here again, language was no problem. There is always someone who can speak English in the shipping office.) The people at the shipping line gave us the number of the dock that we should look for and a description of the area where we would find the business office of the shipping line. Since there are literally hundreds of docks in an enormous area of land, this information is

TIP

Be sure to make your airplane reservations late in the process. Shipping companies can change their proposed sailing dates with very little notice.

absolutely necessary in order to find the right place. You cannot pick up the RV from the dock without specific dock information.

The next morning, we took our luggage—and we had a lot of it!—and had the hotel call for a taxicab to pick us up. We couldn't leave our luggage at the hotel because it was in an area of the city that was closed to trucks and RVs, so we didn't have the option of driving the RV back to the hotel to pick everything up. Our original plan had been to take the cab to the train station and then a train to Zeebrugge. From there we planned to take a cab to the dock. Luckily, we happened to explain this complicated plan to the cab driver who picked us up at our hotel. He immediately pointed out that he could take us—complete with baggage—directly from our hotel in Brugge to the docks in Zeebrugge for a modest fee of $25. That made the entire process much easier, since we would not have to go up and down the stairs at the railroad stations with our luggage. When we had arrived in Brussels the previous day, we had found the different levels at the train station difficult to manage with all those bags. Fortunately, the cabdriver was familiar with the huge dock area and he was able to find the dock where the shipping office was located.

Once we got to the office, an agent was assigned to work with us. It took a while to complete the paperwork. There were quite a few papers needed to pick up the RV in Europe:

- Proof of liability insurance for the RV (the "green card")

- The paperwork supplied by the forwarder before we left the U.S.

- Customs forms

- The title to the vehicle issued by our state's Department of Motor Vehicles

- Our passports and driver's licenses

- Cash (in euros) to pay the port charges

If even one of these had been missing, we would not have been allowed to remove the vehicle from the dock. Copies of everything were made and filed, we signed various other forms, and the agent sent for our motor home, which by then had been parked on the dock.

We had to wait until lunch was over, so that the dock crew would be available to bring our vehicle. Finally, our RV was delivered from the dock area to the parking lot of the business office, where we inspected everything for damage and pilferage. There was none. Before we left the dock, we reinstalled the side-view mirrors and taped on the inside of the rear window the license plate that we had carried over in our luggage. The entire process, from the time we left the hotel until we drove away from the dock, took about four hours. Since we had been in Brugge the night before, we already knew where there was a campground, and we drove directly there.

Although we had reached Belgium early the previous morning, we were glad that we had not tried to pick the RV up immediately after landing. If we had done that, it would have been a race against time. We would have had to carry all our luggage with us while we got from one city (Brussels) to another (Zeebrugge), changed money, and got everything done at the docks during the hours between lunch and closing. Then we would have had to find a campground and get settled on our first day in Europe. If everything had gone perfectly, it might have been possible, but it would have been a strain the entire day. In fact, once we pulled into the campground and found a site, we found we still had to deal with electricity differences. Because we had started for the dock from a hotel just 17 kilometers away, the whole process the next day was a piece of cake.

Our European visit in 2003 was a lot easier. A second trip to Europe had been in the back of our minds during our 2002 trip. So after that trip, we stored our rig in a greenhouse in Amstelveen (close to Amsterdam's Schiphol Airport), where we could easily pick it up and start another journey. (A discussion of storage possibilities can be found in chapter 11.) Before we left home in 2003, we sent an e-mail message to the storage facility asking it to reconnect the battery and get the RV ready. Then we flew into Schiphol and took a taxi to the storage facility. We loaded our luggage into our RV, drove to a

Restaurant at Gaasparplas Campground in Amsterdam.

local supermarket to get enough groceries to get us through the day, and then drove to a campground where we could rest up from the international flight. By afternoon, we had unpacked and were ready to roll.

Suggestions for Day One

As you can see from our description of our first day in Belgium, it is probably a good idea to arrange your trip so that you can go to a hotel the first night. Finding a hotel and reserving a room that fits your budget is quite simple on the Internet. You can use any search engine and there are a lot of sites that will come up. Hotels are universally interested in being available via the Internet, so you can ask for hotels in a specific city and get an overwhelming response. Or you can check one of the Internet travel sites. If you do not have Internet access of your own, you can access the Net through your local library. Appendix F includes several Internet sites that list European hotels. Use them to contact the hotels nearest the port you are planning to use. If you do not have Internet access, check with a travel agent.

Most international flights arrive at their European destinations early in the morning. It is much better to have a day to acclimatize to the time difference without having to deal with a lot of chores. You will need to travel from the airport where you arrived to someplace close to the port area where your RV has arrived. You'll need to get euros so you can pay the port charges. As we explained, picking up the RV from the dock is a long process and will require some time. And you need to find a campground so you can drive there after dealing with the port and getting the RV.

There will be plenty of things that need to be done, and it is less stressful to do them if you begin fresh in the morning. It is also safer, since you won't be in danger of falling asleep at the wheel from jet lag and fatigue.

7
ON THE ROAD

Using the Highways

Being on the road in continental Europe is a little different from driving in the U.S. and Canada. In contrast, it's a lot different in Great Britain, where an American has to get used to driving on the left side of the road, with everything that entails (all of which will be discussed below under the United Kingdom). The rest of Europe drives on the same side of the road as we do, thank goodness. So, driving there is not necessarily harder than driving here. It's just different. Being prepared for the differences can save a lot of stress.

General Information

As you would expect, there are major highways linking large European cities. These are the equivalent of superhighways in the U.S. Such six- and eight-lane limited access highways have different names in different countries. For example, they are called motorways in England, *autoroutes* in France, *autobahns* in Germany, *autostrade* in Italy, and *autopistas* in Spain. On the Continent, where they run from one country into another, they are all designated on maps and road signs by a dual numbering system that uses both an "A" number and an "E" number. The "A" refers to the number assigned to the road by the country of origin, while the "E" means that this is also an international highway that enters other countries at some point. If the "E" is an even number, then this is an east-west highway. If the "E" number is odd, then it is a north-south highway. A highway with a number A2 (E13) would mean that the road is a national highway marked "2" in the local country (say France), while it is also an international highway numbered "13" that runs from north to south. On a continent where the main city of one country, e.g., Paris, is only a little over 300 miles from the main city of another country, e.g., Amsterdam, this is a way to indicate that the highway will continue in another country. It is a bit confusing at first when you look at a map and see a road with two different numbers listed under it. If you bear in mind that international highways have both an "A" number and an "E," you'll have no problem.

These routes are fast. Like U.S. superhighways, they are set out in the middle of nowhere and there is very little to see when you're on them. They are usually limited access highways just like the ones you are used to, although there may be small differences.

Most European road systems use rotaries (known as "roundabouts" in the UK) as a means of keeping traffic flowing in places where roads meet and motorists need to change directions. At the border of a town, where several roads meet, there will be a roundabout allowing the traffic to change direction without a traffic light. In fact, if there are more than three or four roads coming in, there may be more than one roundabout, one after another. This system allows traffic to merge without being slowed down by traffic lights or expensive overpasses and entrance ramps.

Regardless of what country we were in, there was always very heavy traffic everywhere. In fact, a young Dutch man we know who was visiting the U.S. expressed surprise at how little traffic there was going to Cape Cod. Since the roads to Cape Cod are fabled as one big traffic jam, we thought that was an odd comment. In response to our questions, he said that there were always more cars on the road in Holland than he saw on the Cape. Now that we have driven our first 7,000 miles in Europe, we have to admit that may be true!

When we took local highways, there always were cars close behind us as we traveled. We were not quite as guilty of slowing down traffic as were the tractors going from field to field or farm to farm. Farmers were out on the roads because in the spring there is a lot of cleaning up and planting to do in fields that are far apart, and in the fall there is harvest and preparation for the next spring. Fortunately, Europeans are used to passing on two-lane roads.

We should mention that all of Europe looks to an American like a huge farm. Unlike the wilder and more forested U.S., most of the land that we saw in our European travels was farmland. Of course there are areas of the U.S. where there is nothing but farm field after farm field. The Midwest prairie is like that. Areas of California where there are huge "industrial farms" are like that. But there are also huge expanses of forest or just plain unused land all over the U.S. There is very little unused land in Europe, and it is mostly in the areas that are unsuitable for farming. In England there are some large tracts of unusable land in the "uplands," hilly areas like Dartmoor, Exmoor, and the Salisbury Plain. There are also small (to an American) forested areas throughout Europe, but the overwhelming impression is of a huge, well cared for farm.

Wherever you are driving, you will want to look at the map very carefully before you begin each leg of your journey. You need to know what cities lie ahead, including cities that can be reached by roads that intersect with the route you are on, not just those on your route. This is the single biggest key to not getting lost because European destination signs do not indicate direction. Although the numbering for the major highways uses odd for north/south routes and even for east/west, there are no signs saying "east" for example. Instead, signs indicate the cities that lie ahead—both those directly on your route and those that can be reached by roads that intersect with the one you are on. Therefore, it is very difficult to navigate unless you are familiar with the names of those towns.

The difficulty we had in the beginning was that Adelle found this way of indicating direction confusing. (She's not so terrific with maps to begin with!) As long as the signposted cities were straight ahead, she was able to follow our route on the map by locating the city named on the sign. The problem came when the sign indicated a city that was off to the side, sometimes far away and at a 90-degree angle to the route we were following. That made it hard to spot on the map, especially when we were using a book of maps where the city named on the sign was sometimes located far enough off to the right or left that it wasn't even on the page Adelle was following.

The moral of this story is that when you are looking at a map, look not only at the towns directly on your route, but at those around your route. Sometimes you will need to know the names of cities in a large area around the route you are taking, so that you recognize them when you see them on a road sign. If a city is off to the side of your route, you will eventually reach a cut-off for the road that leads to it. Drivers wanting to go there will turn, while you will continue on toward your own destination. So when you see a sign for a city you don't recognize, keep examining the map until you find it. That way, you will be able to avoid what an English camper called "the scenic view."

Knowing the map is important for another reason, as well. In the

U.S., there are signs indicating which road goes to New York City at the border of Connecticut and Massachusetts, 175 miles from New York City. The practice in Europe is to provide signs only for the next few cities on the route. You don't see a sign for a major city until you are quite close to it. The only exception we've seen is in France, where nearly all signs indicate the direction to Paris!

In our experience, European destination signs tend to be smaller than they are in the U.S. and there are many fewer signs in evidence. This means that you have to train yourself to be an excellent spotter in order to see the signs. Frequently the only signs indicating what road we were on appeared on the left hand (i.e., the driver's) side of the road. They were small and close to the ground. Also, because the signs are not as frequent as we are used to, you must learn to have faith that the last sign you saw directed you to the right road. We often found our faith sorely tested, but almost always, after going for a long distance without seeing a sign indicating that we were on the right road, we would eventually spot one. There was always a great feeling of relief at those times.

England has no international highways of course. And, as you will read in the section on the UK, England also has better signs. But they are still different from what we are used to.

A further problem is that so many of the towns you drive through are so small that they do not appear on maps unless the map scale is 1 to 250,000 or better. Such maps are available in bookstores, camping equipment stores, and department stores. The problem is to fold them up so they can be read. We prefer books of maps—such as, for example, a book of maps of Belgium—using the scale mentioned above. These don't need to be folded, but you had better be prepared to turn the page to find the next town on your route when you get near the edge of the page. Fortunately, this is a skill that grows as you use it!

"Ring" roads are common in European cities, even small ones. These are a road or series of roads that route you around the city in a ring, and allow you to exit at different highways without going into the center of town. In Paris, this is known as the *Périphérique,* but ring roads are usually designated with an "R" before the number. If you wish to bypass a city that lies on your path, you can usually enter the ring road from the road you are on and then stay on the ring until it connects with the road you want to enter.

Before you follow the signs to enter any city, "Centre Ville" or its equivalent, however, be sure that you know how high your rig is *in meters.* You may have to make a quick decision when you come to a place where there are two roads leading to the same city. One road

> *TIP*
>
> *You can save yourself a lot of grief by figuring out how many meters high your rig is and posting the figure on your dashboard.*

may include an overpass that can be too low for anything but cars. Sometimes there will be a sign showing a truck with a red slash through it. That's enough of a warning. You won't fit. Sometimes, though, the only sign is a modest one indicating that the "tunnel" is 2.5 meters high. Or, it might just be an exclamation sign ("!") and underneath will be an indication of how many meters high will be okay. For example, the sign might say "3 m." Our unit is over 21 feet long and over 9 feet tall, which means that we cannot go under an overpass less than 2.9 meters high. We learned this lesson the hard way. On our way to Caen, in Normandy, we suddenly came upon a set of road signs indicating that Caen could be reached either by "Centre Ville" or by a "Tunnel." There may have been a modest sign indicating that the underpass would allow only vehicles less than 2.5 meters in height. We didn't notice such as sign, but we wouldn't have known how high our rig was in meters anyway. Unfortunately for our Coleman air conditioner, the overpass was a little less than the height we needed. We didn't get stuck, because only the air conditioning unit was too high, but we certainly ruined the air conditioner that kept the living quarters of the unit cool. This was our single most unpleasant driving experience and it could have happened anywhere.

Buying gasoline was a "thrilling" experience! It was always a shock to see how expensive it was to fill up the tank. But if it was a shock to fill up the tank, it was a pleasure to see where that tank of gas could take us. And the fact remains that although the unit price of the fuel was a lot higher than we are used to in America, distances were much shorter.

Ferries

Ferry service from one country to another in Europe is very common. On our travels, we were impressed by the fact that the ferries were big, beautiful, and pretty new. The prices were high, but you have to take into account how far you might have to drive if you don't take the ferry. If you have a good map of Europe, you'll see ferry lines running everywhere, and not just to the island countries.

Obviously if you are going from the Continent to the UK, you will have to use either the Chunnel or a ferry. You'll need a ferry to get to Denmark and Ireland too. But you can also get ferry service from England to Spain or to Germany. All the ferry companies have web sites and all the information you will need will be on them.

Ferries range in size from small affairs that travel between ports that are near each other to huge vessels resembling cruise ships.

These are usually used for more distant ports. For example, you can take a ferry that runs between England and the islands of Denmark. Or you can go between France and England, Holland and Scotland, Scotland and Ireland. There are ferries that travel overnight to get to Norway or Sweden or even Estonia. The price for travel on these ships depends on how far they go, what kind of a cabin you ask for, and so forth.

The Caravan Club has a comprehensive list of ferries that ply the waters between the British Isles, including Ireland, and other parts of Europe. There are nearly fifty different routes listed. That gives you an idea of how many ferry routes there are.

Obviously, most of the ferries will take motor homes. However, the Caravan Club warns that the number of spaces allotted to RVs may be restricted, at least during the busiest season. When booking space in advance, you will have to give ferry operators the outside dimensions of your rig so that they can both plan their use of space and give you an accurate price. Since there are space restrictions, and since long distance ferries may not travel every day, planning for ferry use requires research and trips should be booked in advance, if possible.

Remember when looking into the ferry situation that these ferries are pricey, but that a ferry that leaves you closer to your planned destination will also save you money on fuel. For example, if you were planning a trip to the British Isles and wanted to start in northern Scotland, it might be advantageous to take a ferry that leaves you closer to that destination, even though a shorter ferry trip might be less expensive.

For example, when we took a ferry that ran between the Hook of Holland (or Hoek van Holland) and Harwich, England, which takes only three to six hours and runs four times daily, the price for the RV and the two of us was $250. (Our trip back to the Continent was another $240 to go from Dover to Dunkirk; there was no price saving for buying a round-trip ticket on one line between the same two ports.) Had we wanted, we could have taken a ferry from Calais in northern France directly to Edinburgh, in Scotland, an overnight trip lasting 17½ hours. This would have been much more expensive—over £500—since we would have been paying not only for the RV but also for a cabin to sleep in or aircraft-style seats in a public cabin. Had our destination been Scotland, however, this more expensive trip might have been more cost effective, since driving from Dover to Edinburgh is about a 500-mile trip.

The only other ferry ride we took was without the RV. We made a day trip from Holyhead, Wales, to Dublin, Ireland. The fare for

Queuing up for the ferry to Harwich, England, in Hoek van Holland.

this excursion was only 18 British pounds for the two of us. We did inquire about the ferry charges to make the same trip with the RV, and found that it would have cost £500. We knew we'd need a lot more time than we had available once we got to Ireland, since we'd want to tour the west coast, so we had to decide against making such a trip. There just wasn't enough time.

In 1996, we took a big cruise-ship ferry from Harwich, England, to Esbjerg, Denmark—a 22-hour journey, but we didn't have the RV with us at the time. We had a tiny, inside cabin, in which we spent only the hours when we were sleeping. We wandered through the huge boat when we were up. There were movies shown, stores where you could shop, arcades for playing games, a casino, and lots of restaurants. The main part of the huge public cabin area was all glass, with easy chairs and tables, so passengers could sit, snack, and see out.

When we got to Esbjerg in Denmark, we disembarked and were transferred to a train that took us to Copenhagen. The amazing thing was that the train went to the end of the island and then was put onto a smaller (but very nice) ferry that traveled first to another island before leaving us at the railroad station in Copenhagen. As we walked around this beautiful new ferry, we passed the very long new bridge that the Danish government was building so that vehicles disembarking from international ferries could drive directly to the capital city! That bridge has since been completed, so it is now possible to drive across Denmark to get to Copenhagen.

We did not use any ferries on our first trip to Europe with the RV. When we returned home, we offered the use of the RV to our daughter and son-in-law for a European vacation. They went in high season (the last weeks of July) and said it was the best vacation ever. They used the local ferry system to go from Holland to Brugge in Belgium. After waiting in a long line about five vehicles wide for an hour and a half, they got onto the ferry and ran up to look at the water, only to find that the entire trip took only about half an hour and they were already almost at their destination. But standing in that long line of cars and trucks they had one of the funniest experiences of their trip.

As our daughter tells it: "Everyone was out and about in the parking lot. There was a lot of activity everywhere. It was summer, and almost everybody was wearing shorts and sports clothes. In back of us, a car pulled up and a man in a business suit got out. He was talking on his cell phone. Strolling around to the front of his car, he suddenly noticed our RV. Still talking on the cell phone, he proceeded to do a close inspection of our vehicle. He looked in the windows, checked the tires, and stared at our Florida license plate a long time. He never approached us, but we heard him speaking into the cell phone as he made his inspection, 'Flurida, Flurida!' "

Tunnels

Getting through the mountains in the Alpine area of Europe is certainly possible. There are mountain passes that require a good deal of driving around on mountain roads, and there are tunnels through the mountains. These tunnels tend to be long and expensive. *Caravan Europe 2004,* the annual guide to campgrounds put out by the Caravan Club, listed over 110 tunnels. These tunnels lead from one country to another and allow easy access to mountaintop villages and other beautiful places.

Gasoline & Diesel

There is no "gas" in Europe, although Spain comes close with *gasolina.* In England, there is "petrol." In many parts of Europe, there is *essence* or *benzin* (or something close to it). The standard for unleaded regular is "95" or "91," equivalent to our 87 octane. It is often identified by a green stripe on the tank. Diesel pumps, on the other hand, have a blue stripe. When looking at the price, you need to remember that it is "per liter," not "per gallon." If the sign reads €1.09, that means that each gallon will cost you approximately $4.13! Diesel fuel sells for considerably less, around €.80 per liter.

There are enough gas stations in Europe to service the very crowded roads. However, there are many fewer than you might expect, given the number of facilities you are used to seeing on American roads. Because there are so many miles between gas stations, you really have to pay attention to how much fuel you use and over what distances. You can't just keep on going until the tank is approaching empty and then find fuel anywhere you look, as you might be tempted to do in America.

The biggest highways on the Continent, the motorways, or the "A" roads, have frequent and very complete rest stops. They include gas stations, restaurants, snack shops, hotels, and many other services you might need. There are many rest stops along the French *autoroutes* that allow overnight camping. Some even have electricity and a place to get rid of gray and black water. We never stayed in one and therefore cannot offer any comments about their safety or convenience.

In fact, we've heard it said that you could drive across Europe and never leave the motorway even at night. Still, there are many more service areas that offer only food and sanitary facilities than there are full service areas that include *benzin* or its equivalent. Motorway rest stops in England tend to be more like those in the U.S.—with fuel being much more expensive at the rest stops than at stations off the motorway.

However, the placement of stations on smaller roads can only be termed idiosyncratic. We passed through a lot of little towns where there did not seem to be any gas stations at all, no matter what country we were in. In fact, coming around Loch Lomand in Scotland, we found ourselves with so little fuel that we had to pay an exorbitant 90 pence per liter. That was over $5 per gallon, but we could not take a chance on finding another station close by, as we would have done in the U.S. Indeed, we drove almost to Glasgow before we found another station!

We finally learned to use the map to locate towns large enough that they were likely to have a gas station of some sort. Our rule was to look at the map and find these larger towns on our route as indicated by the size of the print on the map. There was always at least one gas station in larger places. Even if our tank was still half full, we would stop and fill up rather than wait for later. Later might be too late.

In many countries, fuel is sold two ways: in regular, recognizable gas stations such as we are used to seeing in the U.S. and in crowded facilities jammed into the parking lots of supermarkets. Highway signs indicating that a supermarket is ahead will also indicate whether or not it sells fuel by displaying a line drawing of a pump under the name of the market. Such stations are usually con-

"Even if our tank was half full, we would stop and fill up rather than wait for later. Later might be too late."

siderably less expensive than traditional gas stations, which apparently cater to trucks. Considering that the least expensive fuel was already $3 or more per gallon even in 2002, the cost savings offered by the supermarket stations is worth the extra trouble an RV may have maneuvering their narrow lanes and sharp turns.

The supermarket stations are designed for European cars, which are usually small to make more efficient use of the very expensive fuel. After struggling through many of them in our 7-foot wide rig, we decided that we would have had difficulty maneuvering into the right area even in our standard-sized sedan. Still even 8-foot rigs would be able to get gas in most of these stations, so we suggest that you check them out. We gassed up at them whenever possible.

There are two other "problems" you'll need to be aware of. First, remember that most of Europe (though neither Holland nor Great Britain) closes down for lunch. Including supermarkets. Including gas stations in supermarkets. Compounding this difficulty is the second "problem": you cannot use a credit card at many gas stations. There are stations with self-service pumps that are open twenty-four hours a day, but they take only credit cards issued by the company that sells the fuel, not a regular Visa or MasterCard. That means that you can pump fuel only when there is a cashier on duty. (Incidentally, getting into the cashier's line in a RV is also difficult, frequently requiring very tight turns.) Here again, an ounce of prevention can save a pound of aggravation! In particular, we learned to fill up on Saturday morning, before the lunch break, because on the Continent few regular stations and almost no supermarkets are open on Sundays.

Driving in Europe: Country by Country

We found the driving in each country we visited in Europe a bit different from driving in its neighbors. We'll try to give you some idea of these differences, country by country. (For more specifics about road signs, rules of the road, and required equipment in each country, see Appendix C.)

Driving in Belgium

Major highways in Belgium are free. Since this is a very small country, no city is very far away from any other. In fact, we found that we often could save money by taking public transportation from one major city to another instead of using the RV to go from one campground to another in a different city.

Driving in France

France is one of the largest countries in Europe. It has a very good system of roads. However, in France, all the "A" roads, that is the *autoroutes,* are *péage* (toll roads). Toll roads are indicated by blue signs, while free roads are marked by green ones. There are always signs at roundabouts indicating more than one way to the same city. The blue signs at the crossroads will identify the road that is *péage.* Be aware that even *péage* highways have some portions that are free, usually portions that allow free access into major cities. But when there are tolls, they tend to be much pricier than the tolls in the U.S., especially since a motor home pays a higher toll than a car.

On one 130-kilometer (about 81 miles) stretch of an "A" road in France, we were charged €14.55, plus €2.85 value added tax, (VAT) bringing the charge to €17.40. While this charge is high, the idea that we were being charged tax on a toll was mind-blowing! After paying that toll, we avoided *péage* roads.

Entering Paris, however, we found that we should have transferred to the "A" road, the *péage autoroute,* at the last entrance outside the city. The "highway" we chose from the map turned out to be merely a clogged city street that ran through a suburb on the far perimeter of the city, through other suburbs, and then into Paris. If we had taken the *autoroute* just outside the city, we would have saved time and trouble and paid nothing. At this point in the system, the road is free. Unfortunately, the map doesn't indicate which portions of péage roads are free, but there may be signs at the intersection. Keep your eyes open.

National roads are designated with an "N" on the maps. There is a large network of these two- and three-lane roads that goes from town to town. While they are old, they are generally in very good condition. They are the equivalent of our old Route 66. However, they are mostly in better condition than Route 66 because Europe's roads were pummeled in two World Wars and therefore rebuilt after World War II. The "N" road that winds across Normandy parallel to the sea, for example, is the same route that American troops followed getting off the beaches after the D-Day landing in World War II. "N" roads are shown in thin red on the maps.

Which kind of road should you take? It depends on what you need at that moment. If you are in a hurry to get to a particular place, or have a long journey and a tight schedule, you may want to take the highways. If you are in Paris and need to be in the south of France at a particular time, for example, it might be worth the cost to take the highway and pay the tolls. In addition, even though you may not want to use an "A" road, it may be the only one going in the right direction. But these non-scenic "A" roads are always full of trucks and cars traveling at breakneck speed. Although we sometimes had to use them to get to a place where we could pick up a smaller road, we found driving on them quite stressful.

If you'd like a good look at the countryside, try those two-lane national ("N") roads. They go through every tiny hamlet that lies in their path and lead into every city. When you find yourself entering a town, you will have to travel at city speeds. "N" roads will slow you down, but you'll also see a lot more. You might even see something that you want to stop and visit.

We seemed to be among the slower vehicles in France. But certainly the farm tractors were the slowest, and their drivers in France seemed quite content with their lack of speed. This was pretty funny because the French, like all Europeans, drive so fast. Our theory is that they are all (1) going to a fire, (2) late for an appointment, or (3) practicing for Le Mans.

Sometimes on the main streets of little towns there are not many places that are big enough for a motor home to park in safety. Places where one can park are marked either with a "P" painted directly on the pavement or by a roadside sign with a big huge P on it. You always have the option of going onto one of the side roads and looking around for a parking space. And, as you drive through, there may be unexpected Roman ruins or medieval towns or open-air markets to explore.

Outside of towns, there are rotaries where roads intersect. Within towns and villages there are traffic lights instead of rotaries. The traffic lights in many French towns offer a feature that is puzzling at first, but really is a great boon to driving, especially in an RV. Traffic lights on poles at street corners have the usual large set of red/yellow/green lights at the top of the pole, but there is another set of small lights at just about eye level when you are stopped. Because these lower lights are so easy to see, you do not have to crane your neck upward.

Often, when a city lies in your path, you will reach the outskirts and you will find yourself following signs that suddenly make you change your direction. For example, you are going south, and the city that you are entering is directly in your path. You continue to follow the signs that indicate the city that the map shows should be next on your route. Although this city is directly south of you, suddenly the signs for that city indicate a sharp turn, leading you in another direction. That's because you may not be able to go straight through the town. Cities are very old, and the inner areas may have

"The trick is knowing which towns beyond the area directly in front of you are on the road that you want, and then following the signs for those towns."

narrow streets or low overhangs. Traffic is therefore routed through the outskirts. When you leave the city, you will join the original road again. This process can take quite a chunk of time and may also be very confusing. Here is one place where you can get lost quite easily. The trick is knowing which towns beyond the area directly in front of you are on the road that you want, and then following the signs for those towns. Eventually, you will re-enter the road to your ultimate destination, i.e., the one you were on when you first entered the city.

Rotaries are also a bit confusing. The basic rule, which is new in many parts of France, is the same as it is here. Cars in the rotary have the right of way. But this is not always the case. The rule is in effect only where there are signs at the entrance to the rotary that say either *Vous n'avez pas la priorité* (that is, you who are entering the rotary do not have the right of way) or *Cédez le passage* (those entering must give way to cars in the rotary). If neither of these signs is present at the entrance, the rule reverts to an old rule that gives priority to cars *entering* the rotary! There is no doubt that this is both confusing and dangerous, because one has to notice the *absence* of a sign rather than its presence. Fortunately, not even the French drive fast in this situation. Be careful at rotaries.

Once into the circle, however, you have to take the correct exit, which will be well marked. If you miss it, or if you are not sure which exit to take, simply go around again until you are sure. No one is going very fast in the roundabout, so even if you make a mistake, it's not likely to create a problem. Sometimes your exit is marked *Toutes directions* meaning that you can get to any location by going this way.

Driving in Germany

German roads are good and German drivers are fast. In Germany, speed limits are posted in kilometers per hour (as in the rest of Europe except for the UK). On some of the major German superhighways—called *autobahns*—there is no speed limit at all. In that case, just stay to the right and cars and motorcycles will whiz by you as if you were standing still, no matter how fast you are driving.

But many roads do have limits. A limit of 100 kilometers is equivalent to 60 miles per hour. On some roads in Germany, speed limits are different in different lanes of the highway. We found ourselves on one road that had a speed limit of 120 kilometers (about 75 miles) per hour posted for the farthest left lane. In the middle lane, the limit was 90 kilometers (or 55 miles) per hour, and in the right lane, it was 60 kilometers (or 35 miles) per hour. The Caravan Club book lists speed limits in all countries in kilometers and offers a conversion table.

Driving in Holland

All roads in Holland are free. They are also straight, wide, and flat. There is extensive use of rotaries to keep the traffic flowing. The only problem with driving in Holland is that the signs at rotaries are small and may be hard to decipher from the front seat of an RV.

Here, too, the roads carry no indication of direction. Let us give you an example of how people give directions to strangers in Europe. Consider the following. When we asked in the southeastern Dutch town of Tilburg how to get from Tilburg to Amsterdam, we were told "Follow s'Hertogenbosch, then Utrecht." Strange to say, it worked. As we drove, we followed signs for s'Hertogenbosch. When we got to that city, we watched for highway signs for Utrecht. When we got to Utrecht, we watched for highway signs to Amsterdam. We had to follow signs for s'Hertogenbosch and Utrecht even though we did not go into either city. There were no signs indicating that we were on the road to Amsterdam until after Utrecht. No road numbers were mentioned in the directions. However, by watching the map, we could follow our progress by the occasional road number sign and by noticing the names of the towns we passed by.

There are some other conventions that are different from those Americans are used to. For example, in Holland (and also in the UK) there are the "shark's teeth," i.e., solid white triangles painted

"Shark's teeth." This set, in the UK, marks a speed bump. On many European roads such markers are used in place of stop signs and indicate that your vehicle must come to a full stop before proceeding.

on the road directly in front of you as you come to a crossroad. In a situation where you are coming off a highway but must cross a busy intersection, you may not find a light or a stop sign, but you will see the shark's teeth on the pavement in front of you. This string of solid white triangles is the equivalent of a stop sign It tells you to stop and look both ways before proceeding.

Driving in the United Kingdom

The roads in the United Kingdom almost require a chapter of their own, not only because traffic moves on the left and round-abouts go around to the left, but because British roads are quite different in other ways from those on the Continent. Yes, driving on the left means that the left-most lane is the slowest one, and that other drivers will pass you on your right. As we mentioned earlier, however, we found that—since we were driving our own American vehicle—staying on the left was not a problem. The big trick to driving in Great Britain is that the driver must always know where his own vehicle ends on the left side. Driving an English vehicle with the driver's seat on the right means that you have to get used to the dimensions of that rig, which may be hard to do after a lifetime of driving cars that end at your left elbow!

British road signs are generally much larger and easier to read than those on the Continent, and although there are no poles with road numbers on the side of the road, there are frequent signs indicating direction and road numbers. This makes for much less stressful driving than on continental roads.

Also, in situations where several roads meet and traffic has to enter a roundabout or make turns, the road numbers and city designations are painted in large white letters on the pavement so that you know which lane to get into. This is also a stress reducer.

Road signs conform to the European standard and direct you by listing the names of towns that can be reached by a particular road. You still have to navigate by using a map and finding the towns on your way. But British roads have another custom that is very helpful. For example, if you are on a motorway (the equivalent of a limited access four-lane or more highway), a sign might read like this:

A20
Brighton 12 miles
(London M2 45 miles)

What does the information in parentheses mean? It means that although you are now on A20, and Brighton is just down the road on Route A20, there will be a turn-off from A20 for the M2 sometime ahead and following the signs for that road will get you to London. The parentheses mean that you will be encountering the M2, although you are not yet on it. It will come off this road in the future, and it will get you to that particular destination. Since the road system often uses one road to get to another road, this is very welcome information.

Roundabouts are similar to those you are already familiar with. You must wait your turn to get into the circle. Traffic coming from the right has precedence over you, though once you are in, you have the right of way. But when you enter, you drive left around the circle. In situations where two or more roads flow out of the circle, you always should be in the left-most lane if you are leaving on the first turn-off (that is, the first left off the rotary). Otherwise, you should stay in the inner lane of the rotary until you are ready to leave. Always signal before you make a turn. We found that British drivers are quite polite, especially in roundabouts.

Another great aspect of the British system is that before a roundabout there will be a large sign indicating all the roads and where they are on the roundabout. This allows you to plan ahead! And when you get directions, they frequently will be on the order of "At the Woodside Roundabout, follow the signs for Coventry." This is far more helpful than the small signs on continental roundabouts that come up suddenly and without warning.

The motorways (always shown with the designation "M") are always at least four-lane and frequently six-lane roads. They are governed by motorway rules, which are not too different from the rules governing any other dual carriageway (four-lane highway) except that there are no roundabouts on "M" roads, and the speed limits may vary. While the "A" roads are also often dual carriageways, they have frequent roundabouts to allow traffic coming from the various roads to move on. But you won't notice many other differences between the "A" dual carriageways and the motorways.

However, there are many "A" roads that are not dual carriageways, but only two-lane highways. When we drove through France, we always used the equivalents of these "A" roads. The French "N" roads seemed to go where we wanted to go. These French "N" roads were always two lanes, but they were reasonably wide and straight, and we found them to be no problem. But in Britain, we tried to stay on either "M" roads or "A" four-lane highways. In fact, we tried to avoid "A" roads that were designated by more than two or three numbers. The more digits in the numbers that identified the road, the narrower and windier it seemed to be. So, try to avoid roads with numbers like A3223 if you can. In Britain, minor roads can be hard driving, especially for any kind of camping vehicle, which is always a lot wider than the small European-style car!

Local roads tend to be quite narrow. To make matters worse, they are also frequently bordered by obstacles. Few have even small shoulder areas, and there are often other impediments: three-foot-high stone walls; dense hedges that may hide stone walls but are quite forbidding even without them; and frequently ruts on the sides of the road. Many are literally single tracks that do not even boast a white line down the center. They are too narrow for that, and when two (usually small) cars meet, one may have to back up until the other can pass! Fortunately, if you are a camper van or a truck, or if you are going up a hill, you have precedence. This is white-knuckle driving, however, and you should not plan to travel long distances on such roads. Frequently the roads leading to a campground are these narrow ribbons, but campsites are usually not too far off the main roads.

Several times in our travels, however, we did find ourselves going what seemed like miles on such roads. One time was in Cornwall, where we stayed in a campground on the cliffs of Tintagel. Another was in Kent, where the first campground we tried near the ferry port of Dover was literally miles from the main road. We really had no problem on these narrow roads; we worried about oncoming traffic more than we saw such oncoming traffic. But it does diminish one's enjoyment of the countryside.

In Yorkshire, we decided that driving along the Dales (which are low mountains or high hills) would be pressing our luck. Instead, we opted to take a series of bus rides offered by the local authorities. By getting on four different buses, we were able to see a great deal of the Yorkshire Moors. The bus ride confirmed our original impression. We didn't want to drive those roads any more than we needed to. The roads were narrow, very curvy, and frequently climbed either steeply up or veered steeply down. Also, the beautiful little towns we visited had no parking spaces for vehicles as big as ours. Had we used our RV, neither of us would have been able to relax and enjoy the beautiful scenery of the Dales the way we could on a bus ride.

British roads are not only narrow but also frequently full of curves, many of them blind curves. We laughed nervously when we first saw a sign saying "Oncoming Vehicles in Middle of Road," but we soon realized that a lorry (truck) or other large rig coming the other way could not make the turn without impinging on our lane. This might not have been so bad for someone traveling in a small

TIP

In places where the roads are narrow, curvy, or steep, you'll have a better chance of enjoying the sights if you park the RV and use public transportation.

European car, but it certainly kept us on our toes. And there were times when we were the offending vehicle.

The funny thing is that people in those areas where the roads are worst seem to be quite proud of them. One lady specifically said that the government is spoiling their roads. She seemed to think that there were not so many curves any more. There were plenty of curves for us!

Despite this caveat, however, we drove more than 3,000 miles through Britain, saw most of what we wanted to see and, despite our large size and the roads' small size, we had no problems. We made use of public transportation wherever we could. If the campground did not have good service, we looked for a Park & Ride (P&R). In many British cities there are guarded lots on the outskirts of town. These are set up to encourage people to take bus rides into the city and then bus rides back out to their cars. The fares for these facilities were always very inexpensive, and the service was excellent.

Incidentally, when we returned to the Continent, we realized that there were also P&R centers in many Benelux cities, though there seemed to be none in France. However, public transportation in the cities of Holland and Belgium is so good that we preferred to leave the camper in the campground and take a bus. This was not always true in Great Britain, where we often found that the nearest bus stop was too far from the campsite for us.

There was a problem with some P&R facilities, though. Occasionally there were barriers hung 2.3 meters high. These prevented us from using some P&Rs. Fortunately, there often were other P&R facilities that could accommodate us.

It is worth mentioning that London also has a "ring road"—sort of. It deserves description. We used this "road" when we traveled from the Crystal Palace campground in the southeast corner of the city to the Royal Botanical Gardens at Kew just a few kilometers southwest of London. The instructions on our little map showed the ring road. The reality is that there is no ring road. By the time London planners realized that they needed such a road, there was no room to build one! So they simply designated a series of connected London streets as the ring road and let it go at that. We traveled on really crowded city streets for one hour and forty minutes and never got on a highway.

Road Signs

Because Europeans speak so many languages, the road signs are all international and most of them are easy to figure out. A couple of them, however, did cause us some minor confusion. For example, a circular sign showing two cars, a red one on the left and a black one on the right, is simply a way of advising the motorist that no passing is allowed. A circular sign showing a single car in red means do not enter. Another problematic sign was the one indicating that the town you wanted to reach was straight ahead.

In the United States, all the signs that tell you that the highway continues straight ahead are the same. If the sign is at road level, it shows an arrow pointing to the sky. If the sign is above the road, the arrow points straight down. These arrows follow a convention that everyone is supposed to understand. They tell the American motorist to continue to go straight. Parts of Europe use a different sign for "straight ahead" and it is confusing until you get familiar with it.

Road sign arrows indicating that you should continue to go straight are on the right side of the road and almost at right angles to the road, pointing left. It is very easy to mistake them for signs indicating that the main road turns left and you should take a left turn to your destination. After we made several wrong turns, we realized that the sign pointing left is the equivalent of an arrow pointing to the sky when it is on the far side of the intersection. If it is on the near side of the intersection, it indeed means that you should turn left. This can be quite confusing.

We met several other campers who told us that they had "taken the scenic route" (i.e., gone the wrong way) because they also had not at first realized that "straight ahead" arrows point left.

Fortunately, most other road signs are easily deciphered. For example, as you drive into a city, there may be a stylized tent and/or a caravan displayed on a sign. This indicates a campground. Gasoline stations will be indicated with a stylized gas pump on a sign. Areas where there are industrial installations or commercial malls will be identified by a drawing of a factory and smoke stacks. In France, the distance to a place is sometimes indicated in time rather than in kilometers. A tourist attraction or a supermarket will be "15 mn direction Lyon" for example, meaning that it is a 15-minute drive on the road to Lyon. (Note that there is no route number mentioned.)

Keep in mind the story about directions from Tilburg to Amsterdam. Very little is made of the route numbers in any European country. It was suggested to us that the reason for this is that, in the past, people rarely used to go far from home. So, if you were in Glastonbury and wanted to go to Coventry, you would take the road to Worcester and then go right toward Coventry.

Sometimes, usually in a rotary, there is no sign that shows the name of the town you have been driving toward. In these cases there is always a sign that conveys the information that "this exit from the rotary will take you to all roads going to all directions." In France and in the parts of Belgium where French is spoken, such an exit will be labeled *Toutes directions*. In the Flemish-speaking parts of Belgium, in Holland, and in Germany, the words will be something similar to *alle Richtungen*. This tells you that it is safe to take that exit for the town you wish to reach, even though the town's name does not appear on the sign.

One sign that we found confusing in France was *Tout droit*. Since *droit* is right and *tout* means all, we thought it meant "make a right," but it turned out to mean "straight ahead."

Signs in Britain are much easier to follow than signs in other countries. Further, there are always advance warnings of upcoming changes, giving you a chance to adjust. And, in a situation where you are entering a road, the signs will indicate direction. If you enter a motorway that runs north-south, the sign will not only give you the name of a city but also say "north" or "south." Very helpful when you have to decide quickly which way to go!

Our favorite British road sign.

Our favorite British sign was the previously mentioned warning "Oncoming Vehicles in Middle of Road." But we were also fond of the warnings on some side streets: "Beware of Children," "Kill Your Speed," and "30 is Enough," which had to do with speed limits. Driving on the Salisbury Plain, which is almost all wasteland, we saw signs indicating that there were Army camps just off the highway, and we were amused to find signs similar to the signs you may be used to at home, warning of deer crossing the highway. But here, instead of a deer, there was a picture of a tank! We never saw one, but we certainly would beware of one if we saw it!

Some highways, both on the Continent and in the UK, had large white chevrons painted on the pavement. At the side of the road, there were signs indicating how many of these chevrons you should see between you and the car in front of you. Depending on the speed limit, two or three chevrons visible between you and the car in front is recommended for safety.

Frequently, especially in France, there are signs just saying "!" or *Rappel* (which means "remember"). I can recall at least one "!" (meaning "pay attention") serving as a a warning that frogs often cross the highway (indicated by a line drawing of a frog) and one warning of birds! Usually, though, the sign *Rappel* indicates that conditions have changed and that you are to resume the previously posted speed limit.

There was another interesting set of road signs. In some places in France, we would drive past a sign that said something like "Ten people died on this road since 1996. Be careful." As you drove on, a black, life-size wooden silhouette of a person would appear at the side of the road. It might have a bright red lightning bolt painted across its face, or it might be missing its head or have red marks through its heart. We eventually realized that these were indications of scenes of accidents and how people had died. It was a sobering thought, and probably an effective way to slow people down.

Europeans drive very fast. If you are a bit too slow, they will drive around you, sometimes in amazing ways. For example, while we were driving through southern France, we lost track of the signs that indicated the direction that through traffic should follow. As a result, we ended up in a narrow dead end, at the beach, in an area packed with beach stores and pedestrians. While we were slowly and carefully trying to back up and turn around in a very tight space with sidewalks full of people on either side of us, cars impatient to pass us were driving around us, half on the sidewalk.

On national roads and smaller highways on the Continent, this kind of driving can be a problem. But the rules are really the same as on any two-lane road in the U.S. The traffic that is being impeded by your lack of speed will wait until the road is clear and pull out and around you. On the main motorways there is no problem at all. Since these have four to six lanes, just stay to the right. The left is for passing only, and the other cars will pass in that left-hand lane. In fact, driving along in the left lane is a traffic violation. "Passing lane" does really mean only for passing. Of course, on British roads, you drive on the left and others pass you on the right, but the concept is the same.

You can find a list of standard signs in some map books, in guidebooks, or on the Internet. For signs that differ from the norm in each of the Western European countries, see Appendix C. In addition to listing specific signs that may be different in a given country, the fact sheets on each nation identify the local way of indicating types of fuel and provide a short list of required equipment and national rules of the road.

8
The Campground Scene

Finding a Campground

Many European campgrounds are in cities. This means that once you've picked a place to visit you can almost always find a campground that is convenient to it.

One way of finding a campground is to drive directly into the center of town and get the names of local campgrounds from the Tourist Office. This method may pose problems, however, since it requires driving on streets that may be difficult to maneuver in a large vehicle and parking may be limited.

There are easier ways of finding campgrounds. Camping guides that list a number of campgrounds may be the most useful. In the United States, camping guides are the size of telephone books. This is not true in Europe, although the guides put out by the English caravan clubs do have extensive listings in both their UK publications and those dealing with continental campgrounds (see page 74). The bibliography lists several books offering suggestions about campgrounds. While some may list only one or two campgrounds in a city, the directions are usually good.

It does require a little research to find a campground near the place you want to visit next. The first challenge is determining if there is a campground nearby. The second is physically finding the campground.

First, of course, you need to pick the next place you want to visit. If you are going to visit a city, you will need to consult both a map and a guidebook covering the city and its sights. Both of these sources may also show the names of campgrounds. (Note that in England some public libraries have telephone books for all English cities and you can use these books to find campground listings.) The next thing you'll need to do is consult a guide to campgrounds to see if there are other listings for the city you want to visit. If the city is included in the guide, you should find a roster of campground names with such information as exact location and facilities.

Using the information you've obtained from maps and guidebooks, you can start driving toward the city. As you approach your destination, you may see a road sign for a campground that may or may not be on your list. This sign may include the number of stars assigned to the campground by the government Tourist Office. The stars indicate how fancy the campground facilities are. The range is from one star to five stars, just like the hotel rating system. A new facility with up-to-date sanitary arrangements and such amenities as a swimming pool, a game arcade, or a restaurant will have the most stars. If this campground was not on your list, you'll need to make a decision. You can follow the directions on the sign and find that particular campground or you can continue on your way to the campground you had originally picked.

Sometimes you may make a mistake. Especially on our first trip, we often did not have enough information in the sources we had with us to direct our search. In fact, we once ended up staying at a campground miles outside the city of Lyon, spending $25 round-trip for the suburban bus and then the metro in order to get into town. That was the only time that we stayed so far out of town, and better sources of information would have told us that there are two campgrounds in Lyon itself!

In the U.S., a lack of information might mean that you should rethink your destination. But in Europe, you've got more resources. First of all, if you are lucky, you will see signs outside the city for countryside campsites. In France, we once found a beautiful campground by following a homemade sign that said *Camping a la ferme* (at a farm). In this particular case, we weren't interested in being close to a city. We just wanted a safe and comfortable place for the night. There would be time enough to drive on in the morning! We enjoyed that campsite, and thereafter were very conscious as we approached other cities that there were many such signs along the roads.

A good map will tell you how far away the little town you are passing through will be from the city you want to visit. You can always stop and ask about facilities, costs, and public transit to the city or parking lots that will accommodate a large vehicle such as yours.

> To find campgrounds in Europe, you'll want to use
> - *maps*
> - *camping guides*
> - *city guides*
> - *road signs*

Then you can make a choice. Either choose to continue driving toward some preferred destination or follow a campground sign as you drive in toward the city. If no campground sign appears, there certainly will be a sign for the center of the city (Centre Ville, etc.) and eventually a sign for the Tourist Office (either a sign reading "i" or, in Holland, the circle of inverted "V"s). Here at least one person is likely to speak English. Many offices have printed booklets listing facilities. In any case, they will know where all the campsites in the area are located. In fact, we went into the Tourist Office in several towns where we had been unable to find campsites on our own and were given listings of a good many campgrounds in the area. In England we even found a campground while in the library, where we noticed telephone directories from all over the United Kingdom. The basic difficulty is not a lack of campsites, but the lack of comprehensive listings of campsites.

On our first trip, we had only two inadequate campground guides. As a result, we would often trust to luck. In most cities, we would find the universal signs. These signs would indicate a direction and, if we stubbornly followed that direction without deviation (no matter how long it took), we usually reached a campground, as we have already said. The problem is one has to have a great deal of faith in the authorities that placed the sign there. Signs are used sparingly. If you don't need to make a turn, there will be no further signs. You're just supposed to keep going. Sometimes the campgrounds will be quite far away from the original sign. That's why it is necessary to show stubborn persistence in following the direction indicated by the last sign.

In Europe, where it is even more common to go camping than it is in the U.S., many cities maintain their own facilities. These municipal campgrounds may not even be listed in campsite guides. They range from primitive to comparable to any other facility. But look for them to open for business only on May 1. They cater mostly to Europeans on vacation during the summer months. The Tourist Office will always tell you where they are located and a good number of them will be either signposted at the side of the road or listed in the guides. They usually have two advantages: first, they are within the city limits and, second, they are usually quite inexpensive. In fact, the least expensive campground we stayed at was the municipal campground in Antwerp, which cost the munificent sum of €5.28 per day including electricity! It is important to note that, while we would not expect to find a campground closer than 20 miles outside of Chicago, we would expect to find at least one inside almost every city in Europe.

Our trip to Aix-en-Provence is a good illustration of the difficulties that can be overcome by a good guidebook. We decided to visit Aix because we hated to leave Provence. Also we remembered it because the city figured prominently in a poem we had read in our youth. We had with us only a very incomplete guide to campgrounds, but it listed a campground in Aix. The instructions, however, were awful. We took the "scenic route," going round and round, getting nowhere, and finally decided to bypass the city. When we got home, too late to help on our trip, we found a listing (and a good map) and equally good directions in the Caravan Club directory for an additional two sites. What a difference a good book would have made!

But, having solved the problem of where the campground is, what will you find? There are differences between most U.S. and European facilities. These range from the services they offer (e.g., electricity, water) to the kinds of facilities that they have (e.g., laundry, restaurants, stores). However, there is no one-size-fits-all description of European campgrounds. We stayed in huge facilities like Blaarmeerson in Ghent, Belgium, and in a tiny campground on a pretty river in a rural Belgian community. The latter consisted of the proprietor's house, two cabins, and room for four transient visitors. This "mom and pop" operation was clean and pretty, and the proprietors were very proud that they supplied a full 10 amps of electricity, not like *les Français*. They welcomed us warmly, pleased to have such exotic visitors. Most of their business came from Dutch campers. We were the first Americans to ask for a pitch.

In the section on guidebooks for campgrounds (page 74), we mentioned the availability of the Certified Locations all over the British Isles. These, too, were small affairs, and they frequently had limited services, but they were fun!

Contrast these quiet spots with Blaarmeerson, which housed hundreds of camping units. It had an entire section set aside for tent campers, as well as cabins for rental by backpackers and others. There was a grocery, a bar, a game room, and a "Friterie" that sold *frites* (fried potatoes), ice cream, and fast food. There was even a full-service restaurant. The campground was part of the municipal park system, so it also had all kinds of outdoor sports facilities.

Many campground stores in Holland, Belgium, France, and the UK offered fresh baked bread every morning. One of the delights in the Bois de Boulogne campground in Paris was the very fresh, crispy baguettes that one could have for breakfast each day. It was very pleasant to watch a steady stream of people carrying several of these loaves on their way from the store to their campers.

Electric Service

One of the biggest differences between campgrounds in the U.S. and those in Europe is the electrical service. As any traveler knows, the electric system in Europe is 220 volts. What you may not know is that service in the United Kingdom is 240 volts. On the other hand, all appliances, including the battery charger and AC to DC converters made in America and common in American motor homes, run on 110 volts.

It is possible to buy a current converter in the United States that will allow you to convert the 220 or 240 volt current available in European campgrounds to the 110 current needed to run your RV. We discussed this type of converter in chapter 4, "Preparing the RV for Europe." As we mentioned in that chapter, we thought we could simply plug the RV's electric cord into the converter's socket and then plug the converter's cord into the campground socket. That was not quite true. We also needed adapters, because the fittings in campgrounds in different European countries vary.

The fittings in most campgrounds require a rather large three-pronged plug, with two smaller prongs for the current and a larger one for the ground. The top and center photos on the left show the female socket found in most European campgrounds and the large plug that is required.

While we were in Belgium, we bought an adapter that would enable us to use this type of fitting. It cost us the equivalent of $10. Unfortunately, however, although the fitting we have just described is a standard European fitting, it is not yet universal.

Some campgrounds in France, for example, have receptacles that use a standard household two-prong 220-volt plug. This means that you'll also need a pigtail adapter that has a receptacle for the large, three-pronged plug described above and a wire that can plug into the French two-pronged one. We bought such an adapter in a hardware store in France. We were concerned as we walked into the store that our primitive French would be inadequate for describing what we needed, but apparently the words are similar enough in both languages that the owner was able to give us the correct adapter without a problem. The bottom right photo shows the adapter we bought.

In some of the Certified Locations in the UK, the only sockets available were the standard UK type, which has vertical straight slots instead of round ones for the power and ground. Therefore, if you're in the UK, you'll need to have an adapter that allows you to plug the converter's cord into such a socket.

Once we had all the adapters and pigtails we needed, we thought

The female socket found in most European campgrounds.

The male plug that fits into female sockets found in European campgrounds. The two small prongs conduct the electricity and the single, wider prong is the ground.

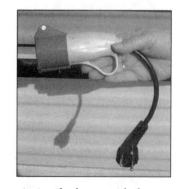

A pigtail adapter with the socket used in campgrounds on one end and a 220 volt household-type male plug on the other end. You'll need to use this type of adapter in many French campgrounds.

113

the electricity situation was under control. We assumed that we could now use the RV exactly as we had when camping in the U.S., using our usual appliances including the microwave and the all-important battery charger. This wasn't quite the case. Two other problems surfaced once we solved the problem of the plugs.

Amperage

Let's start here at home. In the listings of campgrounds put out by Good Sam, Trailer Life, and Woodall, there are often notations stating that a particular campground has 50 amp service, rather than the usual 30 amp that is standard. We never found a campground in the U.S. that offered less than a standard of 30 amp service. Our unit is not a big energy user (unless we use the air conditioner) and we did not require high amperage, so we just never thought about it.

In Europe, on the other hand, we were frequently in a campground that offered 4 amp service, which is approximately the equivalent of 8 amps in the U.S. While this will run your refrigerator and the lights, it will certainly not allow you to run a microwave. When we got what the Europeans call 6 amp service (12 amps), it might run the microwave—but only if it was a full 6 amps. In at least one place that promised 6 amps, the handyman told us that it was really only 5 amps. Needless to say, no microwave there! We tripped a lot of circuit breakers before we figured this all out.

In many campgrounds, you get a choice. Some campgrounds in Holland and Germany have 16 amp service. At 220-volts, 16 amps is about equivalent to American 30 amp service. All the facilities in England listed by the Caravan Club promise 16 amps. On the Continent, though, we were mostly offered 4, 6, or 10 amps, which are the equivalents of a little less than our 8, 12, and 20 amps. Generally speaking, the higher the amperage, the higher the surcharge for electricity. If you don't need to use any equipment that requires "high" energy, you can choose the less expensive option. Just don't try to turn on the microwave and the heater at the same time.

There is a slight chance that 10 amp service may even allow you to run the air conditioner on low! We never actually did this, but we met a couple from Scotland who owned an American Winnebago and they were able to turn on their air conditioning unit one rare hot day in Holland without tripping the circuit breaker.

We also discovered that our converter had a place where it was possible to plug in 220 volt appliances, and we were able to run a European extension cord into that plug. This allowed us to buy an inexpensive European-style electric heater to take the chill off cold mornings in spring and an electric pot to boil water for tea or coffee. We used both to conserve our supply of propane. As long as we had 10 amps, the extension cord was no problem.

In addition to the amperage differences, there are hook-up differences. In America every single site will have its own outlet. This is also often true in the UK, but not always true in continental Europe. Many facilities there do not have a hook-up at every site. Instead, they rely on two or three hook-up panels with six or eight outlets each. We always asked for a site close to the hook-up, but we noticed that most campers carried very long household-type extension cords. Such cords are okay because the amperage is so low. On our first trip, our lack of a long cord was a problem in one or two places. Fortunately, these campgrounds were able to loan us cords when our two 10-footers were not long enough. On our second trip we bought a 25-foot cord in the campground shop at Gaasparplas Campground in Amsterdam. It was usually long enough, although we might have been better off with one that was even longer.

In all the time we were in European campgrounds, we never heard the sound of a generator. There were lots of motor homes, many caravans (trailers), and a lot of people in tents. Everyone made do with the 4 to 6 amps of electricity. Energy in all its forms is very expensive in Europe, so less is used.

Once we had been in Europe for a while, we realized that our biggest problem would not be electricity, but propane.

Propane

If you have shipped your RV to Europe, you will probably be touring there for at least two months and perhaps longer. This may be long enough for you to have to face and solve the propane problem. That is, you will need to maintain a supply of propane so that you can keep your range, refrigerator, and possibly your furnace working. How you do this will depend on whether your rig has a built-in propane tank or, like ours, a removable tank (also called a bottle). In either case, you will need to adapt the fittings on your tank before you can refill it—or exchange your empty removable for a full tank—because European and American fittings are incompatible. You will also need a source for the propane.

If your rig has a built-in tank, the problem is easily solved. In Europe, many cars have been adapted to run on propane (aka, LPG) instead of gasoline to save on fuel costs. So a number of European gas stations sell propane. You can fill your built-in tank in any of

DO-IT-YOURSELF STORES

Unlike most tourists, you may need to visit the local hardware store or one of a large number of do-it-yourself chain stores similar to our Home Depot and Lowes.

The best source of local information is always the office in the campground. Still, you might find these few names useful. (Note that this is not an exhaustive list.)

BELGIUM: Brico, Gamma, Hubo

FRANCE: Bricomarché, Mr Bricolage

GERMANY: OBI, Bauhaus, Praktiker

THE NETHERLANDS: Praxis, EB

UNITED KINGDOM: B&Q, Focus-Wicks, Homebase

these stations—if you purchase an adapter with appropriate fittings to receive the hose. You'll need one adapter for the UK and another for most of the Continent since different countries use different pump fittings. Photos of those used on the Continent, can be found at www.iwemalpg.com/LPGstations.htm, which also lists LPG gas stations by country (see also Appendix E).

The UK seems to be the primary source of these adapters because American-made RVs are much more popular there than they are in the rest of Europe. You can purchase adapters from UK motor-home dealers who specialize in selling American-made RVs and are experts in adapting systems to conform to both UK and continental requirements. (See Appendix E for some names and web sites.) You can also get adapters—and other equipment you may need—through ABP Accessories, which is affiliated with American RV Enthusiasts, or ARVE, a British organization whose members are mainly Brits who own American RVs. If you go to ABP's web site and click on the tab "Accessories" you will find pictures of the various kinds of adapters. Buy one before you leave home unless you are planning to be in the UK. And be prepared to pay a bit. The adapters used in the UK and France, for example, cost about £36 pounds (about $67) last time we looked. But that's a worthwhile investment if you think you might run short of propane during your trip. Once you have the adapter, simply screw it on to the fitting in your propane tank.

A regulator with a fitting that screws onto a typical propane or butane tank used on the Continent. The nipple fitting on the opposite side will be attached to the flexible hose leading in to the motor home's appliances and will be secured with a hose clamp.

Adapting a removable tank is a bit trickier. In the U.S., we take our tank out to have it filled. This turned out to be almost impossible in most of Europe, where the refilling of tanks is confined to wholesale gas bottling plants that don't have the facilities to sell retail. To make matters worse, the thread of the fitting on the pipe that is used to fill American tanks is different from the thread on European tank fittings. That meant that we could not swap our empty tank for a full one as most European and UK campers do.

Unfortunately, we didn't find out about those problems until we were well into our first trip and found ourselves short of propane. Thanks to the chilly March weather in northern Europe, we had used our propane furnace to keep warm and had quickly gone through a lot of gas. We spent many hours trying to find out if one of the numbers of firms that sell "camping gas" would be able to fill our tank—only to discover that the laws in many countries prohibit such refills. We finally found that the Ganda Gas factory in Ghent, Belgium, (see Appendix E) could and would refill our tank. Meanwhile, we learned to conserve our propane by using an inexpensive 220 volt space heater for warmth, heating water for coffee and tea in

A head-on view of the fitting that screws onto European propane and butane tanks.

an electric kettle, and keeping the refrigerator cold while we were on the road with refreezable ice packs. Those strategies worked so well that we had propane to spare when we returned to Belgium after our 77-day trip through the British Isles the following year. Of course, the fact that we visited the UK in a particularly warm summer helped, too.

At the end of our second trip, Ganda supplied us with a regulator, complete with the fitting used throughout Europe on portable propane tanks (see photos at left). On our next trip, we will simply replace our American-style fittings and regulator with the pictured one and replace our tank with a large European tank that we can exchange at most campgrounds and gasoline stations when empty.

Note that the regulator fitting is a nut that is screwed onto the outside threads of the European tank. U.S. and UK tanks have inside threads.

If your propane system uses a removable tank we recommend that you start your trip with a full tank and ask campground wardens to direct you to a place that sells regulators with this fitting. You will find them in stores that sell camping supplies, in propane bottling plants, and in many campgrounds. Use the new regulator to replace the one on your RV. The easiest way is simply to cut the hose leading from the tank to the inside of the RV and replace it by using a hose clamp and the nipple fitting on the regulator. Screw the fitting onto the tank and test for leaks by brushing soapy water on the connections. Assuming that there are no bubbles, and therefore no leak, you are in business for the rest of the trip. Just remember to keep your American regulator so you can refit the tank when your rig returns to the U.S.

After you have replaced your regulator, store or discard your American tank and replace it with a European one. (You can resell the European tank to any campground at the end of your trip). Replaceable European tanks come in various sizes from about one-foot to three-feet high, so you should have no problem finding one that will fit the space available in your RV. Once the regulator and tank are installed, you will have access to as much propane as you may need during your trip.

You will find that in Europe and in the UK you have a choice of either propane or butane. The tanks are color coded but the code is different in different countries. In the UK, propane tanks are red while butane tanks are blue. Your appliances can use either. The chief drawback of butane is that it freezes in cold temperatures. Freezing does no harm to the gas or the tank, but frozen gas will not flow. It is probably a good idea to stick with propane and to use a butane tank only in a pinch and only when temperatures are not expected to go below freezing.

Sewage Disposal

All campgrounds have some kind of disposal system for portable chemical toilets, but we found that not all had in-ground dumps that could accommodate the hoses required to clean the contents of the waste tanks of a motor home. When the people at the reception desk did not speak English, asking if such facilities were available was difficult, but asking for a *vidange* or *vioir* helped in France. We have read that in German the word is *entsorgungskanal* and in Italian it is *scarigare*. However, we usually found what we needed simply by explaining that our chemical toilets needed to be dumped through hoses into the ground.

Most disposal facilities for chemical toilets were designed for portable units and could not accommodate a motor home hose. As we understand it, even a few years ago there were very few facilities for motor homes. However, this has changed radically. According to the French Tourist Office, there are now 17,000 *sanistations* in France alone. There were occasionally places where we could not stay because we needed to dump our gray water and there was no suitable facility. But, most of the time, the campgrounds had in-ground dumps. (Incidentally, in the guides for continental campgrounds put out by the English caravan clubs, the category "mvwaste" will allow you easily to pick a campground with a suitable area.)

In-ground sewage discharge area in Tintagel; England.

Toilets and Showers

We found that all campgrounds except some CLs had showers, sinks, and toilets. But there were a lot of differences among them. In a very few places on the Continent, men and women shared the same toilets and showers. Privacy was not really an issue, however, since the commodes and showers all featured individual stalls with doors that locked and with their own dressing areas.

The Continent

Most sanitary blocks on the Continent were clearly marked either male or female. And most kept the showers quite far away from the toilet area. Some sanitary blocks had commodes in all the toilets, just like the standard in the U.S. Others, however, particularly in France, had so-called continental or "Turkish" toilets in at least some of the stalls. These toilets are porcelain fittings in the floor. They provide places to put your feet as you squat. Not our favorite. These really are not a "problem," just an annoyance. In our nearly six months of traveling, we never had to use one. We discovered that even in those places that had a lot of continental toilets, the toilets marked "Handicapped" had regular commodes in them. (As an aside, we noticed the other day that a catalog devoted to items useful for traveling has a funnel designed to help women with continental toilets, which are apparently quite common all over the world!)

Some campgrounds had toilet seats on the commodes; others didn't. Having only the porcelain to keep clean may be easier and even more sanitary, but such an arrangement certainly requires getting used to if you are accustomed to American facilities. Some places provided toilet paper, but many did not, so it would be a good idea to carry your own. Provision of toilet paper seems to vary by country.

The showers also varied. In many places, especially in France, the water temperature was pre-set. Often these facilities require you to push on the faucet button constantly. It is the constant pushing that keeps the water running. Not as nice as what you can expect at home, but functional, easy enough to use, and usually clean. Some facilities had a cold-water shower but would supply a specified number of minutes of hot water if you put a token into a small heater. It is a good idea, when registering, to ask if tokens are needed for the shower. You may need that token before the office opens in the morning. Again, not up to commercial American campground plumbing standards, but acceptable. In fact, several national parks

Sanitary block facilities in Amsterdam campground.

in the western U.S. also have this sort of arrangement.

Everything seemed to be tiled, so it is a very good idea to bring shower sandals that can be used to walk to, through, and from a shower! Another difference between the U.S. and Europe was the "style" of clothes worn by people going in to take a shower. In American campgrounds, we were accustomed to seeing people wearing sweat suits or lightweight running suits as they headed for their shower. In Europe, we very often saw people dressed in robes and slippers!

In many places, the sanitary blocks had walls that ended short of the actual roof, providing some breathing space to allow dampness out into the air between the posts that hold up the roof. This is okay when it's hot, but not terrific when it is cold.

Besides toilets and showers, every campground had individual stalls containing a sink and a mirror for shaving. All too often, the basins in these little stalls had only cold water. Brrr! Fortunately, motor home travelers always have clean sinks of their own.

The bottom line about all these sanitary arrangements is that while they are unlike what you may be used to, they are perfectly useable and generally clean. Our experience is that facilities in France and Belgium are the least up-to-date, while Germany, Holland, and the UK have more modern facilities.

We can't give you firsthand information on what will greet you if you are adventurous enough to travel in Eastern Europe. The information we have, mostly from the English caravan clubs, suggests that campgrounds there range from modern facilities with up-to-date plumbing to sites where you'd best use your own sanitation facilities. We haven't been able to get a live update from anyone.

The United Kingdom

In general, UK campgrounds are up to American standards and more. The sanitary facilities are equal to those we've found in American campgrounds. The electricity was at least 16 amps of 240 volt electric service, which is more than equivalent to 30 amps of 110 volt current. In the many different campgrounds we stayed at during our second trip, shower valves were turn types, not push types. There were some places that had restaurants and/or bars, but more had small stores that sold a few groceries, some camping equipment, and canisters of propane. Much more like home.

Security

Driving around Europe in a vehicle with an American license plate in the years 2002 and later seems a bit different than it might have been in earlier years. Although we were a bit apprehensive about how people would treat us, we found that we were quite welcome wherever we went.

That does not mean that we were unaware of the problems that might come our way. We adapted our plans in several ways to accommodate to possible dangers.

Although there are many free places where a camper can pull in and stay overnight, we agreed in advance that we would stay only in real campgrounds. This automatically made us feel safer. It is a lot harder for someone to get into a campground than into a field or parking lot.

During the trip, we were careful where we left cameras and our computer. We used closed cabinets to store the obviously expensive stuff so it could not be seen from outside. Our important papers, including our passports, were with us at all times, and were never left in the camper. Since we certainly did not need the passports on an everyday basis, I wore them around my neck in a bag designed just for that purpose. We made and hid copies of all our important papers so that we could replace them if necessary. Fortunately, it was never necessary.

When we left the RV during the day, we always turned on the alarm system. It never sounded an alarm although it was in use well over 70 days on each of our trips. Since we were leaving everything locked in the vehicle, we felt better about the idea of going away for eight hours or more just knowing that the alarm would alert the campground people if anything went wrong.

We had a black-and-white copy of our license plate, as well as copies of our passports and "green card" and a record of important information such as credit card numbers. The license copy came in particularly handy when we found out that in most European countries two license plates per vehicle are required. We are allotted only one license plate in Florida. But we had made a black and white copy of the plate before we left, and we taped it up on the top right side of the front windshield. We were glad we had done so when a policeman stopped us in a small French town because he did not see a license plate on the front bumper. We were able to point to our "second" license plate taped to the windshield. We explained that in *Les Etats Unis, une license seulement* (United States, one plate only). Despite our terrible accent and grammar, he nodded and let us go on our way.

We had heard and read that RVers should be especially careful in parts of Italy and Spain, so we decided we would go no farther than the south of France. However, we met many European RVers who had gone to both countries without incident. After our own experience, we would have fewer qualms about going to those countries now, although we would probably take extra precautions. Europeans who had made such trips were very sure that no one would have any problem as long as they followed the rule to stay only in campgrounds.

Campground Amenities

We found that many European campgrounds had full-service restaurants, snack shops, and bars. Some sold groceries and freshly baked bread. Many had some spaces for transients, but were really what we used to call "bungalow colonies." They catered, at least in part, to large numbers of privately owned mobile homes that had permanent spaces and to RVs that were left for the entire summer in the same place. Many had some rental units of different types for campers and hikers. These campgrounds tended to have playgrounds and other facilities for families. We noticed that the better guidebooks include in their description of the campground information on the percentage of "statics" (i.e., permanent residents) at the facility.

Two other differences between campgrounds on opposite sides of the Atlantic should be noted. First, it is very common to find picnic tables and fireplace barbecues in U.S. campgrounds. Not true on the Continent. Tables are uncommon and you see signs all over the place forbidding open fires. We never smelled anything cooking outside there. However, more experienced campers have since told us that the signs refer to open campfires in the tent areas, and that no one will object if you take out a portable barbeque and use it to grill meat. We think you might want to ask before doing so. Here again, Great Britain was different. We frequently smelled meat cooking over charcoal in campgrounds there.

Second, most campgrounds had rental units in addition to the sites for campers. They ranged from tiny hikers' cabins to mobile homes. Why should this interest someone who is in an RV? Because you may want to have people join you at various times during your trip. If they will need to sleep in quarters other than your RV, these rental facilities could become very important. In the height of the season, you might have to arrange such quarters ahead of time, but that is easily done. The campground guidebooks list facilities that offer rental units, so it is possible to pick out appropriate campgrounds before you leave. If you need to rent such facilities, though, you'll have to plan ahead more.

One other campground service could be important to you. Every site has a central bulletin board that lists emergency information (usually names of local physicians, hospitals, and emergency numbers) as well as information about local attractions and facilities.

At the Reception Desk

Every campground has a clearly marked reception area as you drive in. You must check in here before the barrier is lifted. When you enter, you will need either a passport or an International Camping Card for identification. Usually the staff in Continental campgrounds must keep some ID until you leave, since you pay at the end of your stay. They will also need your license number. In Great Britain, most facilities ask how long you are staying and then require you to pay in advance. That way they do not need to keep your ID.

The daily rate can consist of several separate components, and therefore often must be calculated. The charge will be so much per vehicle, so much per adult, child, or pet, plus charges for electricity. Since many campgrounds open for the day at 9 AM and are closed between 12 and 2 (and often longer), it is wise to get all the information you may need before you leave the office. Here are some of the questions you'll want to have answered:

- How many amps of electricity do you supply?

TIP

If you're interested in renting a unit for guests, it's a good idea to call ahead for reservations— especially in the busy summer holiday season.

123

- Does the fee include hot water?

- Do you need tokens to obtain hot water for the showers?

- Do you need tokens or particular coins for the laundry?

- Is there a dump for a motor home?

- Is there a special place to take on water?

- How do you get from the campground into the center of the city?

- Where is the stop to get the bus?

- What is this bus stop called in the appropriate language?

- What number bus is it?

- How much does it cost?

- Do you have to have exact change for the fare?

- What is the name of the stop where you should get off?

- How late does this public transportation run?

- When is the campground gate locked and how do you get in after that?

- Is there a supermarket nearby and how do you get to it?

Fresh Water

Fresh water is regarded as a more precious resource in Europe than it is in the United States. As a result, there are rarely hose fittings at your pitch that allow you to connect a hose to the faucet and just run the water into your RV as you use it. Even where there are individual faucets, they usually are not threaded to allow you to hook into them. Instead, the campgrounds have faucets designed for communal use set up between sites. You can draw water at these faucets to put into drinking containers. There are also specific areas where caravans and camping cars can fill their tanks. Then you must use your own system to pump the water.

All the water is clean and supposed to be potable, except for some hoses at "camping car" dump sites that are clearly marked with symbols indicating that one should not drink this particular water. However, in our travels we came across places where we were very suspicious of the water, especially in Belgium in the summer. We always filled our large bottle with clean water and used that for such things as drinking and making coffee. That way, it didn't have to sit for long periods of time in the RV tanks before we used it.

Since European campgrounds have areas designed for people in tents, there is always a series of sinks on the outside of the sanitary block where you can wash your dishes as well as specific sinks where you can wash clothes. Sometimes you have to put in a token to get hot water at these places, but most of the time hot water is free. We developed the habit of doing our dishes there; this saved us from having to use our electrical system to heat our water as well as from having to dump gray water frequently.

In fact, we found that these community sinks were also community meeting places. Most of the people doing dishes seemed to be men, so Ron got to meet a lot of people. No matter what country we were in, everyone was quite cordial. We often got to know other campers at those sinks.

We did have one problem with this, however. We noticed that everyone seemed to have wine glasses to wash after dinner—except us. Ron insisted on using plastic cups, because they don't break. Adelle considered this very declassé indeed, since everyone else used real stemware!

Laundry & Laundromats

Many campgrounds have self-service laundromats. Since a great deal of the business at many of these facilities is from people who

The 30-acre campground at Oban, Scotland, is the largest we've ever seen.

park their caravans at sites in the campground for the entire summer, the laundromats are very busy. They are also very expensive. Costs for a single load of laundry on the Continent ranged from €5.50 to €9.50! This explains why there are always lines of towels drying! Washing is done sparingly and dryers are often absent or ignored.

Furthermore, the machines are quite different from what Americans are used to. They are mostly European-made front loaders, which are slow beyond belief. That's because they wash on a different principle in order to save water. The drums are quite small, and the machines fill with a small amount of soapy water and swish it around. Then they rest. And rest. Then they swish it around some more. After a considerable length of time, things do come clean with a minimum of water. But be prepared to wait.

In at least one place in France, we found an American-made set of machines. Indeed, the proprietor was quite proud of them. But this was also a place where the electricity service was very low. As a result, the machines strained through the cycles.

The only place where we found that doing laundry was reasonably priced was in Great Britain. Here the machines were also slow and small, but at least the price was right.

Still, if we were very careful how we used our clothes, washed out things by hand when we could, and made do with less, we were able to get by doing only one load about once a week. We were very glad that we use sleeping bags and had no regular bed linens to clean. Once every week or 10 days, we did have to devote one afternoon to laundry, but we were able to keep abreast of it. At the end of the trip, we washed everything, including our sleeping bags, in a regular laundromat in a town where they had multiple machines. Here the price per machine was on the low end of outrageous!

> **TIP**
>
> *Using sleeping bags will cut down on the amount of laundry you'll have to do, but don't forget to pack a clothesline and clothespins. You won't find dryers in all laundromats. When you do find them, they are expensive.*

9

STAYING IN TOUCH

You'll be away from home a long time when you are RVing through Europe. You will not have a set itinerary and may not know in advance where you will be on any given day. Even if you are disposed to write letters, it is much harder to handle mailing from a foreign country. So, the best ways to stay in touch with home are telephone, cell phone, and the Internet.

Telephone

Differences between U.S. and European telephone service do not loom large when you are on a two-week vacation. But stay two or three months and you'll be singing a different tune. For people planning to ship a motor home to Europe for an extended stay, the peculiarities of the European service and fees require special discussion.

Let us give you two examples. When we were in Brussels, we called the library from a public telephone in the main square. We used a Belgacom phone card and a Belgacom telephone. The library was within walking distance of the square. It cost €1 (which at the time was equivalent to $1). That seemed to be the minimum charge. In Amsterdam, we used a Dutch telephone company card for a phone call from an Amsterdam campground to an Amsterdam bank that lasted all of about 10 minutes. The charge was €3.50!

You have a number of options for phone service in Europe. You can buy or rent a cell phone, or you can simply buy calling cards and use public phones (although these are not so easy to find on the

Continent). All the European telephone companies offer prepaid calling cards with which you can call both the U.S. and local numbers. None of them is inexpensive. Most American telephone companies will issue cards to their subscribers that will allow them to call the U.S. from abroad. None of them is inexpensive either. It is even possible to get a telephone card from Wal-Mart in the U.S. without being a subscriber. But here again, the price is not a particularly good deal, unless you happen to be AT&T.

There are a number of ways to control your phone costs, however. For example, before we left the U.S. we arranged for a special prepaid telephone account with an outfit called Net2Phone, whose network depends on VoIP (Voice over Internet Protocol). This means that the network utilizes the Internet rather than the dedicated lines the telephone companies use. Our account had a European 800 number. After dialing 00 and the 800 number, we were able to call any U.S. number for only 20 cents per minute. That was a big improvement over the prices quoted by major phone companies.

The big disadvantage of this system is the number of digits required to dial a number. You must begin by dialing 00 to get an overseas line. (This was the "exit code" in England, Holland, Belgium, and France. If we dialed 00, our call was directed out of the country. You should probably check this with the operator in each country, however. Dial operator, ask for an English-speaker, then ask how to dial out of the country.) Once we got an overseas line, we had to dial Net2Phone's toll-free 800 number, then the account number (our telephone number including area code), then a four-digit pin. Finally, we dialed the U.S. area code and phone number as prompted by a recording. It all worked fine. In fact, the service is good. Voices are clear and loud. Just don't make a mistake in a number!

Net2Phone is listed in Appendix E. We picked it because it has a Western Europe 800 number that can be accessed by phones all over Europe. While there are other VoIP companies, none as of the date of this writing offer similar services. Since this is one of the fastest changing parts of the telephone system, there may very well be other companies offering this service by the time you read this book. The best way to get an update would be to use a search engine to check the Internet for VoIP companies.

High cost wasn't the only problem we encountered with telephoning on the Continent. Perhaps the most annoying to us was the scarcity of telephone booths even in big cities. We hadn't realized how few public phones there would be. Several times at the beginning of our trip we pulled into a gasoline station expecting to find public telephone booths like those available in the U.S. We were dis-

> ### TIP
>
> *On telephones in most countries, the "exit code" to dial an international call is "00." However, you should probably check with the operator in each country.*

appointed. Then we tried huge malls anchored by the kinds of supercenter markets that carry not only food but also all kinds of other goods. There were no public telephones anywhere. We walked for miles in one direction in one city without finding any telephones. In fact, we soon found we could go most of a day without seeing any public telephones. So, we adapted. If we saw a telephone booth at a time that was convenient, we used it immediately.

We faced another problem when we tried to use the phones in those telephone booths. Some Continental public telephones prohibit connections with 800 numbers. We found these mostly outside the campgrounds, and the fact that we could not call an 800 number was an inconvenience. Despite this handicap, we were able to stay in weekly touch with our scattered family for very little money thanks to the VoIP service.

It is worth noting that, even when you do find a public phone on the Continent, you probably won't be able to use coins to operate it. Most Continental public phones accept only telephone cards. Even to use an 800 number, you often need a calling card to start the transaction. The system works only if you put in a card, even though it won't be charged. Moreover, you must buy a different card in each country. Since we did not know any locals whom we might want to call and would be using the card only to "open up" the line for our 800-number calls, we simply bought the least expensive cards we could find. The cards are sold in lots of places, from newsstands to post offices, depending on where you are. The campgrounds will be able to tell you where you can get them, and the bigger ones often have cards for sale.

Finding public telephones is easy in the United Kingdom. If there were only six visible houses in a village, there was a red phone box. If we were on the outskirts of a popular hiking area, there was a box. Truly, public telephone boxes in the UK could be described as ubiquitous. The cost is low and the phones work with either coins or cards, which gave us a lot of leeway. We soon realized that if we were going to use our 800 number, we didn't even need to put in a coin to begin the transaction. We could just dial.

Of course, phones in the UK are also easier to use because the operators and the automated messages are in English. The only problem we had was with the new information service. Apparently the British government decided to deregulate telephone information services. As a result, you can no longer ask British Telecom for a telephone number, but have to dial one of the new services. We had some difficulty getting a telephone number from them, but we think that it was a matter of our not understanding how to pay for the service.

The telephone dialing system in Europe is different from the system here in the U.S. In fact, it can be quite confusing. It took us a lot of wrong numbers before we caught on to the European system. In the meantime, we found that it was easier to call the United States from a European public telephone than it was to dial people in Europe! In fact, would you believe that, by the end of our trip, if we needed to call anywhere in Europe, we dialed through America? We would call Net2Phone's 00-800 number, dial our account number, our pin, a three-digit number that told the computer we were calling out of the country (out of the U.S., that is), a country code, a city code, and a phone number. Try doing that without a mistake!

In the U.S., dialing long distance means dialing a "1" and a three-digit area code in addition to the seven-digit telephone number. In Europe, you dial a "0" then a city code and then the phone number. The number of digits for the city code and local numbers varies, even within the same country. The largest cities have two-digit codes. However, since every little town has its own city code, the city codes can run up to four digits! When telephone numbers are written out, the European custom is to give the entire number: 0 + city code + local number. This means that phone numbers are long and may have different numbers of digits!

The thing to remember is that you must dial all those numbers unless you are calling from a telephone that shares the city code with the number you are calling. If the city code is the same, you dial only the personal telephone number. Let us make up two examples.

- Calling 020 555-5555 from 0254 444-4444, you would dial 020 555-5555.

- Calling 020 555-5555 from 020 444-4444, you would dial only 555-5555.

There are two exceptions. In Italy, you must always dial all the numbers, including the leading zero. In Spain, all numbers begin with a "9" instead of a "0" and you must dial all the numbers no matter where you are calling from.

Somehow, this was confusing. We didn't understand the system when, on our first day in Belgium, we tried at least four or five times to call Wallenius Wilhelmsen's Zeebrugge dockside office. We consistently dialed the wrong number of digits. Since there was no provision for English on the phone that we were using, we had no idea what the recorded message we got meant. We finally had to ask the manager of our hotel to dial for us. Zeebrugge has a different city code from Brugge, where our hotel was, but we didn't know this, so we hadn't been dialing the complete number.

International direct dialing is also different. If you are going to make an international call, even just across the border, you dial "00" and then the country code. In this case, however, you do not dial the "leading 0" that always begins a written phone number (e.g., 020 555 5555), but you do dial the city code and the phone number. As examples, let's use a fake number in both the UK and in the U.S.:

- Great Britain's country code is "44," So if you are calling from Holland you would dial "00 + 44 + city code + phone number or "00 44 20 555-555." (Note that you did not dial the "leading zero.")

- The U.S. country code is "1." So, if you are calling from Europe, you would dial "00 + 1 + area code + telephone number."

Writing numbers down is hard enough, but it can be frustrating when you go to dial. Of course, the fact that you are unlikely to speak Dutch/German/French/etc. makes it more difficult. When you encounter problems, it'll probably be because you're dialing the wrong number of digits.

As a matter of fact, the lack of public telephones and the enormous number of cell phones being used all around us made us think about buying a cell phone. By the time we really understood the system, it was too late to follow through on this idea on our first trip. Such an investment would have made sense only if we had made it when we arrived. We rarely had to call European phone numbers, and the airtime charge on a cell phone for an 800 number made the cost prohibitive for inter-country calls. But we did meet an American staying in the Paris campground who thought that his portable phone was well worth the money.

Cell Phones

It is possible to rent or buy a European cell phone. As I've mentioned, in 2002 we did not have a cell phone. When we first arrived in the Brussels airport, we stopped at an airport store to discuss the possibility of renting or buying a phone. The airport was a good place to look into cellular telephone service because the people who work in the store need to be linguists. They deal with all kinds of people, many of whom do not speak either French or Flemish, which are Belgium's languages. Since the system in Europe is quite different from the system in the U.S., it was a big plus to be able to understand the sales clerk!

At the time we asked, in March 2002, the price to rent a cell phone would have been the equivalent of $25 per month, with additional charges for airtime. The European system is based on the use of a pre-paid card. Each call is automatically subtracted until the card's value runs out. The same phone can be used in any country, but you have to buy a different card for each country in order to utilize the phone network of the country from which the call originates.

We were not sure at the time we began our first journey if we wanted a cell phone. First, we didn't know anyone local to call, so we were not sure that we needed a phone. Second, without firsthand knowledge of the public telephone system, we were really not positive that a cell phone would be necessary as an emergency tool. As it turned out, we would have used the cell phone very rarely that first trip for telephoning, and we never had an emergency.

Nevertheless, before our next trip, we decided to buy a phone from Roadpost (www.roadpost.com) in Canada and have it shipped to us in the U.S. Our plan was not to use it for calling home, but to have it so that our family could call us in an emergency. As it happens, there was no such emergency. But we never had to worry that we were incommunicado, which we had been concerned about on the first trip. This time, if our family needed us for anything, they could reach us through our cell phone, which is considerably more immediate than leaving us a message on the Internet. And, since we had the cell phone with us, we could easily call ahead for campground reservations throughout our trip, which was handy because we were traveling during the busiest season of the year.

It is possible to buy or rent mobile phones in Great Britain fairly inexpensively and prepay for service. They are available from several different companies. One American camper whom we met had a phone from Orange PCS Limited. He found that the more prepaid service he bought from Orange, the less expensive the service was.

Every U.S. cellular telephone provider has some kind of system for providing service to its own subscribers when they are traveling in Europe. You may, however, need to purchase a special plan or phone to take advantage of it, because Europe uses a digital cell phone technology (GSM or Global System for Mobile communications) while most U.S. mobile phone networks use either an analog technology or a GSM technology that operates on a different band width from the one used in Europe. Your options as we go to press are to purchase a phone that is made to operate on both band widths or to buy a GSM phone that will work only in Europe, which is what we eventually did. However, the technology is changing fast; so there may be other options by the time you travel. Check with your

"Since we had the cell phone with us, we could easily call ahead for campground reservations throughout our trip."

cell phone provider or search the Internet for information.

The Internet

There are lots of Internet cafés and other public Internet facilities all over Europe. Finding them is not always so easy, but most cities have storefronts with signs showing a large "@." In fact, there seemed to be a couple of chains of such stores. One source of information about where such cafés may be found is the government Tourist Office. Other sources include hotels that offer this service to their guests, areas around universities where there are always such facilities, some public libraries, and some campgrounds. Sometimes you can send messages from post offices or communication centers that offer telephone, wire services, and Internet in the same place.

If you are able to take a laptop computer on your trip, you can do what we did. We would type out a letter while we were in the RV, copy it to a diskette in text format, and take that along to the local Internet facility. There we would copy and paste it into our e-mail message. If you do this, you may have to ask the attendant in the café to explain which buttons on the screen to use and which words indicate "copy" and "paste." That will save you a great deal of time while you are on line.

Rates in Internet cafés vary widely, from €1 to €4 per hour. The French government offers Internet service at many post offices for €7.50 per hour! If you are using a diskette, you will have to find a facility that has computers with floppy disk drives and will allow you to use them. When we compared 2002 with 2003, it seemed to us that in 2003 there were fewer places that had floppy disk drives on their computers. Floppies are apparently getting to be outdated equipment! We're not quite sure how the cafés plan to replace this part of their service. On our next trip we plan to explore the use of a USB thumb/flash drive, a device that we found at a number of the Internet access points that did not have floppy disk drives.

Make sure that your computer has an up-to-date program to check for viruses so that you can check out the diskette before you reuse it. But we must add that we never had a virus problem although we must have used twenty different computers to send out e-mail during our two trips. (Our letters from these trips, in Appendices A and B, will give you a feel for life on the road.)

If you have your own Internet provider and it allows you to access your e-mail account from anywhere, you need only go to your provider's web site, log in, click e-mail, and sign in with your password, after which you will find everything exactly the same as at home. While we encountered certain little difficulties—with language, keyboard, and the ability to use material that we had already prepared "at home" in the RV—none of them was insurmountable, and we found it simple to use the Internet as a way to stay in touch with people back home.

Mass Media

If you are media hounds, as we are, you will have to make adjustments in your listening and watching habits. Even if you have a satellite dish, you will not be able to use it in Europe because European television uses a higher definition signal than U.S. television. To make matters more complicated, English TV signals are different from TV signals on the Continent. So, in order to view local TV, you will need to use a local set. Such a set would have to be plugged into a 220-volt outlet on your current converter. Unless you speak French or German, there is an additional problem—very little English language programming! There may be American movies with foreign language subtitles, of course, and it is possible that you may be able to pull in the BBC. We really can't tell. We just didn't bother bringing our TV.

Furthermore, unless your TV is not removable, you probably should take it out of the unit for two reasons: first, its presence in the vehicle may serve as a temptation for dockside theft, and second, removing it will lighten the load and give you additional storage room.

OK. No TV. What about the radio? The automotive radio in your car will work to pull in local stations. Knowing that this would probably be our main source of entertainment and news, we fixed our radio before we left so that we could turn it on without starting the engine. We used the radio every day. The results were mixed. A lot of the programs we heard were music, so we didn't need the narration. The problem was that the European norm seems to be too much talk and too little music. We realized too late that what we really needed was a short-wave radio that could pull in the BBC News. All our little radio was able to furnish was the BBC station—and that only when we happened to be just across the English Channel from the source.

For our second trip, we brought a short-wave radio. It took a while for us to find BBC Radio 4 or the BBC World Service, but we did find them. In fact, the guidebooks of the Caravan Club indicate where such programs are to be found on the dial in each of the European countries. These radio stations carry mostly news and classical music programming.

Newspapers in English on the Continent are all quite expensive, quite thin, and not too informative. The best were the *International Herald Tribune, U.S.A. Today,* and the European edition of the *Wall Street Journal.* These papers are available in all big cities. There were also British papers, but they were even more expensive and still less illuminating, since they had very little about things that were happening in America! As a matter of fact, our favorite of all was the section of *U.S.A. Today* that has a one-paragraph story from every state. This feature kept us in touch and made us feel at home.

On our second trip, we bought a newspaper every day. Since we were in Great Britain, we liked being able to understand what was going on in the country. The English papers are quite different from those we are used to. Almost all of them are published in tabloid format. This means that the pages are small and easy to read, even on public transit. And almost all of them are countrywide papers, unlike in the U.S. where every city has a different paper. We found that we enjoyed the two independent papers the most. Almost all papers in Great Britain are part of huge media conglomerates. Rupert Murdoch, for example, controls a number of papers, including the famous *Times.* We are pretty certain that only *The Guardian* and *The Independent* operate with independent editorial control, although there may be others.

10
SHOPPING & EATING YOUR WAY THROUGH EUROPE

When people asked me why we were going to tour Europe in an RV, my answer always began with food. We have often felt at a disadvantage when we were traveling in Europe and saw the array of food for sale in the open-air markets. While staying in local hotels, we could never make use of those things. No matter how fresh the seafood or how tempting the other foods, we could not store much in our hotel room, so we could buy very little. Unlike other ways of traveling, using an RV allows you to really taste and enjoy the food, wine, and beer that Europeans have at home.

Our two trips allowed us to shop like Europeans. The only problem was that we couldn't eat or drink nearly enough of the wonderful things that we saw for sale. We cannot even begin to give you a good description of everything we saw. It is important to understand that there are big differences between the kinds of foods you can buy in Europe and what is available in the U.S. as well as differences in what you can enjoy when you have a kitchen where you can store food and cook what is available.

The Continent

Among the many treats in store for you when touring continental Europe in an RV is going to open-air markets wherever you happen to find one. Furthermore, you can do more than just look at all the delightful things for sale in these markets. You can buy the same foods that they are offering to the locals. The variety of food for sale in open-air markets is huge. It ranges from baked goods, cheeses made by local farmers, local wines, and all kinds of fresh fruits and vegetables to local specialties like cassoulet or fois gras in France, and even Asian specialties made by more recent immigrants to Europe. Meals cooked at "home" can be really easy yet exotic. There are a huge number of ready-to-eat products, such as pork and prune stew and *choucroute* (French sauerkraut), and they are very different from anything offered in the U.S.

We loved shopping at these markets. We frequented them as often as we could. First of all, it was fun just to walk through and hear all the men and women shouting out their wares, even if we could rarely figure out what they were saying. The experience was like being in an old movie about Europe. It was quite exhilarating. Even months after our return, we could clearly remember the markets we had walked through!

If you are adventurous, you can go into little specialty food stores. There are full-range butcher shops, and butcher shops that sell only pork and have a delicious looking array of sausages, hams, and pâtés that were probably made on the premises. A bakery may sell both breads and cakes, or specialize in one or the other. The bakery may also make its own chocolates. Some stores sell only cheese and milk products. Most of these little stores are considerably more expensive than the supermarket, but buying from them and eating in the RV is still much less expensive than eating at restaurants. A small town in Europe will always have a bakery and a café, and often a butcher shop, even when it has no real grocery store as we know it.

Even shopping in a supermarket (*hypermarché* in France) is a whole different experience for an American. More European supermarkets follow the supercenter model, selling everything a department store sells along with the groceries. The food and grocery selection is different, too. There is an aisle containing cereals, but it is nothing compared to the 60-foot refrigerated case displaying different kinds of yogurts! A 15-foot case of herring and smoked fish is barely smaller than the case holding hard cheeses. An equally vast display of soft cheeses can be found in the next aisle, and the numbers and kinds of pâtés and sausages available are mind-blowing. In contrast, the space dedicated to cleaning supplies and paper goods is tiny compared to what Americans are used to. In fact, we were in stores where we could not find a single package of paper napkins. Part of the fun of supermarket shopping is trying to figure out what things are, since, if you're like us, your command of the language is unlikely to include all the things that you'll find on the shelves. Everyone we know who has been able to shop at a supermarket in

Europe agrees: there are very few experiences that are more fun!

Before you head for the store, though, remember two important things. First, nothing is sold in pounds. Every price that you see is based on the a kilo, which is about 2.2 pounds, so the price per pound is about half what it says on the sign. If you want a pound, ask for a "demi," which is half a kilo (a little more than one pound). If you just want a small sample, you can ask for 100 grams, which is a little less than a quarter pound.

Second, in many supermarkets, you not only pick out your own fruits and vegetables but also bag them yourself and get a price for the bag. Look around for scales that weigh the goods and issue stick-on labels indicating their cost. In such supermarkets, there are no scales at the check-out counters. If you come to the cashier with a bag without a label, you'll be sent back to get one—and hold up the entire line.

For us, the open-air market is one of the few things that can be more fun than shopping at a supermarket. These markets are as big a tourist attraction as anything else that is to be seen in Europe. No matter where you go, there are open-air markets with what seem to be miles of individual stalls full of the most amazing displays of food you can imagine. A stall might sell thirty kinds of olives, most of them fresh and less salty than those you get in bottles or cans. This stall might be next to one containing fifty kinds of nuts and hard candies, licorice, and other sweets. The stall that sells chicken, chicken parts, and other fowl may also sell rotisseried chickens, but, if not, you are sure to find a stall that sells only chicken, pork roast, and perhaps two kinds of pre-cooked potatoes, all cooked on the spot. In one open-air market in southern France, a huge Spanish dish called *paella* made of chicken, seafood, and rice was cooking right in the booth in a pot that was at least four feet across. If you stood anywhere near this gorgeous dish, the heavenly smell would make your mouth water. Portion sales were brisk.

The market may also offer Italian and Greek specialties, really fresh fish, large varieties of cheeses, yogurt, and eggs, and very inexpensive flowers. In Holland, you're sure to find fish stalls selling fresh fish for cooking, as well as many kinds of fried and smoked fish, and *nieuwe haring* ("new herring") in season. Some markets, also offer clothing, leather goods, cloth, kitchen supplies, electronics, and even livestock—poultry, rabbits, pigs, and other animals.

Of course, you'll find large numbers of vendors selling beautiful fresh fruits and vegetables in all the open-air markets. You will find it very interesting to try the produce. We discovered that many things tasted very different from the same items bought in the U.S. Asparagus, artichokes, and strawberries usually were much better

TIP

In European open-air markets, you should not try to pick up the items you want, because the seller is the only one who handles the fruits and vegetables. You can, of course, point out the exact pieces you want.

tasting in Europe than what we buy here in America.

Note that you should not try to pick up the items you want in the open-air markets; the vendor is the only one who handles them. Instead, point out the specific pieces you want and the vendor will serve you. Although the vendors rarely speak English well, they use the same Arabic numbers we use and they will write out your charges on a piece of paper and show them to you. They are used to dealing with foreigners who do not speak their language.

In addition to standard restaurants, which are everywhere, there are cafés and tiny specialty take-out places all over Europe. In a small town where there may be only a couple of stores, there will be four or five cafés. Every café and take-out place serves delicious coffee. In most places, your luncheon sandwich can be ordered on a really crisp baguette. You can buy Middle Eastern specialties, Greek specialties, and Italian specialties as well as local specialties such as pancakes and crêpes, and everything Asian.

Every country offers a variety of exotic fare, but each has its own flavors. In the Netherlands, for example, cheese stores sell enormous numbers of special cheeses, and herring and other fish—whether salted, smoked, or cooked—are sold everywhere by vendors in freestanding booths called "Haring Handlers." The fish are all wonderful. Dutch pancakes are worth trying, too. These little taste treats are made in a pan with silver-dollar-sized depressions and are served with a variety of toppings; our favorite, of course, is Dutch chocolate. While Dutch cuisine isn't fancy, you'll find plenty of restaurants and take-out places that specialize in the cuisines of Holland's former colonies in China, Indonesia, and Suriname (a dot on the map of South America that the Dutch got as a consolation prize when they had to cede Manhattan to the English after losing to them in a seventeenth century war). Most of the Asian food served here is Indonesian, and the Indonesian specialty called *rijstaffel* is especially good. It is a meal that consists of an unbelievably large number of individual small dishes, each with different flavors.

In Belgium, the dish of choice is what we in America call French fries. This is a misnomer. They really are Belgian fries, *Vlaamse frites*, and in their home country they are much better than most of what passes for fried potatoes anywhere else. The Belgians are very particular about their *frites*. They cut fresh potatoes—no frozen potatoes here—and flash fry them in advance. When you place your order, they finish the frying in very hot oil, cooking the potatoes until they are crisp and golden brown. The *frites* are frequently eaten with large quantities of mayonnaise, but anyone will be glad to give you an order without that extra fat! Ketchup is also available,

TIP

Although prices in specialty food stores are higher than those in supermarkets, remember that the things you can buy and eat in the RV are much less expensive than what you would spend eating in restaurants.

as is a variety of other dressings. But most of the people one sees eating fries do eat them with huge dollops of mayo.

The most amazing food we saw in Belgium was a *frite* sandwich! It was prepared as follows. First, the vendor opened a baguette by cutting it in half lengthwise. Then he laid down two big ropes of mayonnaise on the bread. Next he put in something that looked like a hot dog that had been breaded and fried in deep fat. Then came an entire order of frites on top of this sausage, followed by three more ropes of mayonnaise. Needless to say, we did not try this specialty, but it was certainly an interesting experience to watch it being prepared!

Waffles are sold in many forms, from mouthwatering to not worth the calories! Belgian waffles range from so light and airy that you can't believe it to baked and sweetened to be sold and eaten cold. Of course, Belgian chocolate is arguably the best in the world and there are little chocolate shops everywhere. And Belgian beer is universally acknowledged to be among the world's best. It's not only among the best, but the bottles with XX and XXX on their labels have a very high alcohol content, 10 or 12 percent versus a little over 5 percent in American beers. The Belgians call these potent beverages "double" and "triple" beers.

Germany is the home of the wurst (sausage), and of incredible numbers of lunch meats. In the supermarket, we wanted to taste a few of the great numbers of different lunch meats. We had no idea what was in them, but we were able to buy them by simply pointing to the displays in the case and indicating with our fingers the number of slices we wanted. We were able to get a sampling this way. Actually, we did not always get our exact choice, but it was always interesting. German cooking, like Dutch cooking, is plain, but the specialties are still not what Americans are used to. Even something as plebian as sauerkraut is made differently.

The French are justly famous for their obsession with food and it shows. France is renowned for its great restaurants, but the food that is sold for home consumption is equally good. All the food we bought in France was delicious, especially the bread. The French are decrying the decline of the baguette, but believe us, even the bread in the supermarkets is crisp and good. You have to buy it every day because it goes stale so fast. It creates a storm of crumbs, but it is delicious.

In France, many street vendors sell crêpes with different kinds of fillings. There are Middle Eastern specialties for sale everywhere. And every province has its own special dishes. In some parts of France, we found great quantities of cassoulet (a bean, sausage, and duck stew). As we got closer to Alsace, in the east, we started seeing *choucroute*—fresh sauerkraut, smoked meat, and wurst in the form of a hot dog. Americans are accustomed to thinking of France as one country, but it is really a conglomeration of very different areas that were once quite separate and had cultures and cuisines of their own centuries ago. So each area has its own delicious specialties.

The French apparently do not believe in sliced cheese. A *tranche* (which translates to slice) does not indicate a slice of cheese suitable for a sandwich, but instead a wedge of cheese. Fortunately, even supermarkets honor the deli tradition. They will gladly give you a taste of the cheese that you are thinking of buying.

We found prepared crêpes in the refrigerated case in supermarkets all over France. You heat them up in a pan and put a topping on them. (They were uniformly delicious.) In the northeast part of the country, we found crêpes that were sold with the baked goods. These Breton crêpes were even more delicious than the refrigerated ones we had already tasted. Discovering these kinds of differences was always interesting—and delicious.

Although we were not able to really explore the other countries in Europe in the same detail, we've had enough experience to have learned some things.

Spain has its own cuisine. It is known for its delicious Serrano ham, shops that specialize in very young lamb, and restaurants that specialize in *tapas* (a selection of many kinds of prepared foods, served in small portions). In recent years, the idea of *tapas* has spread to the U.S. as well, and there are restaurants that serve this kind of smorgasbord. In Spain, as in France, different areas specialize in different foods.

Foods and wines are as important in Italy as they are in France, and they are equally delicious, even though the cuisines are quite different. Italian cuisine is remarkably varied, and as in France and Spain, many dishes are associated with specific regions. For example, although there are numerous different—and delicious—kinds of pasta served in Italy, the tomato-based cuisine that is most familiar to Americans is really southern Italian cooking. There are always local specialties for sale in small towns.

The Scandinavian countries have amazing collections of salmon for sale. There are markets selling fresh fish and fish salted or cured in ten different ways, most of which are totally unfamiliar to us!

In all these countries, there are different wines, beers, and regional beverages. Some are famous, others aren't. All are quite interesting. There are the usual selections of sodas and other soft drinks, many imported from the U.S., as well as soft drinks you'll probably find in only a single country. Here are some of the things we learned as we shopped and ate our way through Europe:

- In France, Germany, Spain, Italy, and many other places, everything closes for lunch. And this includes the supermarkets. Don't plan to go to the store between noon and 2 PM. The restaurants and cafés that cater to the lunch crowds are open, but many restaurants stay closed until 7 PM. In fact, in Spain, the dinner hour really begins at 9 PM, and if you go into a restaurant at 9 o'clock, you will likely be the first customers.

- Sundays are a day of rest for stores in many countries, so make sure you stock up on Saturday. In Germany, everything closes at 2 or 3 o'clock in the afternoon on Saturday and does not reopen until Monday morning. In France and Holland, stores close at 6 PM or so on Saturday and frequently stay closed until Monday. In Belgium, they close early Saturday evening but are usually open on Sunday. We found that Sunday was the day for the weekly open-air market in many countries. It doesn't conflict with the retail stores that way!

- Open-air markets usually are a one- or two-day-a-week event, although there are permanent markets in many places. You can ask at the Tourist Office or the campground office about schedules.

- There is more pork than beef, and we saw about fifteen kinds of ham in every market. The displays were mouth-watering.

- In France, the markets identify all beef by the breed of the animal and indicate its country of origin. The prices are often quite different for different breeds, but all of the beef is tasty.

- There are all kinds of prepared foods and mixes available at supermarkets. They differ not only from American products, but from each other. For example, in the area of France where cassoulet is the local specialty, there were many kinds of cassoulet available in the supermarket. You could buy it from the deli counter, freshly made, or try it from a can or a jar, or buy the ingredients in a cold pack.

- Prepared soups are quite different from those we find at home. Many are sold in plasticized boxes, and the varieties are unlike those in U.S. supermarkets. Most are nowhere near as salty as the majority of the ones available in America.

- Bakery goods, even in supermarkets, are very good.

"In Spain the dinner hour starts at 9 PM. If you go into a restaurant at 9 o'clock, you will likely be the first customers."

- In France, there's no onion powder in the *épices* (spices) section, not even in places that specialize in herbs and spices. This surprised us, because there is lots of garlic powder.

- You can't buy the cans of chicken broth or beef broth that you might use at home to make sauces. But in Europe you can buy dry powders for making a sauce. They don't taste at all like the stuff you buy at home, since the European versions are much less salty.

- The most interesting thing that we noticed was the difference in the meat. In the U.S., if we try to grill a steak in a pan, it weeps. Everywhere in Europe, it comes out beautifully—dry and perfectly browned on the outside and juicy on the inside. We have a theory about this. We think it is a result of the way cattle are slaughtered. In the U.S., the steers are probably put onto feed lots and given lots of salt, which makes them thirsty. They then drink a lot, which makes them weigh more. This may be cost effective, but it's certainly not taste effective. And it's not done in Europe. We also found that the fresh beef, chicken, and pork just plain tasted better there than at home.

- As we mentioned, often you can buy a fresh baguette for breakfast in the campground. This is great bread, although it is a cleaning lady's nightmare. Crumbs, crumbs, crumbs everywhere. But do not expect that it will be good tomorrow. You have to buy it fresh each day. This is not a problem, because freshly baked bread is remarkably inexpensive and readily available, even in campground stores. No matter what country we were in, we always saw people returning to their campsites from the campground grocery with freshly baked loaves of bread in their hands.

- Exotic foods are not as readily available at supermarkets on the Continent as they are at home. After searching many French supermarkets, for example, we finally found one that carried a small selection of Oriental food. Of course, exotic in France means a lot of things that don't seem so exotic to us, like taco mixes.

- There are extraordinary numbers of pâtés and similar mixtures in all butcher shops. And real charcuteries, either in regular stores or in the *marché* (market), also have a lot more kinds of fowl available than we are used to seeing. There are pheasants, pigeons, quail, goose, ducks, duck parts, turkey parts (though we never saw a whole turkey), and two or three different kinds of chicken. The meat on sale often includes goat and rabbit.

The United Kingdom

Sign in a restaurant window in York, England.

There is a lot more that could be said about the food in continental Europe. There is very little to be said about food in England, however. England has never been celebrated as a place for great eating. Things are (we are told) much better now. Food in restaurants is considerably better than in the past and the small stores that used to sell food have been replaced by supermarkets that are equivalent to those we're used to in the U.S. But traveling in England is not a gastronomic adventure. It's more like being at home.

The specialties in England are things like sausage rolls, Cornish pasties, "bubble and squeak" (sausage, cabbage, and potatoes), and other high fat, high salt items. The lamb is good, although somewhat expensive. We were introduced to a local specialty called a "Scotch Egg," which really was delicious. It is a hard-boiled egg with a sausage covering. You just warm it up in the oven. We had good food in England at various times and places, but, in general, you don't travel in England to sample the delicacies.

Prices in England generally were also more expensive than we were willing to pay. You have to keep the value of the pound against the dollar in mind when you look at prices, especially in restaurants. A good example was a store in Oban, Scotland, where we saw a lot of people lined up to buy what looked like really good fish and chips. This English take-out specialty cost 7.95 (7 pounds 95 pence), which is pretty expensive for take-out. When you figure that each pound was worth $1.60, this take-out lunch cost about $13.00. Not what we'd consider a good value! Around the corner in Oban, we found a reasonably priced Chinese restaurant and had a sit-down lunch for less than that amount per person. By the end of our trip, we were taking our own sandwiches with us when we went out, since we did not relish paying large amounts of money for mostly mediocre food.

We don't want to give the impression that there is no food worth eating in England. We had lovely meals in various places. Several pubs where we had dinner offered excellent meals. The tea and scones with clotted cream we had in one tourist attraction was so delicious that we'd like to go back again just for that. And a real English lunch served in a National Trust Tea Room was quite memorable and reasonably priced. Some of the small places where we had lunch were as good as anything anywhere. But, if you are interested more in food than in the other treats of traveling, England should not be your first choice.

Milavsky's Culinary Laws

Here are some of Milavsky's Culinary Laws, drawn up as we ate our way through France, Belgium, and Holland. Feel free to add your own.

- French beef tastes better than it looks.

- The same is true of French chicken.

- French pork and veal taste much better than they look.

- If there is anything better than a fresh French baguette it is a fresh French baguette with poppy seeds.

- French pastry is marvelous—even if bought in a supermarket.

- Belgian chocolate is the best.

- So is Belgian beer.

- Smoked eel in Holland is even better than Nieuwe Haring.

- Nieuwe Haring in Holland is not new, unless it is sold during strawberry season.

- No one knows what is in an andouille.

11
EUROPEAN HORIZONS UNLIMITED

Despite the fact that we have already traveled in Europe many times, and that we have toured a total of six months in the RV, we have a lot left that we want to see. We're already planning our next trip, and we're thinking of going first to Scandinavia, despite the distances involved.

While arranging in 2003 for the ferry crossing between the Hook of Holland and Harwich, in England, we discovered what seems to be the only true bargain in ferry crossings. If we drive through Germany and then up the Jutland Peninsula of Denmark to Frederickshaven, we can take the Stena Line Ferry to Oslo, Norway; the fare is unbelievably inexpensive. So, on our next trip we will probably begin by taking the ferry to Norway and then driving to Sweden. From there, we'll return to Germany and possibly even visit France again.

Traveling "in Europe" takes in a lot of territory. Still, any American RVer who has spent time driving across the United States will find that Western European countries are small in comparison to the U.S. Even the largest countries, France and Spain, are much smaller geographically than the United States. But since it is not possible to see all that Europe can offer in a three-month trip, you do have to make choices about how much driving you want to do between stops.

The difficulty is not really the distance. Rather, it is the time required to go these distances. We found ourselves saying that cities only a few hundred miles away were "too far." They certainly were not far in distance. But there was a problem. It would take several days driving to get there and an equal number of days to return. The six days of traveling would have probably been somewhat interesting, but why should we waste our time with "somewhat"? If we went in a different direction, we could count on something special all along the way. Since we had to make a choice, we preferred to organize our trip so that there was something interesting to see every day. We knew we'd have to get back to the plane at a specified time, so we planned our trip to see as much as possible before we had to leave.

That's why we tend to think of each trip as a circuit. In an RV, you can begin and end in a different place in each country, giving you the opportunity of seeing as much as possible. The Tourist Offices in many European countries offer suggestions for such circuits in their respective countries. (For a web site that has links to all the European Tourist Offices, see Appendix F.) If you don't have Internet access, check the individual countries in Appendix C for the telephone numbers of tourist bureaus.

When planning, keep in mind that, although France borders both Spain and Italy, there are many miles between the disembarkation harbor of Le Havre in France and Madrid, Spain. If Spain (or Italy) is an important destination for you, you may want to select an RO-RO company that serves ports closer to Spain or Italy. That way you begin and end closer to your ultimate destination.

Just remember that there is so much to see and do that you have to make these choices ahead of time in order to plan your trip well.

On our travels and in making plans for future trips, we have collected a large number of books and accumulated a lot of information from them and from various organizations in different countries. We've also learned a lot from talking to other camping enthusiasts (mostly from Great Britain) who have been all over the Continent.

What follows is a quick run-down of selected relevant facts about the different countries of Europe to help in your trip-planning process. We have been far more specific about the countries of Western Europe than about the countries lumped under the heading of Eastern Europe simply because we know more about the Western European countries. But many Europeans spend vacations in the much less expensive Eastern European countries. Generally, their facilities are not as modern, they are not yet truly tourist oriented, and they are unlikely to have road systems as good as those in the much more prosperous Western European countries. We did meet a lot of British and Dutch people who had traveled through these countries, however, and learned that there are campgrounds in every country.

THE HOLIDAY SITUATION

Western Europe celebrates many more holidays than we Americans enjoy. We were surprised to find that many stores (and gas stations and even some restaurants) were closed not only for multinational holidays like May 1 (Labor Day) and national holidays like July 14 in France (Bastille Day) but also for religious holidays like Pinksterdag (Whitsun) Sunday and Monday in Holland and Ascension Day in various countries.

To get the most out of your trip, be sure to check at the local Tourist Office for upcoming holidays. You'll need to be sure that you've got enough food and fuel to carry you through.

Western Europe

Austria

Austria is a small country and a great deal of it is mountainous. The Austrian Alps run along its southern border. Its road system is modern and good. Many of the highways are toll roads and there are tolls at tunnels and bridges.

If you go to Austria, you will need to have a tax sticker called a *vignette* that you paste on your windshield. *Vignettes* can be purchased in gas stations and at tollbooths on the highways as you cross into Austria. A two-month sticker costs about $25.00, which is certainly reasonable. There's a hefty fine if you don't have one.

Most of this country's cities probably are unfamiliar to you, although Vienna (Wien) and Salzburg are certainly well known. Both have multiple campgrounds that are quite modern and very clean. Because of Austria's mountainous topography, even driving into campgrounds may present small difficulties such as difficult turns.

A large number of Austrian campgrounds impose a connection charge for your electricity in addition to a charge for the use of the electricity. This would affect you only because it could cost you a little more if you move every day, since the charge is imposed only once in a stay. The Caravan Club notes that the electricity is often offered in locked boxes, which the campground personnel unlock. Since the boxes may be situated far apart, campers should be sure that they have a long cord and that they are properly connected immediately upon arrival. They should also make arrangements in advance to disconnect if they are planning to leave very early in the morning.

Austria, and especially Vienna and Salzburg, are famous for both music and the good food and incredible pastries that are the pride of Austrians. Besides wanting to visit the three biggest tourist city attractions of Vienna, Salzburg, and Innsbruck, most tourists in Austria are interested in seeing the Alps and the natural scenery. There are other attractions, of course. You can, for example, tour the area where *The Sound of Music* was filmed, and you might want to see the many elegant architectural remnants of Austria's long history as part of the Austro-Hungarian Empire.

There are plenty of modern, comfortable campgrounds, although they may not be evenly spaced throughout the country. Camping is a popular pastime in both summer and in winter when ski slopes are open. A large number of campsites are situated in areas where the chief attraction is either the Alpine scenery or one of Austria's beautiful lakes. Generally speaking, sanitation standards in Austria are very high.

Belgium

Belgium is quite small, and yet it is divided into two language zones. As you drive along, you will suddenly notice that the language on the signs changes from French to Flemish (which is similar to Dutch and German). Fortunately for the American traveler, many people in Belgium are tri-lingual, and their third language is English! It is worth noting in passing that this same duality exists in the names of cities as well. The city of Ghent is also Gent, for example. Brugge is also known as Bruges, and Brussels is Bruxelles. Sometimes the two names are less easily deciphered. For example, Kortrijk is Courtrai! Fortunately, the Belgians always display both names on the direction signs.

Every city has at least one campground, and all cities have the usual good public transit system. Campgrounds may vary in size and facilities, but we found them all to be quite modern and clean. Even the cities that are not tourist areas (like Liège) have campgrounds with public transit to the interesting part of the city ("Centre Ville"). Brussels is a large, very modern city with a seventeenth-century core. Many of the other cities are even more interesting. Brugge and Ghent were both powerful cities many centuries ago. Once seaports, both became backwater cities as the seacoast changed, so there was no impetus for modernization. The result is that the interesting architecture was saved for future generations. Antwerp is a huge modern port, but it has managed to preserve a lot of beautiful old buildings and art from its Flemish past. All these cities are very close to one another, and it is possible to find a campsite and remain there, visiting the cities by public transportation.

The Belgian train system allows "pensioners" to travel from one city to another on any weekday for a round-trip charge of only about €2.50. If you show them your passport proving that you're 65 or older, they'll include you in the "pensioner" category! The charge, even if raised, will certainly be a lot less expensive than the gas that would be required to get from one city to another. And the trains are clean, modern, and easy to use. The cities are within an hour or so of each other and trains will bring you directly into the center of each city, which is where a good tourist wants to be.

Many of the cities seem to be on the sea, on a river, or surrounded by canals. There are a number of places that you may have heard of in histories of World Wars I and II, places like Bastogne,

Malmédy, Ypres, and the Ardennes Forest, where you will find museums devoted to the history of the war and the battles that took place in those locations.

Belgium was part of the battleground in both World Wars. As a result, there are a lot of military cemeteries in Belgium. Many Allied troops who died in those wars, as well as their German foes, are buried here. As we drove through the country, I found my mind constantly quoting the lines from John McCrae's famous World War I poem:

> *In Flanders fields, the poppies blow*
> *Between the crosses, row on row.*

It is a sad poem, but the country is lovely and we enjoyed being there. The Belgians are justifiably proud of their medieval heritage, their fried potatoes *(Vlaamse frites)*, the variety and taste of their beer, their chocolate that is arguably the world's best, their lace, and their beautiful old cities. The battlefields are interesting and emotionally moving. It's a great place to visit.

France

We found France was the most interesting country on the Continent, despite the well-known French penchant for speaking only the French language. Although we knew a few French words, we found it impossible to think about what we wanted to say as quickly as was necessary to speak normally. Instead, we spoke a kind of fractured English—with a few French words thrown in. It worked. Not because we spoke French, but because people in the tourist industry speak English!

Everywhere you look you will find something of historical interest, from ancient cities to places which figured prominently in two World Wars. Even if you are not a history buff, you'll find that much of what you see reminds you of something you once read or knew. If you are a person who has always been interested in history, it is particularly exciting to see all the places where "things" happened! From the walled castle city of Carcassonne, built between the ninth through eleventh centuries, to the Normandy beaches where World War II's allied invasion force landed, there is history everywhere.

France's reputation for culinary excellence is well deserved. The food in every kind of market is mouth-watering. Making dinners at home is just as French as eating in France's fabled restaurants, even when home is an RV. Every town—no matter how small—has its market days when the main street is full of stalls selling all kinds of food, including cooked dishes. The supermarkets are a joy and a pleasure. The inexpensive French bread sold everywhere is simply delicious.

You'll find a tremendous variety of cultural traditions in France because the nation is composed of many areas where discrete cultures flourished for thousands of years. The differences in such things as architecture and food specialties from one area to another make France fascinating. In addition, the French have always considered France the artistic capital of the world, and they have the museums and architecture to prove it.

Besides all this, France is one of the most diverse countries in Europe in terms of its topography. There is the northern seacoast, including Normandy and the famed beach towns of Honfleur, Trouville, and Deauville; the Atlantic seacoast down to famed Biarritz; and the Mediterranean coast better known as the the Riviera, with areas such as the Côte d'Azur. In between there are mountains and plains, with fields of grain and enormous vineyards and olive groves, as well as cities large and small. Despite the ravages of time and war, you'll find walled cities from every era, Roman ruins, huge castles, and ancient monasteries.

France is one of the largest countries in Europe and anyone on a motor trip is bound to find gems of towns and villages unknown to the world at large. We visited world-famous cities as well as small towns we had never heard of before. If you asked us to pick our favorite, we could not do so. The entire country is one beautiful huge farm, and the back roads take you through village after village. There are signs everywhere for thirteenth-century monasteries and fifteenth-century chateaux. There are also enormous numbers of campgrounds.

Every town seems to have at least one campground, which accounts for the boast we saw in several books claiming that France has 10,000 campgrounds. Some of these are only *Camping en ferme* or *Camping a la ferme* (camping on or at a farm), but since the government rates facilities by assigning stars and has standards to which every campground must adhere, most are at least passable. We did in fact go to one farm. It was early May and the campground was not really open, but the owners were glad to let us stay. Although the farm had space for 10 campers, there were only two of us there. The farmhouse was a beautiful old stone building that could have come out of a travelogue! When I went inside to pay the camping fee, I felt as though I was walking on a stage set for a play. The farmhouse was a beautiful eighteenth-century home!

The campgrounds vary in the kinds of amenities that they offer,

> **TIP**
>
> *Since many of the campgrounds in France open only in mid-May, be sure to check on the opening date when you look up a campground.*

but we never found one that did not offer some electric service, although frequently it was a very low level of amperage. Most had reasonable sanitation facilities. Although there were a lot of continental (or "Turkish") toilets, there were always standard commodes in the toilets marked "Handicapped." Perhaps the biggest problem in the campgrounds was the way the showers worked! You had to keep pressing the button to keep the water coming, and this often became very annoying. The annoyance was not a deterrent, however. We learned to take a shower while pressing the button, and the fact remains that people in motor homes always have the option of using their own facilities if the ones supplied by the campground get too difficult.

We spent time in campgrounds all over France. Some had hundreds of sites, others no more than ten. A large number of them open only in mid-May, so you'll want to check on the opening date when you look up a campground. Don't be discouraged if you don't finding a listing for the place you're headed. You'll see signs for camping establishments as you drive into almost every town.

Germany

Although Germany is also one of the large European countries, it does not boast as many campgrounds as France. This is really somewhat surprising, because the majority of the motor-home-style camping vehicles we saw in Europe were made in Germany, and a very high number of them were occupied by Germans. You can tell where a vehicle is from by looking at the rear bumper, where an official oval sticker must be affixed. A large percentage of these signs said "D"—which stands for "Deutschland." On the Côte d'Azur, we saw RVs lining the sides of the water—and most of them had a "D" on their rear bumper. But where France has the storied "10,000" campgrounds, Germany has only about 3,500. They are usually very modern, always very clean with good electrical service, and usually located near public transportation.

All the major cities in Germany have at least a couple of campgrounds. A great many of these have a heavy concentration of "statics," units that are permanently parked in the campground and used only on weekends and vacations. But all the campgrounds have room for transients.

The German tourist industry has put together a number of themed vacation routes for tourists. For example, you might drive "The Romantic Road," (220 miles of castles and river running from Würzberg on the River Main to Füssen in the Alps), "The Castle

Road," (a 600-mile route from Mannheim to Prague), or "The Fairy-Tale Road" (a 400-mile drive in the north of Germany from Hanau to Bremen). Each features interesting sights related to the theme. Of course, you may want to head directly to such cultural and historic centers as Bayreuth, Heidelberg, Stuttgart, Köln (Cologne), Dresden, Nuremberg, Munich, Frankfurt am Main, Bonn, and Berlin, or check out the Black Forest, the Roman ruins, or the spas. All of these areas have plenty of campgrounds. Of course, there is a difference between the facilities in western Germany and those in the area once known as "East Germany." Even the roads in the western area are better, but the Germans are bringing the others up to date as quickly as possible.

In our opinion, German food is not in the same league as the food in France. However, Germany offers an abundance of wursts (sausages of all kinds) and amazing numbers and varieties of cold cuts, as well as traditional kinds of delicious pastries.

Germany has always been celebrated for its organization, its cleanliness, and its order. Americans may feel more at home in Germany than in the more exotic southern countries like Italy and Spain! We talked to German campers in campgrounds from southern France to Scotland. We asked them all what places in Germany they would recommend. Would you believe that all we got from anyone was a shrug?!

Greece

The English love Greece. It is one of those sunny and warm places where English tourists have always longed to go. Greece is a very beautiful country and it is most assuredly one of the most interesting countries in terms of history and culture. The several books we have found on the subject agree that the campgrounds are very modern and clean. It is also a very mountainous country, and although its roads are reported to be good, they would be difficult for the four-cylinder Toyota engine that does its best to keep our RV moving along. Adding to this difficulty is the fact that Greece is also a country of islands and ferries.

In fact, Greece may be a place that might be best seen by people driving only a European-style car—and then they would have to be aware of two other challenges. First is the fact that the Greek alphabet is different. At least one visitor suggests in a book that you might want to get two different maps—one that uses the Roman alphabet and another that will show you what the signs look like in Greek. The second problem is that Greece reportedly has the highest number of accidents in all of Europe. When you consider the great distance you would need to drive to get to Greece from a disembarkation port, you can see that visiting Greece in an RV requires a great deal of planning. You might be better off touring it a different way.

Ireland

Ireland is a favorite destination of American tourists. However, for an American RVer there are several difficulties. One is the cost of ferry service to Ireland. Another is the fact that roads in both the Republic of Ireland and Northern Ireland are reported to be narrower and less modern than roads in other European countries. As Ireland prospers, the government is building a new and better infrastructure, but that process takes a long time. In addition, there are far fewer organized campgrounds than you'll commonly find in other places. It is possible, however, to ask local farmers for a space to park overnight, and if Ireland is an important destination for you, good planning will allow you to enjoy your trip.

Italy

Italy is a great destination. It is beautiful, historic, and enchanting. Its cuisine is world class. And its fabled artistic works, beautiful medieval cities, and original Roman ruins make the country a must-see for travelers from around the world. Moreover, a great many Americans can trace their ancestry to Italy. It is, however, quite far south. To get there from any of the Atlantic ports requires a journey of several hundred miles, through several other countries. According to Mapquest Europe, the distance from Amsterdam to Milan is about 669 miles. Rome is 358 miles farther south.

If you have only two or three months and you wish to visit Italy with your RV, you have two alternatives. You can plan to ship directly to Italy (see information on Mediterranean ports in Appendix D) or you can go directly south as soon as you disembark at an Atlantic port. If you do, you'll see a great deal of Europe on the way.

Camping is very popular in Italy. In fact, Italian motor homes are among the best of those manufactured in Europe. We always saw Italian rigs in the campgrounds we were in. During the past few years, campgrounds throughout Italy have been upgrading their facilities. Nonetheless, we have a number of reservations about making Italy your primary destination, especially if you plan to disembark your rig in northern Europe.

An Italy-only trip has a number of what might be termed general problems. Northern Italy is very mountainous, and getting there from France or Switzerland requires a great deal of driving through Alpine mountain passes or else through long tunnels—which may be quite expensive. Because the region is so mountainous, even driving to a campground may require difficult turns. The *autostrade*—or multiple-lane highways—often charge tolls.

Italy also has a reputation as a land of highway robbery—literally. We found warnings in many sources about gangs of thieves who target tourists in cars, a situation that would be even more difficult for an RVer. Specific warnings in various official publications as well as the Caravan Club publications told of gangs of thieves who use ice picks to puncture tires on targeted cars while tourists are stopped at roadside gas stations and restaurants. Then, when the tire goes flat on the road, one of the gang "helps" the victim change the tire while the others rob the car. The warnings all say that the farther south you go, the more problems you may encounter.

We have talked to RVers from all over Europe who have been to Italy and encountered no problem. We have also spoken to a couple of others who either experienced the ice-pick ploy or a similar rip-off or knew someone who had. So, if you are seriously considering Italy as a destination, be prepared. Know in advance what campsite you are going to and plan to drive directly there. Once you are parked in the campground, you are perfectly safe. If you do leave the RV unattended anywhere else, be alert and extra careful.

Also, do not try to drive through cities. Since Italian cities tend to be very crowded (and full of Italian drivers), they are better visited by public transit. Bear in mind that traffic in cities includes the "mosquitoes"—motorbikes that drive around in complete disregard for everyone else on the road. If you do not drive in cities, you will not have to worry about them. Rome has narrow streets, terrible traffic, and lots of motor bikes. But it also has seven campsites that are convenient to the city and to local ruins in Ostia. All seven have full facilities and electricity, although it is low amperage (3 to 6 amps), and many include a motor vehicle dump for gray water. Sanitation facilities may not meet your expectations, however, so it is worth looking carefully at the descriptions of the campsites to see if their facilities have only so-called continental or "Turkish" toilets. Several of the sites do have this old-fashioned fixture, but others have standard commodes.

As for other cities popular with tourists, Florence has four or five campgrounds convenient to the old city and Pompeii has three close to the ruins. Even Venice has a campground; in fact, it has two: one located at the far end of its lagoon and the other, on the beach between the lagoon and the Adriatic Sea!

There are campgrounds not only in all the major cities but all over the countryside—particularly in mountain areas and on lakes and rivers. The more urban campgrounds seem to have more modern facilities, but there are resort-type campgrounds all over the country. Per night charges are about the same as anywhere else on the Continent, although gas prices are a bit higher.

It would be wise to check to see if the camp you've picked is difficult to get in to. Where there are mountains, there are hairpin turns and other difficulties that you may not wish to navigate, especially if you have a large rig. Be sure you know where you are going and how to get there. Plan to go in the spring or fall. Italy is very hot indeed in the summer.

Luxembourg

Luxembourg's campsites were highly recommended to us by several people in Belgium. The tiny (51 miles by 32 miles!) country abuts Belgium and has 120 officially listed campgrounds, which are reportedly clean and modern. (You can get an information booklet on the facilities from the Luxembourg Tourist Office; see Appendix C.) The country is very mountainous and is said to be very beautiful. Apparently there are good facilities, good roads, interesting museums and castles, other tourist sights, and lots of tourists—mostly from the Netherlands and Belgium.

The Netherlands

Although the Dutch are not very numerous among the ancestors of Americans, they have had a big impact on this continent. Everyone knows that the Dutch settled New York, but not many are aware that Flushing, the Bronx, Harlem, Hoboken, Brooklyn, and many other familiar New York area place names are Dutch. And in the Netherlands you will find many other places with names familiar from World War II. Even better, rarely do you find people in the Netherlands who cannot speak at least a little English.

The entire country has a rich tradition of art, architecture, and unbelievable engineering feats to keep out the ocean. There are lots of canals, dikes, and windmills as well as all kinds of wonderful museums. And the food is delicious. If you've read the previous chapter, you know we are big fans of its cheeses, fish, chocolate, beer, and open-air markets. Traditional Dutch cooking is very down-home and plain, but being in the European Common Market means that the food offered in all the markets is up to the European standard. Everywhere we went, we found open-air markets full of fruits and vegetables from all over the Common Market. The stalls that sold flowers had a huge selection and the prices were low. We had fresh flowers in our RV from the day we arrived!

If you are there in the spring, be sure to visit the beautiful tulip garden at Keukenhof. It is open for only about eight weeks, during the tulip season. Flower markets (including the largest wholesale flower auction/market in the world in Amstelveen) and cheese markets can be found all over. This is a very cosmopolitan country, so you will find restaurants and little markets with all kinds of Oriental and other exotic foods.

These markets and the cities were always very crowded, but the countryside was deceptively "empty"—full of farm fields and farm animals—with bike paths everywhere. As we drove along, we often saw lines of people of all ages pedaling along at a modest pace.

The campgrounds are uniformly clean, modern, and convenient to public transit, with good electric service. Often they had huge areas for campers in tents as well as stationary buildings—yurts (permanent tents), huts, mobile homes, and so on—for rent. This is good biking country. Everyone in these campgrounds (except us) had bicycles!

Amsterdam is one of the three top tourist attractions in Europe, and it is packed with visitors all year long. In fact, it's hard to believe how small a city it really is, because you see so many people on the streets. But its relaxed atmosphere makes it an interesting and easy place to spend time in, and it is possible to take public transportation to places all over Holland from your campground in this city. Someone pointed out to us that the original Haarlem is just as far away from Amsterdam as New York's Harlem is from the original New Amsterdam (the southern tip of what is now New York's Manhattan Island). It was easy to get to Haarlem, Delft, Naarden, and many other tourist destinations by public transit from Amsterdam.

Scandinavia

Americans find the four countries that make up Scandinavia very interesting. Because of the geography of these countries, there are many tunnels and ferries that must be used to get from one place to another. Some of these ferries are quite expensive, so if you are planning to camp in these countries, you need to plan for that.

While you can drive through Germany to the Jutland Peninsula of Denmark and then cross over a long bridge to the island of

Copenhagen, the distance, combined with the cost of fuel, may make such a trip prohibitive. It is only 180 miles from Hamburg, Germany to Copenhagen, but Hamburg is quite far north in Germany. To get to the other Scandinavian countries, you must generally use a ferry, although you can drive between Copenhagen, Denmark, and Malmö, Sweden, on a new bridge.

English is widely spoken in all the Scandinavian countries. The roads are good, and the tourist facilities are generally clean and modern. There are ample campgrounds in rural areas and areas of natural beauty, since camping is a popular summer pastime in Scandinavia. The facilities vary widely, as does the electrical amperage. Many of the campgrounds require an International Camping Card, while others offer discounts to those who carry the card.

Despite the fact that these are far northern countries, their summer season coincides with a time when mosquitoes are very prevalent, so campers are always advised to bring some form of repellent! The camping season is short (June, July, and August) because the winter sets in early so far north. But during the summer, there is daylight through most of the night!

Denmark

The infrastructure in the tiny country of Denmark is so good that it will give any American pause. The roads are excellent and the superhighways are free. The beautiful new ferries compete with the equally beautiful new bridge that crosses many miles of water between the Jutland Peninsula and Copenhagen. The buses and trains are new and up-to-the-minute. This whole country has a population of about five million inhabitants—less than that of New York City—so the big mystery is how they can afford this and the extended social welfare plans for which they are famous. Saying that taxes are very high simply is not enough of an explanation!

Most American visitors to Denmark stick to the lovely city of Copenhagen and its environs. The northern part of the country is quite rural. There are over 500 campgrounds in this small country and the government rates them with one to five stars, depending on the facilities offered.

Because the country is so flat, touring by bicycle is easy. In fact, the bike lanes here can get an unwary pedestrian into trouble! You'll see racks of unlocked bikes everywhere. Copenhagen even has a system that allows you to borrow bikes: there are specially marked bikes that you can simply get on and ride away, leaving them at another rack when you are finished. Copenhagen really does seem to the visitor to be virtually crime-free.

TIP

If you're planning to visit Scandinavia in the summer, make sure to pack mosquito repellent.

Finland

Finland is a large country, mostly rural. It does not have large numbers of campsites, but those it has are reported to be generally high quality, modern sites. Helsinki, the main city and capital, has an excellent public transportation system, and the campground is convenient to this system. The second largest city, Turku, also has what is reported to be a very nice campground.

Most of the country's other campground sites are on lakes or rivers. Although the highways are generally good, many of the minor roads are still gravel. This can cause problems during the spring thaw. But that shouldn't be a problem most years because most campgrounds only open in June.

Finland is intriguing for several reasons. There are herds of elk and reindeer that roam free. It is always exciting to see the twenty-four-hour days of summer sun in the northern area, and it is fascinating to drive into the Arctic Circle. Helsinki has a number of tourist sites and a really interesting open-air market—particularly if you like salmon!

Norway

Norway is the most scenic of the Scandinavian countries. While the other three countries are mostly flat and rural, Norway's combination of mountains and fjords (cliff-bordered inlets of the sea) is famous the world over.

We discovered in 2003 that the ferry ride to Oslo, Norway, from Frederickshaven on the Jutland Peninsula of Denmark is quite inexpensive and we hope to take that ferry on our next trip. Since Norway is very mountainous, we are a little hesitant about driving there, even though we managed the Rockies and the Cascades without too much of a problem. With our four-cylinder engine, however, it is embarrassing to drive through mountains because we are so slow!

There are more than 1,200 official campsites in Norway, all of them rated on a government system. In general, the urban ones have more modern facilities. Most have a short camping season.

Sweden

Driving to Stockholm, Sweden, is a very lengthy affair, because the city is on the far eastern coast of Sweden, many miles from the mainland places where you are likely to begin. But the city itself is well worth a visit. Several other cities in Sweden are also interesting to visit and the bulk of the country is flat and easy to drive.

Although the distances are not great when viewed from a country as large as the United States, the difficulty is putting Stockholm on your itinerary. It would be a considerable investment of time to get there if you were driving from one of the more popular north Atlantic ports, which is where a camper from the U.S. is likely to begin. But if visiting the Scandinavian countries is your priority, you can ship your RV by sea to Gothenberg, Sweden's principal port. The RO-RO ships do not go up there, but it is possible to ship your rig from Amsterdam to Gothenberg on a smaller vessel. Transhipping, of course, adds to the cost.

Sweden has fewer than 1,000 officially listed campsites.

The Iberian Peninsula: Spain & Portugal

Here again, there are two ways to get to these countries. One is to ship directly to a Mediterranean port and then fly to a Spanish city and spend your entire time RVing in the Iberian peninsula. The alternative is to ship to ship your rig to one of the Atlantic ports and drive to Spain.

Keep in mind that it is about 990 miles from the northern port of Calais to Madrid. To get there, one option would be to spend two or three days on the main highways (*péage* or toll roads) through France and then drive on Spain's *autopistas*. Using big, fast highways you could get to a starting point in Spain in two or three long days of driving. Alternatively, you could choose to use smaller, slower roads and make the drive in four or five days. You'll see a lot of Europe as you drive by if you opt for the slow way, but either way, you'll have a long drive south.

Keep in mind that unless you have booked "open jaw" tickets that let you fly into one airport and out of another—and also have a place to store (or ship) your rig at (or from) your southernmost destination—you will have to backtrack at the end of your stay to fly home. That means that you will have to spend a total of four to ten days of your trip driving south and returning north.

If Iberia is your destination of choice, of course, you will want to ship your RV directly to Spain. Appendix D has a listing of the three Spanish ports on the Mediterranean with RO-RO service, along with a few campgrounds near those ports.

Although Spain is a large country by European standards, it does not have a lot of cities compared with France, which is close to it in size. Madrid, Barcelona, Seville, and Toledo are the most famous, and they are more than 400 miles apart. In the United States, that is not a terribly long drive, but when compared to the distances between cities in other European countries, it seems a bit daunting.

Because they were originally in different countries, Spain's cities are quite distinct. For example, Madrid was once part of a small country called Aragon, while Barcelona was part of the kingdom of Catalonia. In fact, the people in Barcelona still speak a different language—a twenty-first-century version of the medieval language the French call "Lange d'Oc." This name translates to something like "land of the people who use *oc* instead of *oui* to mean yes"! If that name sounds familiar, it is. Languedoc is now the name of a region near Provence in southwest France.

Over the past few years, both Spain and Portugal have become popular winter destinations for people who live in northern Europe. (If these campers were in Florida or Arizona, they might be called "snowbirds.") Many campgrounds have been built for them, mostly on the seacoasts of both countries. A number of these newer sites are really resorts that offer extensive facilities as well as entertainment. Still, although Spain is the third-largest European country, it has considerably fewer campgrounds than other countries.

Many tourists go to Spain and Portugal more for the sunshine than for the cultural high spots, but if you should decide to spend some time in the sunshine and on the beautiful beaches, don't forget the cities. Madrid, in particular, has one of the finest art museums in the world. Called the Prado, it boasts the art collected by the powerful kings of Spain during the country's heyday.

Though very interesting, the cities in Spain and Portugal are much less accessible to the camper than cities in northern Europe. Nevertheless, there is at least one campground in each major city. Campgrounds are reported to vary widely in terms of facilities.

Free camping is allowed in a number of places, but it is much safer to camp in more secure sites. Most of the problems campers have in Spain occur when they are not camped in regular sites. Furthermore, both the U.S. State Department and the Caravan Club warn motorists of highway "pirates" who target tourists. Specifically they suggest that you ignore "official looking cars" on the highway whose occupants "suggest through gestures" that there is something wrong with your vehicle. If you are concerned, drive until you can pull into a service area. Do not just pull over on the highway.

Both Spain and Portugal have good roads, including new highways. The international highways tend to be toll roads, and they charge high tolls. Fortunately, the secondary roads are very good, too.

The road to **Gibraltar**, or "the Rock" as it is often called, is through Spain. Although it might be quite difficult to drive your own rig through the pass to Gibraltar, it is possible. There are long delays at the border in both directions, and you won't want to take

> *"The cities in Spain and Portugal are very interesting but much less accessible to the camper than cities in northern Europe."*

your rig into the town itself because the roads are narrow and the overpasses low. You can park safely on the outskirts of Gibraltar. It is probably not a good idea to park for the day on the Spanish side. You can also make the journey a day trip. We are told that there is a campground in Spain about seven kilometers from Gibraltar, with public transit nearby. The Rock is notable for VAT-free shopping, an English-style supermarket, and much less expensive gas, as well as for its tourist attractions, such as the monkeys that roam it freely.

And once you are in Spain, there are ferries leaving for North Africa and the Canary Islands, among other places.

Be sure that your insurance includes bail coverage if you decide to visit Spain. If your rig is involved in an accident, the Spanish police have the authority to impound it if you do not have such insurance.

Switzerland

Switzerland is a popular tourist destination because of the natural beauty of its mountains and lakes. It has a good road system, which includes Alpine mountain passes and lots of tunnels. You must have a *vignette* (a toll sticker for the highway network in Switzerland) to drive on many of the roads. You can get one as you cross the border into the country. Slow vehicles are required by law to use the highway turn-outs and allow faster moving traffic to pass them, especially in the mountains.

Most campsites have a high percentage of statics (permanent residents), but there are some spaces reserved for tourists. Switzerland is very environmentally conscious and growth is highly controlled. Since the mountains surround the country, and since air pollution from vehicles has become a concern to the Swiss, the campgrounds leave only a few spaces for touring vehicles.

Campgrounds are clean and modern, and many are reported to have facilities for dumping waste water from RV tanks. As in any mountainous territory, there may be problems with hairpin turns. English is frequently spoken in the campgrounds.

The United Kingdom

As we've said before, the United Kingdom is a special case. Since America has always shared British history and literature, there are a lot of place names that will be familiar to every American. Even if you are not a student of English history, you've heard these names, often because towns here in the United States—places like Truro and Glastonbury—were named after the English towns from which the colonists originated. There are also many towns with funny names. Some are derived from Celtic names. Others convey information: towns that include the word "Chipping," for example, were once market towns. Towns situated on rivers frequently share the name of the river, as Exeter shares the name of the Ex River.

We found that campgrounds in England always had the equivalent of the electricity provided in U.S. sites. There were no prohibitions against grilling meat on barbecues in the UK, and the sanitary facilities were always up to modern standards.

There are not many open-air markets in England, although we did see a few. The many covered market areas are similar to indoor flea markets in the U.S. Even in these markets, however, the food in the UK doesn't measure up to French standards (reminding us once again that no one goes to Great Britain for the food!).

The villages and small cities seem remarkably clean. Most of the farmland is beautiful and the roads are clear of litter and have no billboards. Every little village has lovely hanging baskets of flowers everywhere.

Driving on the "wrong" side of the road makes driving a bit more difficult, but—as we've also said before—driving your own vehicle and driving from the side of the RV that you are used to make it much easier. Touring is also easier when you and the natives speak the same language, and the British really are much friendlier than their reputation might indicate. The entire island is tiny by American standards, and every village is accessible. Road signs are easy to follow and the major roads are as good as anything in the U.S. Although there are many narrow, winding roads leading to small villages, they are all manageable. If you've been to Great Britain and driven a rental car, you'll find that driving your own RV is easier, since you know how to judge your size. All in all, driving around England is really a pleasure.

Eastern Europe

Our information about this part of Europe is sketchy at best. But we have met English caravanners who have traveled throughout the countries of Eastern Europe. In general, the information that we have received is that there are campgrounds in Hungary, Slovakia, Poland, Slovenia, the Czech Republic, and Croatia. The facilities vary widely in their amenities. There are limited numbers of campsites where motor vehicle dump areas are available. A modest percentage of these facilities have proprietors who speak English. Most

Eastern Europe

campgrounds offer toilets, showers, and electricity, though there are many where you must provide your own sanitary facilities.

The countries of Eastern Europe only recently became part of the European Union. This means that border guards and customs barriers are still in the process of disappearing. These are the less prosperous parts of Europe, so the prices are usually lower. Eventually, these 10 new member countries will be eligible to join in the single currency (euro) system, but that will take time.

Most camping guides suggest that a complete inventory of the contents of the caravan or motor home be available for border guards. An International Driver's Permit is suggested as necessary, since it has a picture of the license holder on it.

Although British campers seem to be at ease with traveling in these areas, a motor home with United States license plates is more likely to be regarded by a small minority as a target. The police have issued various warnings about gangs of men who prey upon foreign vehicles, and an American RV would certainly attract unwanted attention.

There are many beautiful medieval buildings, UNESCO World Heritage Sites, and cities worth seeing in Eastern Europe. In fact, there are several cities—particularly Prague and Budapest—that we are personally anxious to visit. Instead of using our motor home for this purpose, however, we are thinking of leaving the vehicle in a convenient Western European campground and taking the train into the less developed areas. For the time being, this seems to be the most prudent way of visiting Eastern Europe.

12
TO BE CONTINUED...

Storing the RV in Europe

If you, like us, should find that touring Europe in your RV is an experience that you don't want to end, you may want to store your camper in Europe for the year. Then you can make another trip back, pick up the RV, and continue your travels.

Once we decided to store our RV, we were concerned about leaving it in an outside storage area. We preferred the idea of inside storage, thinking that it would be better for the brake system of the RV to be inside, protected from the weather. We were lucky to meet another American RVer who knew about storage in Holland. He told us about a storage solution there.

One of the streets in the town of Amstelveen near Amsterdam's Schiphol Airport is lined with storage facility after storage facility. Legmeerdijk (that's the name of the street) is only a few blocks from one of Amsterdam's campgrounds, Het Amsterdamse Bos. This campground is in a park on the southwest side of the metro area.

On Legmeerdijk you can find any kind of storage you are interested in—everything from a fenced-in outside space to a climate-controlled building. All the storage facilities are convenient to the airport. On our first trip, Mr. De Wit, who owns the greenhouse our RV is stored in, drove us in our camper to the bus station in Amstelveen, and we took buses to get to Brussels to fly home. On our second trip, he drove us to nearby Schiphol Airport.

Earlier in this book we mentioned that we opted for a green-

A view of the Amstelveen facility in which we stored our RV.

house that has been put to a new use. Although it is not climate controlled, the temperature and the humidity seemed perfect to us. We put up our rig after a very rainy couple of days. Everything inside was damp because there was a leak that hadn't been fixed. But when we picked up the RV months later for our second trip, it was dry and there was no sign—or smell—of damp or mildew.

There are numerous storage facilities in England as well. Since the English use far more caravans than they do motor homes, a good many of the storage places are outside. Many more facilities advertise "hardstanding" sites (not grass) than inside storage, but it is certainly possible to find inside storage. We found storage advertised in the monthly magazine of the Caravan Club as well as in the magazines devoted to caravanning that we bought on our trip. Storage is probably available everywhere. In Appendix E, under "Storage Facilities in Europe," we've included information for Holland, where we are familiar with the facilities, and for England, where information is easily available and in English.

Should You Get European Plates?

If you are seriously considering leaving your RV in Europe for future touring, it is also possible to get European plates for your vehicle. To arrange it, you'll have to get in touch with the local authorities. At the least, you'll need all the papers that the freight forwarder gave you, the title to the vehicle, a way to prove the value of the vehicle, and an address in the country in which you are going to store the vehicle. A friend's address would probably do, or perhaps the address of the storage facility, if the owners are willing to allow it. You will have to ask to have the vehicle's status changed. If it is no longer a visitor, you will have to pay an import duty on the value of the RV, and there are other legal implications. Once you have taken this step, you may even decide to sell the RV in Europe when you are done touring. There is a market for American RVs. Other campers have approached us in campgrounds asking us if we wanted to sell. They said that they would be interested in buying our motor home if we decided to sell it!

We plan eventually to bring our rig home, so we haven't changed our plates.

Shipping Home

On the other hand, if you wish to bring the rig home after your first tour, it is not hard to do. Just call the shipping company that brought you over. They will be able to advise you about finding a freight forwarder who will handle the transaction. Seabridge for Motorhomes in Dusseldorf, Germany, routinely handles RVs going to America. They are listed under "European Freight Forwarder" in Appendix E, but it may be easier to deal with a firm based in whatever country you are shipping from.

Beyond the "Nuts and Bolts"

A good deal of what we've written in this book has been "nuts and bolts." We've tried to describe how to go about planning an RV trip to Europe and the actual process of shipping. We've provided information on driving while in Europe, following road signs and reading the maps, as well as finding campgrounds and knowing what to expect once you've found them.

We've tried to explain what a great experience RVing in Europe can be. But to get the real flavor of the experience, perhaps even to feel the experience, there is no better guide than reading the letters we sent home from Europe. These letters are in Appendix A and Appendix B.

Before leaving on our first trip, we were surprised to discover that a lot of people wanted to be on our e-mail list to receive letters. So we set up a group e-mail account that allowed us to send a letter to one person and a blind copy to twenty-five others. This way, no long list of addresses would appear on anyone's computer. The letters were written in the evenings after long days of touring, and they tended to ramble. We've edited them for this book, but we think we've left enough in them so that you can get a realistic sense of what our travels were like. The 2002 letters from the Continent are in Appendix A and the 2003 letters from the United Kingdom are in Appendix B. These letters are as important as the first part of the book, because they'll give you a real "feel" for both of our trips.

They will give you a flavor for where we were, what we did, and what problems we encountered. The letters chronicle the things we saw and how we felt. In some ways, those letters made it possible for our family and friends to travel along with us.

Is This Kind of Trip for You?

The experiences we had while traveling led us to formulate some sets of "Milavsky's Laws." You've already seen those on food. Here are the rest:

1. It is always easier to get into "Centre Ville" than to get out.

2. Luggage (and food purchased in an open-air market) tends to grow in weight as the day progresses!

3. Bicycle lanes can be nearly as dangerous to the unwary as cars on the road.

4. Europeans swear that everything in Europe is a ten-minute walk from wherever you happen to be.

5. Nothing in Europe is closer than a twenty-minute walk when we are the walkers.

6. Since we've left England, no one will ever call me "Luv" again.

7. Never go on a trip like this until you've gone on a trip like this. You need to know the territory!

Actually, that last law applied to us, but it doesn't really apply to you—because, having read this book, you already know the territory.

When we first began thinking about traveling in Europe in our own RV, we had a lot of questions. It took several months for us to get all the answers to these questions. After looking very carefully into all the costs, we discovered that such a trip was not only feasible but also the least expensive way to spend such a long time in Europe. We found out how to ship our RV and what needed to be done to prepare the rig for the trip. We organized our lives at home to allow us to be out of the country for such a long time and to have all the things we needed when we got to Europe.

Once we were in Europe, we bungled along, learning about the road system, navigating between destinations, and finding campgrounds. We soon realized that there were campgrounds everywhere and public transit was convenient and common. It also became clear early on that this was a great way to travel, that the roads were excellent, and that we could use the RV just the way we had on our trips in the U.S., although we had to make adjustments to the electrical system first. We figured out how to stay in touch with home, use the telephone system and the Internet, and keep up with world events as we went along.

When we got home and had some time to think about what we had done right and what we had done wrong, we decided we ought to write the book that we wish we had read before our trip. And that's what this book is.

We hope that we have succeeded in explaining why there really is no comparable way to travel. Perhaps the only comparable experience would be to rent an apartment in a city and live there for a while. That is a good way, for example, to become a temporary Parisian, but it is a lot more difficult to become a temporary Frenchman. Driving an RV allows you to be a tourist and yet participate in the community life around you. You can shop for food the way everyone else does, drive the same highways, and see how people spend their leisure time.

In this book we have tried to explain what is so interesting about the kind of camping that allows you to visit cities all over Europe, learning firsthand about the cultural and historical treasures of the Old World or visiting the beautiful mountains, lakes, or seaside areas that you have heard about. We hope that we have given you enough information to make an informed decision about whether this kind of travel is for you.

The information we have presented can be of use not only to people planning to spend several months traveling around but also to those who have only a shorter time available. Obviously, if you only have a two-week vacation, you would not ship an RV to Europe. But there is a lot of information here about such things as renting an RV in Europe, driving it there, and what you can expect. We feel that information like this will be of help to anyone spending any time at all in Europe.

We have tried throughout the book to illustrate our comments by using our own experiences. Don't forget to read our letters!
BON VOYAGE!

"When we got home . . . we decided we ought to write the book that we wish we had read before our trip. And that's what this book is."

APPENDICES

WESTERN EUROPE

NORTH SEA

Baltic Sea

NORWAY
SWEDEN
FINLAND
Oslo
Stockholm
Helsinki

SCOTLAND
NORTHERN
IRELAND
UNITED
KINGDOM
EASTONIA
LATVIA
LITHUANIA

DENMARK
Copenhagen

Dublin
IRELAND
THE
NETHERLANDS
Amsterdam

WALES
ENGLAND
London
Berlin
GERMANY
POLAND
BELARUS

Brussels
BELGIUM
LUXEMBOURG
CZECH
REPUBLIC
UKRAINE

NORTH ATLANTIC OCEAN

Paris
FRANCE
Vienna
AUSTRIA
SLOVAKIA
MOLDOVA

Bern
SWITZERLAND
HUNGARY

SLOVENIA
ROMANIA

PORTUGAL
SPAIN
ITALY
CROATIA
BOSNIA
AND
HERZ.
YUGOSLAVIA
BULGARIA

Lisbon
Madrid
Rome
MACEDONIA
ALBANIA
TURKEY

Mediterranean Sea
GREECE
Athens

GIBRALTAR

SICILY

APPENDIX A

Letters from the Road: The Continent

Note: Because these letters were written during our 2002 trip, certain things, such as prices, have changed since then. Also, in these letters, "I" refers sometimes to Adelle and sometimes to Ron. Our method is generally for Adelle to write the letter and then for Ron to put in his two-cents' worth. This means that you may or may not be able to figure out which one is "I" in any particular reference, but most of the time it will be obvious.

LETTER #1—BRUGGE, BELGIUM, MARCH 25, 2002

When we arrived in Brussels, we got our baggage—three duffels, all quite heavy. We not only had 10 days' worth of clothes (for a 90-day trip), but also books, a few tools, all the medicine for 90 days, and lots of extras—as well as the computer, camera, camcorder, etc. that had been in our carry-on luggage. We put it all in two carts and got into elevators to get to the train station. There we purchased the tickets that would take us from the airport to the Brussels train station and then to Brugge. Unfortunately, the same train didn't go all that way. We had to change trains.

First, it is important (Ron says) to mention the mysterious growth of the weight of our luggage from a manageable 250 pounds to at least 10,000 pounds at the Gare Nord in Brussels. So long as we were in the airport, there were carts available. Once we got on the train, all amenities vanished. Whatever happened to the porters who were always available to the hero and heroine in 1930s' movies?

Actually, there were carts available for rent in the station—but they worked only with Belgian francs, and there are no Belgian francs anymore! What other coin would work? No one knew (or cared). So we carried the 10,000 pounds for miles on train platforms, up and down steep flights of stairs, on and off trains, and finally, after arriving in Brugge, from the farthest platform to the taxi stand. To add insult to injury, the taxi drivers are not allowed to come onto the huge pedestrian area in front of the station, so we had to carry the luggage to the cab. But all things come to an end, and we finally got everything into the taxi and were driven to our hotel. Much later, we discovered that it would have been possible to use either a token or a small euro coin to get a cart.

[Note: See Letter #17, written at the end of our stay, for how we managed to make going home slightly easier than getting there.]

We spent the day in Brugge like any other tourists. We ate wonderful Belgian waffles and looked at the beautiful northern Renaissance buildings and the shops full of lace and chocolate. Then we went to the hotel and slept for a couple of hours.

The next morning we called a cab, dreading a repeat performance of hauling the luggage into the station to get a train to Zeebrugge. Fortunately, in our conversation with the driver, we discovered that he could take us right to the dock for 25 euros (about $23 at the time). Was that ever the right decision! Eventually we got to the right dock. We spent four hours there! First they had to find our RV, then there was paperwork, then there was a minor problem, then there was lunch—during which no drivers could be found to bring us the RV. Finally we were pleased to see it appear, and all was really quite well. No damage. Nothing stolen. We unpacked a bit and started off for Brugge and the campground. Only got lost once or twice. It helped that Zeebrugge is only about 12 kilometers (9 miles) from Brugge, and that Brugge itself is pretty small.

The campground deserves some description. When we pulled in at 2 PM, the reception office was closed. So we went to the attached bar and . . . well, here's Ron's list of information on the campground:

- Has a bar attached. Never saw such a thing in the U.S.

- Bar filled with bleary-eyed locals at 2 PM.

- Very "helpful" denizens.

- Two tried to supply us with one plug needed to plug into electricity.

- One of the locals supplied plug—for 10 euros. And worth it.

- Campground has no sewer dump; water at only a few spots.

- Electric current 220 volt at 5 amps! Blew two campground circuit breakers. But the 220 to 110 converter worked! We have the ability to run everything from the battery charger to the microwave. Since we need more than 5 amps to run the heater, though, we're using the propane furnace, which keeps us very comfortable. Don't know where we'll be able to get propane refills or at what cost. But we're keeping a positive attitude.

- Campground has beautiful, clean showers, but they are housed far from the beautiful, clean toilets in another building. It's a strange arrangement.

About Brugge. It's a beautiful city. After the Renaissance, it never had another boom time, so it still has a lot of its pre-Renaissance thirteenth-century buildings left! It's quite small, with two beautiful market squares, a lot of lace, tapestry, and chocolate shops, and cobblestone streets and canals lined with old houses. The architecture is distinctive. A seemingly endless line of beautiful, high-stepping horses doing a very fast clop-clop parades through the streets, pulling carriages filled with tourists. The horses have bags attached to them to prevent manure from soiling the streets. We also saw a pair of huge jet-black Belgian work horses with hairy hooves hauling an enormous trailer full of beer kegs that the two uniformed drivers were delivering. The city has quite a few museums with lots of Flemish paintings. We visited a thirteenth-century cathedral that has a Michelangelo madonna and child statue as well as a large Caravaggio painting.

That's it for now, except to say that today we got to the old square and found our worst fears realized. There was a market today, but we weren't able to buy anything because we weren't going right home. Flowers, food—everything looked great. R&A

Letter #2—Ghent, Belgium, April 4, 2002

It has been quite cool since we picked up the RV in Zeebrugge. We have been using our propane heater to warm up the RV—mostly just in the evening and morning, but occasionally all night. In just the first week, we used a half a tank of gas! Worse, while visiting some friends in Tilburg, in the Netherlands, we found out that our whole system is different. Everyone says it will be impossible to refill our tank in Europe. So one day we drove all over Ghent until we found a gas company that could sell us an adapter and fill our tank. We ended up seeing more of the workaday industrial area than anyone would want, but we hope that we're all set now—and we know the RV is no problem on the roads.

Tilburg is an industrial town—mostly solidly built brick houses. But it has a wonderful open-air market, which we loved. Everything for sale except old things—meat, fish, fruits & vegetables, clothes, hardware. Bought white asparagus and wonderful strawberries from Spain, cheese from local makers, fish smoked by the dealer, etc. We had a wonderful time in the market on Saturday.

Easter is a two-day holiday around here. We left Tilburg on Monday morning and drove the 2 to 3 hours to Ghent in Belgium. That day there were lots of caravans (small trailers) in the campground. Now it's nearly empty! It's a terrific campground. Among its wonderful attributes: good facilities, including a dump for waste water from the RV holding tanks, a nice restaurant, a grocery, a shop selling *frites* (French fries). In fact, it's so nice here that we'll stay through tomorrow when we'll take the bus to the station and the train to Brussels. Why struggle with a new place when Brussels is only 40 minutes away by train?

Bought gasoline for the first time since we got here. It was, as Ron says, a "thrilling" experience. We bought 10 euros worth of gas (about $9) in Holland at 1.17 euros per liter (which works out to about $4 per U.S. gallon) and then another 30 euros worth in Belgium at 1.01 euros per liter (a bargain), for a total of about $36, which brought our 12-gallon tank up to about 3/4 full! Of course, for this $36 we've been to Zeebrugge, Brugge, and Tilburg. It's a good thing distances are shorter in Europe.

Ghent is another medieval town. Lots of canals (we took a boat tour), an inordinate number of cathedrals, including one that boasts a van Eyck masterpiece—a twelve-part altarpiece that is truly a thing of beauty. Buildings on the canals date back as far as the eleventh century. All are quite interesting and often beautiful. We had our coffee and pastry, walked many, many miles, and even had time to find an Internet shop, where Ron deleted 140 messages from his e-mail inbox. Tomorrow Brussels and Friday, if all goes well, Paris.

Interesting tidbit: We find that the meat we buy here cooks better than the U.S. equivalent. There's no water in the meat, so it browns much better when being pan-fried. The asparagus and strawberries were both outstanding. Even eating in the RV is a pleasure. The weather has turned warm and sunny and pleasant. The coffee is wonderful, the pastries are scrumptious, the bread is crisp, the waffles melt in your mouth, the beer is delicious, and the chocolate is outstanding. So far, so good. R&A

LETTER #3—PARIS, FRANCE, APRIL 8, 2002

We left the RV parked in the campground in Ghent and took two buses to get to the railroad station, where we took a train to Brussels. The cost for two round-trips was less than $25, and we were there within an hour of leaving the campground.

As soon as we got to the Brussels train station, we noticed a big difference. The language had changed from one that is Dutch-like to French. Even the lady who collected money for the toilet in the train station spoke French. Brussels is much more of a standard international cosmopolitan city, but it still has an exquisitely grand market! It's a newer market than any we've seen before. These buildings seem to be mostly late 1600s. Much newer!

Went through the enormous Beaux Art Museum, then walked around the city until we found an Internet café and worked on our e-mail mailbox. After an hour, we left and went next door to a take-out store to buy a rotisseried chicken. We were very sadly contemplating the painful walk up the hill to the railroad station. A bus pulled up. Ron asked the driver if any buses went to the station. "Yes," he said, "I do." So we got on the bus and asked what the fare was. When we tried to pay, all the driver would say is "It's just two minutes up the hill." A free bus ride. Never happened before! When we left, we said *"Merci beaucoup"* with great feeling.

The train to Ghent was quite full, because apparently people commute to Brussels! But we got home quickly. Went to the campground snack bar and ordered one large order of fried potatoes. We were given a huge package, but it cost less than $1.50. The package was 9" by 11" by 6"! Good thing we didn't order two!

It's about 180 miles from Ghent to Paris. The trip took us about 4 hours and we used 60 euros worth of gasoline (about $54). At one point during the trip, there was a sign that said "Take a ticket." We were on a toll road. It had never occurred to us to check that aspect of the route. We won't let it happen again. We were on the A2 for about 130 miles—and the toll was 17.40 euros (about $15.50). As you can see, the cost here is about triple the cost in the U.S. That's bad enough, but when we looked at the receipt, it got worse. They charged not only a high toll but a 19.6 VAT (value added tax) on the toll. That really added insult to injury.

Paris seems much more crowded and has a much more diverse population than when we were here last. We arrived on Friday. The traffic in Paris is not only heavy but also aggressive, frighteningly so. You enter a roundabout and all of a sudden a car buzzes up on your left and gets in front of you, missing you by inches. And the motorcycles and motor scooters buzz around you like a swarm of angry mosquitoes. Our little RV is slow and a bit unwieldy. It was not a fun trip to the Bois de Boulogne where we are now camped. We got into the campground in late afternoon and just chilled out for the rest of the day.

After lunch, we visited the Musée d'Orsay, a converted railway station full of Impressionist paintings. Adelle felt as though every time she tried to leave, she was faced with yet another room full of paintings or etchings or statues that she just couldn't ignore. The place was huge.

Coming home we got on the right metro line and got off at the right metro station, but walked out the wrong metro exit—which was a mistake that was hard to repair. We had no idea where to get the bus that would take us to the campground and we didn't recognize any landmarks. We had walked underground when we had come in and hadn't even realized that the Arc de Triomphe was our neighbor. After wandering all over, we finally found some security people at the huge indoor mall where we had somehow ended up. They had no idea where we should go, but were able to tell us (1) where the regular buses came in and (2) where the *Périphérique* (ring road) lets traffic out into this area. With that information, we were able to find the bus. And you better believe that we watched where we went into the subway the next day, so that we could come out the same way. That's a difference between Holland, Belgium, and France—or at least, Paris. In Belgium and Holland people go out of their way to give you all the information you need, but in Paris you're pretty much on your own. The reputation that the French have for being unfriendly is pretty well deserved, at least in our experience. If they would just tell campers to be sure to follow the signs to a particular gate when they get off the train, people wouldn't get into difficulty. But no one bothers. Another difference between Holland and Belgium and France is that more Dutch and Belgians speak English. In that respect, the French are more like we Americans, who also usually know only our own language—more's the pity.

We spent several days in Paris, going to museums, just looking at various areas—Les Halles, the West Bank, the old Jewish quarter, etc. We did a lot of walking, and found that there was a noticeably heavy police presence at all times in all areas.

We're preparing other letters on special topics that we think might be of interest, but we're too busy to do more tonight. Got to cook the wonderful food we bought—and then eat the great things we picked up at the patisserie. It's easy to get used to this life! R&A

LETTER #4—AZAY-LE-RIDEAU, FRANCE, APRIL 15, 2002

This is small-town France—not Paris—and finding an Internet café is very difficult. In the meantime, we should mention that our French is still rudimentary, but enough people speak English for us to get by—and we do get help from a little hand-held electronic gadget that provides translations in a pinch. It took us a while to discover that the gadget translates from English English, not American English. For example, "elevator" is not listed, but "lift" is.

We left Paris Tuesday morning and began a very traumatic trip to Normandy. Just a few blocks from the campground we got lost and floundered around a bit. And we had a slight "adventure" on our way. We both saw the sign that read "Tunnel to Caen" to the left and "Caen through Centre Ville" on the right. Ron chose the tunnel to avoid the narrow streets. Unfortunately, there was no tunnel. It was an overpass, and it was not quite high enough for our RV. We hit the plastic that covers the air conditioning unit and it broke. The cover fell off shortly after. Got to Normandy without further incident.

Once in Normandy, we were looking for a particular park. We saw a campsite from the road and got off the road, but couldn't figure out how to get back to the site. So we drove a little farther and saw a municipal campground. We pulled into it at 5:15. The sign said *"Ferme a 17h"*—and although one of the permanent residents rang the bell for the caretaker, no one came down. We left. Eventually we found the campsite listed in the book, but it turned out that that campsite took only mobile homes. The proprietor was nice, however, and gave us a flyer from a real campground. We followed the instructions he had given us in French and, after some problems with one-way signs, found the street. We drove into a campground, but it was the wrong one. The man there said *"Fermé"* and waved us on. Finally, after 6 PM, we found a campground in a hamlet called Hermanville. They took us. They couldn't give us electricity, however, because we needed yet another adapter! Some of the *"campings"* (as they are called) have "heavy duty" plugs and others just use the equivalent of a house outlet.

We drove all through the Normandy invasion beaches and visited the American cemetery at Omaha Beach, which was a very emotional experience. It was cold and windy. Very nasty; so we didn't linger long outside.

We stopped near Avranches in Brittany at about 5 PM and pulled into a very nice, modern, clean campground in a tiny town called Genets. In this campground, as is quite common in Europe, the showers are in one building, the sinks in another, and the toilets in still another. The water wasn't really hot, the building was way too open to the cold air, and the "lavabo," where there are sinks for shaving, was ice cold. Ron shaved in the RV! It was really nasty—cold and very, very windy. St. Malo, which had been our planned next stop, looked considerably less appealing because of this. We decided to head directly south.

We are now at our next stop, a little town called Azay-le-Rideau in the Loire Valley near Tours. The *"camping"* is clean, new, and in the middle of a very pretty little town. The water, thank goodness, is *chaud* and so is the shower building . The town has a fifteenth-century chateau and a big tourist trade, so there are restaurants and other services. Since we can easily walk to any one of the restaurants, we went out for dinner.

Today we visited another city with a chateau. Loche's chateau is considerably older—old enough so that Jeanne d'Arc really did stay there. Our next stop was to be a town named Descartes. We wanted to see the philosopher's home, which is now a museum, but we couldn't find the house. The French apparently believe in inconspicuous signs. Driving through France has been an education in how good the signs are in the U.S., even where they are bad.

We returned to Azay-le-Rideau. Adelle visited the local chateau, which had been built somewhat later and was considerably more elegant than the first one we had visited earlier that day. This one is Renaissance style and looks just beautiful—like a set for a swashbuckling movie.

One more thing. In the Paris letter, we said that the French deserved their reputation for being unfriendly. We take it back. It's really the Parisians who are unfriendly, not the French. Here, people say hello and do their best to help us. R&A

Letter #5—Toulouse, France, April 17, 2002

We drove through Limoges (where porcelain is made), but there didn't seem to be any campgrounds open anywhere. So Ron decided to keep driving until we got to Périgueux, where we knew from a guidebook that there is an open *"camping."* We'd been driving a long time, but we didn't see any other choice. And we were worried that we'd get to the campground too late to get in. About 50 kilometers north of the city, we saw a sign for *"Camping en ferme"*—camping on a farm. Because the sign said it was so close, we decided to try it. It turned out that the owners live there, so it was open. The hot water wasn't on, but there were clean bathrooms and electric service. It was a good port in a storm. Of course, it was a little hard to arrange, since we speak so little French and the farmer spoke no English at all. Fortunately, though, another camper-car (as they are called here) had pulled in ahead of us, and those folks spoke not only their native German but also English and French. Between us, we found a safe haven.

We went into the farmhouse to pay. It was just what you'd expect—old, with beamed ceilings, very little daylight, a huge fireplace, etc. The farmer's wife was very nice and even knew a few words of English. In the summer, in that beautiful setting, and when they have hot water and a swimming pool, it must be heaven.

Sunday morning marked the beginning of our third week in Europe. We drove into Périgueux (40 miles east and a little south of Bordeaux). We found a parking space and saw a lot of people carrying empty baskets and heading down the street. Show Ron a scene like this and he'll find a *marché* (market). And he did. It was a wonderful market—flowers, meat, fish, many vendors selling the local specialty, foie gras, baked goods, fruits, and vegetables. Despite a bad case of "eyes bigger than our stomachs," we managed to buy only a fraction of what was available.

It was still pretty cold, so we decided to head farther south. Périgueux also has a medieval city, but it has become obvious that you can't stop to see every one of those in the southern part of France. That would be a life's work! The guidebook had suggested that Périgueux would be a good stepping-off place for the Cro-Magnon cave paintings at Lascaux, so we set off for a small town near the caves. The original caves have actually been closed to tourism. Too many visitors had inadvertently started various things growing on the paintings, and the government decided to close the caves in order to save the paintings. But they made exact replicas for tourists to see, and that is where we were headed.

After describing the way the new caves had been constructed and showing us all the paintings, the guide turned off the dim lights. He then asked everyone to take out lighters so we could duplicate the way the cave was originally lit with the animal-fat lamps that were found on the floor. In the wavering light the animals looked as if they were moving.

Our next stop was Martel, a lovely little medieval town. We parked in a lot and climbed a hill road to the medieval city. On our way we found a covered new marketplace (built in the 1700s), the Tourist Office, and the house in which Henri Court-Mantel (Short Coat!) died. Henri should have been Henry III of England, but he died before inheriting the throne. His father was Henry II and his mother was Eleanor of Aquitaine. We're sure you remember them and their other sons—Richard the Lion-hearted and John of Magna Carta fame—from *The Lion in Winter,* even if you're not a student of English history.

The town was probably old when Henri died, and it looks it. We were there on a Monday, and everything was closed. And we do mean everything. I think people in this town take Monday off for lunch. But we did manage to find a place where we could have a cup of coffee, and we videotaped a lot of medieval streets and buildings. *Très intéressant.*

The lady in the Tourist Office marked off a bunch of local campgrounds for us. Since this is pre-season, a lot of them are closed. But we found one that seemed close and is open all year, so we set off for it. We didn't have far to go, but when we came to the road leading off the highway to the campground, we were a bit dismayed. It was a single-lane road with gullies instead of shoulders—and there didn't seem to be any turn-outs for use in case you met someone coming the other way. But we decided to chance it. We'd gone several kilometers and were despairing of ever finding the place when we came across a truck that had misjudged one of the many turns and was now half off the road in a ditch. He said he'd already called for help, and we managed to get by him with literally inches to spare! Not too long after, we did find the campground and pulled in. I tried to tell the proprietor about the truck, but couldn't find the word "truck" on my translator. Later, Ron had the brilliant idea of trying "lorry" and the word *"campion"* appeared. Anyway, we finally said *"Accidente"* and he went to look. When we left the next morning, the truck was gone, so they must have come to get him.

This campground was clean and had all new facilities. It was beautiful and the birds were all singing. It must be paradise in the summer here when everything is in bloom. Very nice. R&A

Letter #6—Carcassonne, France, April 18, 2002

We arrived in Toulouse on the 16th and found the campground within the city limits, a bus ride away from the city center. The architecture is more modern than in other places we've been and the houses are actually painted in light pastel colors, kind of like what you find in Mediterranean cities. The city's economy in the past was based on *"pastel,"* which in this case means a spectacular blue dye that is used to make gorgeous cloth.

We stopped here primarily because it is almost as far south as one can go in France—which means it's warm—and because we wanted to find Internet access. We were successful in that. The city has a beautiful square, of course. It also has a wonderful private collection of art and an enormous chapel that houses the remains of St. Thomas Aquinas.

After leaving Toulouse we headed for Carcassonne because the guide-books said it had an old walled city. We got a little lost trying to find the campground, overshot it, went around a curve, and there the city was, right in front of us, about half a mile away. We were stunned. Literally. Mouths open, chins hanging. It was as if we had traveled through a time warp. There in front of us was a city from hundreds of years ago. A movie set could not have created a more fantastic sight. In fact, we were looking at a real city that had served as a movie set for the 1990 movie *Robin Hood, Prince of Thieves,* starring Kevin Costner. It stretched before us from left to right, girded by an uneven wall of stone with towers topped by black cones. Behind the wall there was was a square tower, then a taller wall, and then more towers. The city is situated on a hill, and it occupied two-thirds of the view in front of us. A fascinating place. When we leave, it'll be for either Provence or Spain. Stay tuned. R&A

Letter #7—Arles, France, April 22, 2002

It was Saturday when we left Carcassonne. After much discussion, we ultimately decided not to go to Barcelona, which was pretty close—less than 200 miles away. Both of us had been there and Adelle wasn't anxious to go back. And we were quite near the Camargue region and Provence, where there are a lot of promising things and places.

The Camargue is on the Mediterranean coast. Native white horses roam free on the flat marshland, flamingos crowd the bays, and black cattle with long white horns graze in the fields. We headed for the area of Arles, Nimes, and Avignon. It has been our practice to use the roads marked in red in our maps. This time, we opted for one of the yellow roads—rated even worse than the second-rate red roads. But this road followed the sea. We passed a strip of beach about 10 kilometers long. The water was actually an azure color, even though the Cote d'Azur doesn't begin until farther east. The road was totally lined with cars, motor homes, and caravans, but though it was right next to the beach, few people were actually on the beach. It was a warm day, but not quite beach weather yet. Many of the motor homes and caravans were from Germany. I guess if you're from that far north, this beach is heaven. It certainly was nice to look at.

We arrived in Arles, where the artist Van Gogh cut off his ear and had episodes of madness and painted some of the most beautiful and striking pictures ever painted by anyone. We found a campground that turned out to be both inconvenient and expensive. (We found out about the inconvenience only when we discovered that there was no hot water for shaving, unless you used the little tub for washing babies.) So, the following morning we checked out and found a different "camping."

After the move, we took the bus into town. Our first stop was at the Tourist Office, where we bought a guide outlining several walking tours. Arles center contains all the things that would interest a tourist. It is small and walkable, even for us. We started with the Van Gogh walk, looking for the places where he had set up his easel and painted. The first stop on the tour was the café (Café Étoile) which he painted in yellows and bright blues. We found it with little trouble.

This town is filled with ruins from Roman times. There is an amphitheater dating from 80 BC and a theater dating from 10–20 BC. Both are still in recognizable shape and still in use. Bullfights are held in the arena, which turned out to be one of the scenes that Van Gogh painted. A copy of the painting hangs in front of the entrance. There were other assorted ruins—a piece of the forum, the remains of an elaborate bath complex, walls of various sizes, a circus, and what looks like an aqueduct, among other things.

For the next day, Monday, we had several things on our agenda—Internet, groceries, the bridge that Van Gogh painted (no, he didn't paint the bridge, he did a painting of the bridge) and the Museum of Antiquities. We took the RV and found the Internet shop by following directions given to us (in French!) by a young man at the campground. Unfortunately, they didn't have a disk drive we could use to copy our letter, so they gave us instructions (in French!) to another Internet place.

So for the second time today, we drove off into the "wild bleu yonder"! Wonder of wonders, we found the next place too. It was closed until 1 PM, but the garage next door was open and willing to change the oil in the RV. So we made an appointment to come back for the oil change after lunch. Someone there gave us instructions (again in French!) to get to the Museum of Antiquities—and we set off. For the third time in one day, we got where we were going without a problem.

This museum was something really special. It was filled mainly with artifacts uncovered in Arles, beginning with those of the earliest inhabitants from 5,000 to 6,000 years ago, extending through the Ligurians in the sixth through fourth centuries BC and then into the Roman period and the early Christian era. Most interesting to us was the Roman period, partly because there were so many artifacts from that period. This is one of the best museums we've ever seen. It is small and dedicated only to things found locally.

We left the museum, ate our lunch in the RV in the parking lot, and were on our way again. First we wanted to see that Van Gogh bridge and then we needed to get back to the Internet shop/garage on the other side of the river. The bridge was no longer useful, so the city had built a modern one over the Rhone and moved the old one to a canal at the edge of the city. There it sits, looking just as it did when Van Gogh painted it.

We found it with no problem, then headed for the other side of the river. A miracle. For the fourth time in one day, we found our way without a problem. We accomplished both remaining errands. While we sent off our letters and read our e-mail, we had the oil changed. Would you believe they charged us 35 euros ($32) for the oil change? Of this, $7 was for topping off the windshield washer fluid!

We went back across the river and drove to a different suburb where the supermarkets are. No problem! After shopping, we wanted to buy gas, but the Geant where we had done our shopping was remodeling its gas station. So we went to the smallest Intermarché gas station that we've ever seen. Nevertheless, we got back to the campground without having to back up. We must be getting the hang of it!

As for a description of French gas stations, that's going to have to wait. In

the meantime, everybody do your level best to stay well and enjoy.
R&A

LETTER #8—AVIGNON, FRANCE, APRIL 25, 2002

Having done everything that we wanted to do and seen everything that seemed important in Arles, we left. But we both felt a bit sad. We really liked this city. One hundred years later, Arles is not quite as lovely as it seemed to Van Gogh. It's grown and the new buildings are not as charming as the old. And the traffic is a nightmare—but it's a really nice city. We discussed where to go next, and finally Adelle suggested Aix-en-Provence because by going there we'd be able to both visit a city and stay in Provence. So off we went.

A campground was listed in one of our books. The directions seemed simple enough.... They *seemed* simple, but no matter which way we turned, it was wrong. Over a sandwich in a supermarket parking lot, Ron suggested that we forget Aix-en-Provence and move on to somewhere else. So we took off again, aiming for Avignon.

The N7 takes you between Arles and Avignon quite directly, if you can manage to avoid the toll road, which is always an "A" road. This is carefully engineered to connect with the N road in such a way that it may confuse you into taking the "A" road and paying a toll. While we managed to stay off the *autoroute,* we had quite a discussion about the way they had gone about trying to get you to take the *péage.*

Got to Avignon and had the same reaction we'd had to Carcassonne. Wow! A walled city looming up out of the hills. We followed the outside wall, came over the Pont Edward Deladier, and found ourselves at the Bagatelle Camping, which was right on the banks of the Rhone and only a short walk across the Deladier Bridge to the old town. And here we stayed.

From this bridge you can see the Pont d'Avignon sticking out about three-quarters of the way across the river and abruptly ending there. We could see people walking on it, but they weren't dancing. Apparently, the song is somewhat incorrect. The dancing really was "under" *(sous)* the bridge at Avignon, not "on" *(sur)* the bridge of Avignon.

Our first question in the camping reception office: Is there a bus? The answer: No. It's only 500 meters across a bridge to the city wall. From our bridge, we also could see the Palace of the Popes (who lived in Avignon for more than a hundred years in the fourteenth and fifteenth centuries). It's a very imposing structure.

The city is built on a hill. Every time you go anywhere, there are steps. Lots of steps. This morning, after stopping in at the Internet café, we looked for a way to get up to the Palace of the Popes. From the walk we had taken yesterday, we knew that any set of steps (and the city has probably forty or more sets) would lead us to that level. So Ron took the first set he saw, and when we reached the top, we were a bit startled by a street sign that read "The Street of the Ancient Jews." Somehow, the idea of Jews in the city of the popes seemed a bit odd. In fact, I think Ron took pictures of the sign, which was very close to the Palace of the Popes.

Then we saw a sign for a synagogue. We decided to follow the sign and soon found ourselves at a seventeenth-century synagogue. While we were looking around, the rabbi came out and invited us in. He gave us a tour of the building and told us the story of the Jewish community in Avignon. He said that there had been Jews in Avignon since the first century, and when the popes arrived a thousand years later, they became the protectors of the Jews! That's why the Jews here were called "the pope's Jews."

After touring the Palace of the Popes, we decided to have a cup of coffee in a local brasserie that we had found near the Internet place. We each had a wonderful cup of what used to be called *café au lait* and is now *café crème,* and Ron bought a newspaper—all for less than the cost of a single cup of coffee in Paris!

The next day we went south a little ways at the suggestion of a caretaker in the Arles campground. He had told us that a town called Les Baux was worth visiting. He explained that it had been declared the most beautiful village in France last year and next year would be declared the most beautiful village in the world! He didn't know who the declaring agency was, but one cannot ignore such a grand recommendation, especially if the place is only 15 kilometers away.

This village truly is a beautiful place, high up on a hill in the Alpilles Mountains. At one time a Roman outpost, it has stone quarries nearby and was clearly a natural stopping place for traders. Now it has the usual glut of restaurants (several in gorgeous settings), souvenir shops, food shops, an *église* (church) and a chateau, and many ruins from the Roman fort. After a couple of hours of walking around, we were tired and drove to a nearby campground, where we relaxed for the rest of the afternoon—one of the few times we did that.

The next day we had two objectives. One was to see the Pont du Gard and its nearby Roman aqueduct and the second was to visit a mountain village north and west of where we were—and south and west of Lyon— Le Chambon sur Lignon.

First, the aqueduct. This is an amazingly large and beautiful segment of a part of the aqueduct built in the first century to carry water to the Roman city that is now called Nimes. The aqueduct is simply stunning, in terms of both size and engineering.

From here, we headed into the mountains for Le Chambon sur Lignon. Some of you may have heard of this place, which was the subject of a documentary on PBS a few years ago. It is a Huguenot village whose townspeople took in as many Jews as they could handle between 1939 and 1945 to protect them from the Nazis. Why? The pastor of the local church said it was the right thing to do!

Getting there was a tough drive up mountain roads, as bad as the worst we climbed in the U.S. last year. We went from sea level to 4,000 feet in a very short distance and over a very long time. The speed limit was 20 to 25 miles per hour—sometimes 10 miles per hour—and there were lots of hairpin curves. The drive took forever and Ron was pretty tired when we finally arrived—only to discover that the campground there was closed until May 1. We parked near it in a school parking lot and stayed there overnight.

That night it rained and the mountains got very cold. The temperature was probably in the thirties and there was a strong wind. Regrettably, we had to leave because it was so cold and there was no place to park without a very hard climb. So, we headed back down the mountain.

This afternoon we got to a town called Anse, north of Lyon. Tomorrow

Our "home on wheels."

we will bus into the second largest city in France and spend the day there. Then we'll set out for Dijon, where I think there is a fair chance of getting some mustard. After that we'll set out for Alsace-Lorraine and and Germany. More in a few days. R&A

LETTER #9—DIJON, FRANCE, APRIL 30, 2002

Our next stop was the city of Lyon. Although the bus schedule on Sunday is "not very interesting," as a previous campground owner had told us, there was a bus to Lyon at 9:25. So we hurried to leave in time to walk the 20 minutes we knew it would take us to get to the bus stop, even though the owner had assured us it was only a 10-minute walk away.

The ride into the city was long and expensive, but we were glad not to have to fight the traffic in the camper. Our inquiries of the bus driver— How do we get to the Old City? How do we get back? *(en français, n'est-ce pas)*—got us a few grunts and the word "metro." Easier said than done when all you have is a 50 euro bill and everything is automated. But Ron eventually found a news agent who would change the 50 if we bought a newspaper—and off we went to the Tourist Office via Lyon's lovely new-looking subway system.

When we came up out of the subway, we were really pleased we'd come. The Vieux Ville (the Old City) is beautiful—and there seemed to be a huge hill with beautiful buildings on it. It's quite spectacular. The young woman in the Tourist Office said there are two main tourist areas. One is the beautiful Old City. The other is the area far up that hill, which you reach by funicular. We opted for the funicular, so we walked toward the Bonaparte Bridge to find it.

The trouble was that the bridge was the beginning of a huge market— and despite the fact that we wouldn't be home until evening, we bought a lot of stuff. It didn't start off too heavy. How much can one chicken (cooked), green beans, peas, tomatoes, two kinds of olive melange, new garlic, bread, and a few flowers weigh? Not too much at 11 AM, but by 2 PM, the weight of it caused Ron to think we might have also bought a case of beer, and by 5 PM he said he didn't think we should have bought a case of wine too!

But at 11 AM, I was very happy to shoulder the load. We started looking for a place to eat lunch. Then it took a while to find the signs for the funicular. After riding it up to the top we arrived at the Lyon Cathedral of Notre Dame—a wildly ornate nineteenth-century building standing high on a hill overlooking the city. Interesting. Great views from the terrace. Then, since the map indicated that the Roman theatre and the museum of Roman Gaul weren't too far away, we headed there.

A lot of the theater is left—and an odeum (a small roofed concert hall) is next door. On the other side, there is a wonderful museum built into the hill. It has a huge amount of information and many objects from Roman and pre-Roman times.

We decided to take the funicular down from the other side of the area so that we could walk through the theater. Before attempting the bottom set of stairs, which had no railings and had been built in 43 AD, we sat for a while on the seats. Afterwards, we both were struck by the fact that we'd just sat where many other people had sat in the first century!

Sitting on the funicular allowed a little rest, but when we got back down, we realized we didn't have any change for the metro. So we did a very French thing. We sat down in a café. Ron had a beer and I had an ice. Very nice, indeed.

We had a wonderful dinner, all from the Sunday market. Rotisseried chicken, wonderful country wheat bread with poppy seeds, fresh peas, the first grape tomatoes we've seen here, and spectacular-tasting fresh olives prepared two different ways—Provençal and Mexican. Since they are fresh olives, they have very little salt in them, and they taste just wonderful. It was a perfect ending to a perfect day.

The next morning we left our campground in Anse. First stop, Fleuri. The campground owner said the best Beaujolais comes from Fleuri. So, we stopped at the town, tasted the wine, and bought some. Then we got back on the N6 and headed for Dijon. Next stop, the supermarket. As usual, we had a really good time in the supermarket. We've got a refrigerator full of strange and wonderful things to eat.

An hour or so later, we got lost in Chalon le Grand because the navigator (Adelle) didn't realize that, in the absence of signs for Dijon, one should follow signs for Beaune. As a result, we went south instead of north, and ended up making a huge circle before we finally figured it all out. Why there were no signs for Dijon is one of the mysteries of the French information system. Why our navigator didn't realize we had to follow signs for Beaune is (she thinks) quite understandable.

When we corrected the error, however, we drove straight through Beaune, which has a wonderful medieval city wall complete with ramparts and funny little guardhouses with gothic roofs, and into Dijon. We were now in Burgundy, home of the "grand cru" wines. Beaune is at the heart of this region. We even found the new campground without too much trouble. So, if all's well that ends well, all is well. More later. R&A

LETTER #10—MAINZ, GERMANY, MAY 5, 2002

We drove to Mainz through Dijon, Alsace, and the small German border town of Freiberg. On every long trip, a little rain must fall. On this trip we had almost no rain for the first five weeks or so. But it has been raining since May 1. Today is May 5 and the rain stopped before noon, but it is still overcast and threatening in Mainz, Germany. We think nature has more than caught up. And, in the process, it has caused us to miss what may have been several nice experiences.

In Dijon we washed clothes but could not dry them because the *sechage* (dryer) wasn't working. So we put up a line and hung the clothes out to dry—in the late afternoon. Of course, that night it started to rain. Ron got up and brought in the clothes, which were still damp. We discovered that we were not equipped for sightseeing in the rain. Ron had not brought any rainwear and we had no umbrellas.

We spent only a day in Dijon. It was nothing spectacular as far as great big medieval buildings and/or Roman ruins are concerned. It's a really big city, with a small area of tourist interest. However, it does have a terrific market area, and we certainly did enjoy that. We didn't need a lot and didn't buy a lot, but we had fun walking through the market for several hours before buying a couple of things and having a sandwich in a park nearby.

By the time we finished with all the things we wanted to do in Dijon, we'd had it, so we went back to our campground to do the laundry and rest. The rain started up again early the next morning. We weren't planning to stay another day anyway, so we left in the rain for Besançon. Unfortunately for us, the needle on the gas gauge was nearing empty as we approached Besançon. No gas stations were open. To make matters worse, the signs on the way into town were confusing and we drove around needlessly, endangering our supply of gas. So we decided to concentrate on finding the campground before empty found us! And we did.

Besançon is about 80 kilometers to the east of Dijon. We got there on May 1, a big holiday in France, and waited there for France to reopen so that we could investigate the ancient citadel on a great hill in Besançon and go on to our next stop, Colmar in Alsace.

Talk about taking a holiday. On May 1, France is literally closed. This means stores, supermarkets, gas stations, all government and other offices. The only things that were open were flower shops and bakeries. And the heavy rain that had begun in Dijon continued.

We've driven a long way in France, and it's been one big farm wherever we've gone. It is certainly beautiful. Today in the cold, pouring rain we traveled on a road that looked like the beautiful roads in Oregon—a river on one side and forested mountains on the other. Alsace is interesting in other ways too. For nearly the first time, we're seeing towns in France that have painted, clean houses with yards and flowers. Occasionally we've seen that before, but always at the edge of big cities, in new suburbs. In Alsace, we've found ancient little towns look that way. The fields, the farm animals—everything—is picture perfect. In our campground in Colmar, the radio station that comes in strongest is in German.

We spent a very wet day in Colmar. The town can be described as Hansel & Gretel-ish. It is lovely, with many old, half-timbered houses—very German-village looking. It was not pleasant outside, but we saw a lot. After lunch we visited the Unterlinden Museum and then went grocery shopping before getting the bus for "home."

Incidentally, the bus stops in Colmar are equipped with electronic sign boards telling you how many minutes it'll be until the bus arrives. When we got to the bus stop, the sign said 11 minutes; it counted down to 1 and then suddenly the word *"ARRIVE"* appeared. At that moment we looked up and saw the bus coming!!! The same thing happened on the way home. Talk about the trains running on time in Fascist Italy!

The campground in Colmar is on a river. It has two levels, one near the water and one higher up. We were told not to use the spaces on the river. In the morning, after so much rain, we could see exactly why those spaces were not to be used. The river had risen high enough to flood them. Swans were swimming in some of the spaces.

It was a short trip into Germany. When we left the flea market in Freiberg, Germany, it was still raining, so we decided to continue north to Karlsruhe in Baden-Wurttemberg. We took the equivalent of the "N" road, which winds through a great number of towns on the German side of the Rhine. It's an interesting drive. The countryside is flat on our left, which is the east bank of the Rhine, and there are mountains on our right. The towns look like they did in Alsace: painted houses with lawns and flowering shrubs—very different from the utilitarian gray look of French villages. The buildings are somewhat baroque, with all kinds of curves, curls, and embellishments. The fields have been freshly plowed and have a lot of standing water in them. Everything is very neat. With any luck, the rain will stop. We have said that for four days now.

Driving in Germany is considerably different from driving in France. First of all, the much heralded great *autobahns* are free, unlike their French counterparts that, as we have noted, are very expensive. German drivers are considerably more restrained and we are almost comfortable with them, which we certainly were not with the French drivers. Germans drive very fast on the *autobahns* but not on the national roads. They don't tailgate as much and they don't try to pass as often—certainly not when going into a rotary. Actually, they do not use the rotary system anywhere near as often as in France, so there are a great many lights and stops instead. The *autobahns,* which we somewhat feared going on, were actually great for us. Where necessary, they set different speed limits for the different lanes, e.g., 130 kilometers per hour in the far left, 90 kilometers per hour in the middle lane, and any speed at all, i.e, as slow as you want, in the right lane. So we could amble along without pressure. The only thing to get used to is the cars that roar by, and especially the motorcyclists who scream past you at 80-plus miles an hour, wearing their leather suits (which a friend once described as their personal body bags).

Compared to France, there seem to be many fewer gasoline stations. Furthermore, supermarkets do not seem to sell gasoline. In France, the supermarket stations were up to 10 cents cheaper per liter than brand stations. When you are taking on 45 liters, that makes a difference of 4.50 euros per tank. At gas stations, gasoline seems to be the same price here as in France. It takes some getting used to, though. We filled up today and a man who was ahead of us paid 69 euros to fill up his Mercedes. That's about $63.00!

Another difference is that siestas are even longer here than in France. They last from 12 noon, or 12:30, to 3 PM, instead of until 2. And most stores, including about a third of the gas stations, close at 2 PM on Saturday and don't reopen until Monday morning. R&A

LETTER #11—AMSTERDAM, HOLLAND, MAY 11, 2002

On Tuesday, May 7, we were in Aachen, Germany, near the borders of Belgium and Holland. We were continuing on our way north. After our day in Mainz, we were not so anxious to spend another day in the pouring rain in a German city. So we decided to head for Holland. But first, there was one "must see" destination in Mainz. Not the cathedral, not the Gutenburg museum (which was closed on Monday, the day we left Mainz), and not any other old buildings—but the Wal-Mart Super Center! We found it while driving around on Sunday, trying to find the Old Town. In order to do business in Mainz, even Wal-Mart apparently has to close from Saturday afternoon to Monday (this is the law in Germany).

It is a big store, with lots of American goods made specifically for the German market as well as many local brands—totally different brands of clothes, but similar to the styles we're used to. We literally spent an hour and a half in the store, and then we paid our usual Wal-Mart bill (huge!)

and left, intending to go either to Aachen or Köln (known to us Americans as Cologne). As we got closer, we decided to go on to Aachen, which is not too much farther than Köln and is nearer to Belgium and Holland. Both cities had campgrounds listed in our camping book.

Our first stop in Aachen was at an enormous store called Bauhaus. We figured from the outside that it might sell building supplies. Ron needed to buy a few things to fix a new leak in the camper. He was in the store a very long time, but he finally came out with the things he needed. I asked why it had taken so long. He said it was the biggest store he'd ever been in—and it really was a Home Depot. The signs, the positions of the goods, everything was familiar to him!

The two campgrounds we experienced in Germany were quite nice, and invidious comparisons with the French ones we have written to you about are in order. At the German campgrounds where we stayed, the grounds were well kept, the shower rooms and the WCs were warm in the morning, and they were clean. Instead of the taps that one has to push for a few seconds of warm and cold water mixed to a set temperature, the water appliances had hot and cold taps that one could set for whatever temperature one wished. The commodes had seats and toilet paper was there in the stall. At the camper site, electricity was 10 amps and 16 amps respectively in each of the two campgrounds. And the charges for electricity were less than in France.

Based on our experiences with roads, electricity, and campgrounds, it certainly seems that France's infrastructure is somewhat more backward than Germany's—and (based again on our limited experience) than either Holland's or Belgium's. The electricity advantage might be explained by the fact that we saw only one atomic plant in France, and no wind generators. But in Germany and in Holland, we saw several of both, and we drove many more miles in France than we have so far in the other two countries.

Our campground for the past two days has been in Oisterwijk, near Tilburg—a huge place with hundreds of campers, many children, and lots of dogs. It reminded us of what used to be called a "bungalow colony." Most of the campers seemed to have put down roots here, for the spring and summer anyway. Very few were transients, like us.

This evening, May 10, we are in a campground in Amsterdam, on the metro line. We just successfully phoned a former student from the University of Connecticut who is in some unknown hotel in Amsterdam with his new bride. We will meet them in the Tourist Office tomorrow at 11 AM. It's worth mentioning how we phoned them. We used a public phone and dialed an 800 number in the U.S. Then we dialed our account number and pin, a number indicating we wanted to call overseas, plus country code, city code, and phone number. In other words, to reach his cell phone, we called from Amsterdam, Holland, to the U.S., and from the U.S. called a Swedish cell phone that is with its owner in Amsterdam, Holland. Ah, the wonders of the twenty-first century.

And it may also be worth mentioning that tonight we had visitors. We had noticed a group of men sitting in the camper across from ours. They certainly noticed us. One of them came over to talk to us. He had seen our license plate and asked where we were from. We told him our story, and he told us his.

He is from a small town in northern Austria, traveling with a group of men including the Burgomaster (the mayor of their town). He told us quite proudly that their wives were all home, working! We had a nice—if difficult—conversation with him since his English is limited and our German non-existent.

Half an hour later, there was a knock at the door, and all the rest of the men appeared on our doorstep, wanting to meet us, delighted that Americans were interested in spending so much time in Europe. Much laughing and good humor. The Burgomaster even kissed Adelle's hand. All of them had been drinking throughout the afternoon and evening and were, as my mother used to say, quite *faschmushket*. Very mellow indeed. R&A

The patio at the campground restaurant just outside Amsterdam.

LETTER #12—AMSTERDAM, HOLLAND, MAY 14, 2002

We arrived in Amsterdam on Friday afternoon. We're at a campground at the southern border of the city. It is a 15-minute walk to the metro line which gets to Central Station in less than 20 minutes. Central Station is the hub of the city's very good transportation system—trams, buses, the metro, and trains.

Amsterdam is quite exotic in lots of ways. There is a museum here devoted to marijuana, and stores sell it legally. There is a red light district. There are street-stands that sell herring—fat little lightly salted filets served in a small tray with chopped onions, with or without bread, to eat on the spot. Some of these also sell other kinds of fish, usually fried and served in little trays with sauces. Houses in the city are of brown and red brick, accented with white stone, generally tall and thin, with decorated step gables literally being propped up by the houses on either side. Most have booms sticking out of the top gable with pulleys and ropes and hooks. They were originally used to haul goods up into storage attics and now probably are used to bring up furniture. The city is built mostly on sand dredged up when the many canals circling the city were dug. This soil does not provide a very firm foundation for the buildings, many of which date from the seventeenth century. As a result, a row of houses often takes on the look of a bunch of drunks leaning this way or that and being held up by countervailing leaners on either side. Adding to this look is the decided forward lean that many houses have. They were built that way in order to ensure that the goods being hauled up to the attic on the pulleys would not hit the front facade and perhaps break a window.

The center of the city is charming, very pretty, and—alas—also very, very dirty. Trash is all over the place. There are always amazing numbers of people on the streets, including more tourists than we have seen anywhere else. We've seen people just throw their trash down wherever they are. "Don't litter" is a phrase that might not have been spoken or posted here ever. The canals are not quite open sewers, which is what we were told they once were, but they are still pretty dirty. Part of the problem may also be the very small trash containers on the streets. They seem always to be filled to overflowing. Also, just as in Paris, people do not curb their dogs and do not pick up after them. So this queen of cities has to learn how to be a bit less slovenly and to wash her face a little.

Amsterdam is loaded with museums—art museums, history museums, church museums, war museums. We went to as many as we could possibly crowd in!

Internet access is easy and cheap here. We found a place right near the

Central Station that charged €1 for an hour, but you had to order a drink. We spent a good hour there sending stuff to you all. We both had a cup of coffee and the bill was still only €1.90. And they had computers with disk drives, Microsoft Word, AND the same kind of keyboard that we use in the U.S. Now we are spoiled rotten.

Many of the large supermarket chains in the U.S. are owned by Dutch companies, so we expected to see new, beautiful markets with lots of goods in the stores on their home turf. So far, though, they are nothing to write home about.

One great thing about supermarkets all over Europe, though, is that the cashiers at the checkout counters sit down while working. And they never bag, even if bags are supplied. In the U.S., as you know, checkers have to stand and usually bag also. Why isn't this considered cruel? Where are the unions when you need them? R&A

Letter #13—Amsterdam, Holland, May 19, 2002

We've been bumming around northern Holland for five days now. After leaving Amsterdam, we moved the camper closer to Haarlem, (almost as close to Amsterdam as Harlem is to what was New Amsterdam, i.e., lower Manhattan in New York City), which boasts a number of things we wanted to see. Sounds reasonable, but it turned out to be a great hassle.

In short, after moving to different, inconvenient campgrounds, we ultimately decided we should have stayed put in Gaasparplas to the south of Amsterdam, right on the metro line. From there we could have gone everywhere we wanted to go—primarily Haarlem and Floriade—by public transit. The problems involved navigating badly-marked roads, campgrounds in very inconvenient places, and changing buses often.

Haarlem is a small, friendly city. It has a wonderful old church (1300–1500) with several great features. Both Handel and Mozart played the huge organ, which has 5,000 pipes. We were lucky. Someone was practicing on the organ when we got there. You could feel the sound in your belly.

Also in town is a long row of houses originally constructed in the seventeenth-century as homes for the elderly. In the early 1900s, some were rehabbed into private homes. But they left one of the main buildings and turned it into the Frans Hals Museum. It houses a lot of his portraits as well as a number of painting by other artists of his era. One room contains a series of his paintings of the local militia done over a twenty-year span. You almost had to stop yourself from winking at some of the militia or going up and patting a shoulder and asking, "How's it going?" A bunch of good old boys, looking rakishly alive and obviously eager for some fun.

In another part of the museum there was an extremely well-furnished doll house from the seventeenth century. It's about seven feet square, not a child's toy, but something put together as a hobby by a young woman of wealth. This miniature house provides a glimpse into the reality of the lives of the wealthy at the time.

This brings us to Friday, May 17, the day we decided to go to Floriade, billed as "the horticultural show of the decade" because it is a once-every-10-years show. We were there for six hours and saw about half the exhibits—and did nothing but complain through it all. There were beautiful gardens throughout, but none so exceptional that the word *"Bellissimo"* would pass one's lips. Not in the league of Keukenhof (the tulip extravaganza of Holland) or of the Canadian Buchardt Gardens. One English lady we met said she'd enjoyed her day at Keukenhof much more. And we certainly believed her.

But the tulips were very beautiful and the two buildings we managed to find at the end were almost worth the hassle. One was a huge hydroponic greenhouse in which were growing, red, yellow, purple, orange, and green peppers (called paprikas here), and the long cucumbers, and three kinds of tomatoes—all the things we buy in the U.S. (mostly in winter). A tape recording explained how the whole thing worked from seeding through to harvest. The second building had indoor plants from different parts of the world, including hundreds of gorgeous orchids and lilies and bonsai—you know, the stunted Japanese plants.

The designers of Floriade built a 100-foot hill that is intended to be the crowning glory of the show. Since we live in a place where 100-foot hills are the norm, we were not impressed. But the Dutch, who live in a very flat world, seemed to like it.

Speaking of flat, lets talk bicycling for a bit. The Dutch, like the Belgians and many French, use bicycles a lot. Every city has huge numbers of them standing around, especially at transportation stations. And the streets in every city here have bicycle lanes with their own separate traffic lights. Perhaps this dependence on bikes is responsible for there being very few fat Europeans. And there is a great deal of walking on the city streets as well. So one result of the high cost of fuel in combination with the flat land is that people get a great deal more exercise and there is much less obesity here. This is something we envy.

There's only one problem with all these bicycles. Often, when we're walking on what in the U.S. would be considered a sidewalk but here is a bicycle lane, we wander from side to side, endangering both ourselves and the cyclists. Although I hear the bell when I'm being warned that someone is coming, it rarely registers. I have become "Adelle Milavsky—Menace to All Bicycles"! In fact, at one Amsterdam campground, we found ourselves with bicycles, motor scooters, and horses, all using the same "sidewalk" as we were.

After locating an Internet café and waiting for the right terminal to get free, we sent you the last e-mail letter. Then we had lunch and looked for a supermarket where we could buy supplies. None around. We knew of one that had been open the previous Sunday, which is rare here. After spending quite a while figuring out how to get to it, we arrived to find it closed. On the door was a sign: "19 and 20 May closed for first and second Pinksterdag." Another holiday! Since we have been here, France and Holland have collectively had the following days when work stopped and everyone was off: two days for Easter, May 1 (Labor Day), Ascension Day, and two days for Pinksterdag. That's about 10 percent of the days we've been here.

What percent of the days since March 24 were holidays for you guys back home? We suspect that in the U.S. we're just not living right.

At any rate, we started for the metro. On the way, we saw a convenient ATM. We put in the card, asked for €300, got a receipt for that amount—but no money. We were fiddling around when someone in line said something, so we explained the problem. Everyone spoke English—and we all talked about it. Then another man tried the machine, and he got his money. By now, we were livid. We copied the phone number we found on the wall for emergencies and went to look for a phone. Eight blocks later, not having found a phone, we decided to continue walking toward the metro, so that we could at least go back to the campground. On the way we finally found a phone, but nothing we tried worked. And we tried everything, including dialing the number with and without the zero. Finally, we gave up.

As we were walking away, we saw two taxi drivers at a taxi stand. We showed them the phone number and asked them if we had the right number of digits. Of course we didn't, and when we explained what had happened, one of them picked up his cell phone and called the right number. He was assured that the bank would find the error, and the lady on the phone suggested that we call on Tuesday, because tomorrow, Monday, was second Pinksterdag, so no one would be at the bank to answer.

Much of this day was not fun, but our Good Samaritan taxi driver saved it from being a disaster. R&A

LETTER #14—AMSTERDAM, HOLLAND, May 25, 2002

On Sunday evening in the Gaasparplas campground in Amsterdam we had a visitor. A man stopped by to ask if that was really a Florida license plate on our RV. It was lucky for us that he did. He's been touring Europe in an RV for years—six weeks at a time, twice a year. He and his partner have been all over, and they know a great deal more than we do about how to manage things. They store their RV here and told us about the facility they use. The only problem for us was that the place is closed on Sundays and we had reservations for our flight home on a Monday. But we were able to change the airline reservations to the previous Wednesday. So now we'll be able to drop the RV off on Tuesday morning, travel to Brussels, and fly home on Wednesday, June 19.

Visited Delft where there is a beautiful campground with a city bus right outside the camp. Loved the two old churches, the museum, and the charming square. Did a lot of walking. When we got tired, we just did our grocery shopping and then went back to the campground.

From Delft we drove to Antwerp, Belgium. We had a lot of trouble finding the campground, but eventually we did. This is the most inexpensive campground yet—€5.33 per night. It is convenient to town, pretty clean, and has adjustable hot water in the showers as well as hot water in the basins and in the dishwashing sinks.

Antwerp is famous for diamond trading. There is a metro station named "Diamant" and Saturday marks the opening of a new Diamond Museum (which we will skip). We visited the Royal Museum of Art and saw many Pieter Paul Rubens paintings, as well as many paintings by unknown (to us) but excellent (also to us) artists.

This is Rubens's hometown and the house in which he lived and worked is still here. We visited it today. It is a large, elegant house that has an enormous studio. We learned that in the course of his career he produced 2,500 paintings, many of them huge. "Produced" is the right word, because he worked much like a producer—he designed the paintings and then had a staff of specialists execute the details.

For four days there was a book fair very close to the campground. Ron went in on day two of the fair. He found a huge hall brimming with books, many of them in English as well as in other languages. One whole section was on travel. Ron found one book on Great Britain, for our next trip, and one for France. And he also found some novels and mysteries that were pretty inexpensive—much less than in the U.S. New paperback novels were priced at between €.99 and €2.25. So today we both went to the fair and came back with a treasure trove of books that we will leave in the RV for the next time we come.

On Sunday we visited the Antwerp Zoo—which is right in the center of the city and apparently the oldest zoo in Europe. We saw a lot of wonderful birds and fish, as well as some large animals, all of which looked like they were well cared for.

We inquired about one-day excursions into Brussels…and found that on Monday, after 9 AM, the cost for the over-65 set (that's us) is €2.50 per person round-trip. We'll stay here another day, ride the train into Brussels, and look around a bit more. It certainly wouldn't pay to move to a Brussels campground (which is bound to be more expensive). Then we're going back to Ghent to have our propane tank refilled. We're still talking about where else we want to go in the time remaining.
Having been in Belgium and the Netherlands for an extended period of time, we've developed a new maxim, which might be of interest to others. Maxim #1: Never worry about taking suntan lotion on a visit to a place that has shops selling only umbrellas—and seem to make a go of it even though they sell nothing else. Most days here it has rained. When the rain hasn't been heavy, there have been rain showers or it has been very overcast. (Incidentally, there is no Maxim #2, but one may come up!) R&A

LETTER #15—PARIS, FRANCE, MAY 30, 2002

We spent Monday in Brussels and made the best €2.50 purchase imaginable: two 40-minute round-trip train rides for €5.00. Not much like the Long Island Railroad.

Our first order of business was to make reservations in a hotel for the night before we fly home. This accomplished, we went to an Internet place and then we walked around.

Tuesday we drove to Ghent—where we had a "housekeeping day," grocery shopping and having our propane tank filled. There seemed to be nothing much that we wanted to do in Ghent, which we had visited near the start of the trip, so we decided to leave for Paris.

The trip was not uneventful. As usual, we did okay for a while, but then we were following N17 in Arras when it apparently disappeared. In retrospect, it probably went straight when we turned left, thinking it would intersect with N39. Wrong, wrong, wrong. But the question remains. How much would it have cost the French government to put a sign at the roundabout indicating that N17 was ahead?

After floundering around a bit, we got onto a *péage* (toll road) for one exit, and caught the N17 as it crossed a tiny little town. We prefer the smaller roads because you can see France when you're on them—unlike when you're on the major highways, which could be on the moon, just like the highways in the U.S. There is something to be said for Route 66! About an hour after we got back onto N17, we drove through a town called Pérrone. It was a nice looking place and had a couple of signs that intrigued us, so we stopped. The town has a small medieval area and a "Historial," that is, a museum devoted to World War I. The city had been held by the Germans throughout that war. About 45 kilometers away, another site still has trenches preserved so one can see what living in them was like. But after the Historial, we lost any desire we might have had to pursue this experience.

We found a photographic exhibit about a group called CARD, American women who had come to Picardy after the war to help rebuild a devastated area. Although the exhibit was in French, it was intelligible even to us! And the pictures were terrific. My favorite was the photo showing the women giving the peasants new "livestock"—i.e., rabbits. Although I (Adelle) cannot eat *lapin* even if it's cooked in a delicious sauce, the picture gave me a new view of the value of rabbits as food in a ravaged area. And two rabbits are an easy, light, and simple way to begin a "herd"! R&A

LETTER #16—PARIS, FRANCE, JUNE 3, 2002

We are now in our end game, winding down and looking forward to returning to friends and relatives, easily obtained showers, bathrooms with clothes hooks, commodes with seats, bathrooms with toilet paper, directions in an understandable language, highways with (comparatively) little traffic. It would also be nice to be provided with directions that refer to city blocks, not meters, and be in places that don't close down every couple of weeks because of yet another religious holiday.

Which is not to say that we won't miss being here. Bread is always fresh and crispy; meat is lean and tender and sears without weeping in the pan; and vegetables and fruit—even when bought in supermarkets—taste great. Here cities and towns with very long histories and cultures have wonderful museums devoted to illustrating and explaining those histories and cultures. Public transportation systems are good, and using them is more convenient than using automobiles. There are streets that one delights in walking because one never knows what beautiful building or monument or sculpture or park one may come across around the next corner. Except in Paris, the people are as comfortable to be with as the nicest Americans. Parisians live up to their reputation as unfriendly.

Europeans are governed by policies that appear to be more enlightened than American policies. Probably the most un-American aspect of Europe is that social policy seems to take precedence over economic policy. Social integration of the races is arguably further advanced here than in the U.S. This judgment is based on how many interracial couples and families one sees here and by the comfort level of all concerned in racially mixed situations. On the other hand, some ethnic groups, mostly Middle Easterners including Turks, seem to be having a problem.

We spent three days visiting the Louvre and were very impressed with how much better the experience is now compared with the impression we had on a previous visit, when everything seemed very disorganized, with displays that were dark, dirty, and hard to view. This Louvre is now clean, bright, and a pleasure to visit, except for the exhaustion.

We walk around Paris a lot and we've made massive use of the metro system. However, Adelle in particular frequently curses the persons who designed the subway system. We have climbed and descended unbelievable numbers of stairs to get from from one line to another. One day we added to the strain by going to Sacre Coeur. That required hundreds of steps; even though we took the funicular up to the cathedral, we walked down the 200-some steps afterwards.

After five nights in Paris we left, heading north and east. We wanted to visit St. Denis, a northern suburb that has what is supposed to be a very interesting basilica, with transitional architecture between the heavy-walled Romanesque and the thin-walled Gothic styles. We got to the basilica but could not park anywhere near it because on that day there was a large open-air market set up next door. So, a double disappointment—no basilica and no market! We continued on toward St. Quentin, our objective for the night.

On the way we noticed a road sign that said something like "Clairière de l'Armistice." Ron wondered what that was, so we followed directions to it. We found nothing less than the museum housing the infamous railroad car in which the Armistice was signed after World War I. That's the same car that Hitler used when France fell to the Nazi onslaught and the Paris government had to sign a surrender agreement.

That night we stayed at a campground in St. Quentin and made plans to visit Bastogne and Liège on the way to Tilburg. The next night we stayed in a campground in a tiny town in southeast Belgium. We were a source of great excitement to the couple who ran this little establishment because we came from America. Apparently their most exotic visitors are usually the Dutch! The next day we got to see Bastogne, the place where General McAuliffe responded to Nazi demands to surrender with the eloquent and never-to-be-forgotten single word, "Nuts!"

A great deal is remembered here. The town has two museums, as well as a Sherman tank with holes in it that sits in the town's main square. This tank was part of the unit led by General Patton. His army broke through Nazi lines after a three-day push from Verdun in the southwest to relieve McAuliffe and his men, who had foiled the Nazi plan to reach the Meuse and then Antwerp and force an Allied retreat.

Bastogne was severely damaged during this battle. The small museum near the town square has a booklet with photos of the buildings around the square taken after the very fierce fighting and other photos on facing pages showing the exact same spots today. Both of us remembered vividly hearing about this battle and seeing pictures of the exhausted American troops in Bastogne in 1944.

After leaving Bastogne we went through a town called Noville, which had been the northernmost defense line set up to stop the Nazi assault. In front of an ordinary house on the main road were the turret and gun of a Sherman tank. An unofficial memorial.

Next stop was Liège. There were no campgrounds for this city listed in our book, but the Tourist Office in Bastogne had given us information on a few pretty distant locations. We decided to try for a particular one in a suburb. We had one hell of a time finding the town—and an even harder time finding the campground. Why? No sign! You gotta know the territory! But it's turned out to be a very nice campground, and we've been here a couple of days. It's about an hour's ride by bus into the city. Yesterday, on the way home, there was a man on the bus in obvious distress. When we got out of the city and into a more rural area, the man ran up to the driver and said something. The driver stopped the bus, the man got out, the driver waited until the man had a chance to pee, the man climbed back into the bus, and then we returned to the scheduled service. Something like this would never happen in the U.S.!

We plan to go to the museums on Saturday and spend at least Sunday morning at the huge flea market that is a tradition here. Of course, we don't need anything, but if this market is anything like advertised, it'll be a fitting end to our stay. We'll be back to Tilburg in just a few days to say goodbye to our friends, and then we'll spend a few more days in Amsterdam getting ready to return to the real world. R&A

LETTER #17—LIÈGE, TILBURG, AMSTERDAM, JUNE 16, 2002

We spent Saturday in Liège. Walked a lot, but found that the things we wanted to see were simply not open. We tell you this not because we are cranky, but because this is a typical problem. Most of the things a tourist would want to see are within the small area of the city's center—but "small" still means miles of walking every day. We really don't mind the effort, though, because both of us are finding that this unaccustomed exercise is good for us!

We stayed so that we could go to the traditional market on Sunday. It was by far the largest we've seen, stretching literally for miles along the river Meuse. They sell everything—fruits and vegetables, dairy products, raw meat, cooked meat, sausages, nuts, candies, cakes and breads, olives, clothing (including shoes and pocketbooks), fabric by the yard, and all kinds of small livestock (ducks, pheasants, chickens, roosters, chicks, ducklings, baby pigs, etc.) We only bought one backpack and one shopping bag's worth! Then we took the bus back to the campground, ate lunch, and left.

We drove a couple of hours and then decided to try a new way of finding space. Instead of using our camping guide, we opted for a campground shown on the map. It's an interesting operation. Most of its business consists of daytrippers—families with kids who come for the day. When we pulled in there really were hundreds of people, including huge numbers of kids. Most have now gone home, leaving the twenty-five or thirty campers (in a space usable by hundreds) and a number of people who own non-mobile homes that are permanently parked here. Like the campground in Oisterwijk, this one reminds us of an old "bungalow colony." But the huge number of people are gone.

We returned to Tilburg to say good-bye to our Dutch friends. Afterwards, we drove on to Amsterdam, winding our trip down. Our hope is that the rolling duffels we bought—plus our new backpacks—will make going home slightly easier than getting here. And we think we figured out a way to do a lot of traveling with very few staircases. Instead of using the train to get from Amsterdam to Brussels, we're going to take the much slower bus. And to get to the international bus, we're going to take a city bus. In fact, we've arranged to be driven in our camper to the bus station, and then everything should be on one level, at least until we get onto the train-to-the-airport in Brussels. Then we'll see! But we may just be lucky!

It's all very well to say people should "travel light," but we've been here for three months. There's a lot of stuff to take home. Even the printed stuff that we want to take home is pretty hefty. We'll be getting ready on Monday, traveling to Belgium most of Tuesday, and flying all of Wednesday. Talk to everyone after that. R&A

LETTER #18—MISCELLANY FROM THE MILAVSKYS

We had lots of other thoughts that didn't quite fit with the geographical letters. So we've made a long letter out of them and sent it along.

Camping Notes

Since we appear to be in a minority among our acquaintances with respect to living in a recreational vehicle, we thought we'd put together some random thoughts on camping and campgrounds that might interest other people. And before beginning, we want to tell all the French word for campground: *"Le Camping."*

Our first impression of camping really came from the old Frank Capra movie *It Happened One Night.* The 1930s "campground" looked more like a motel room, and you had to stand in line for a shower.

In all the time we've been in Belgian or French campgrounds, we've never had to stand in line for anything. In fact, we rarely meet anyone at all in either the showers or the toilets. That's because we have done this mostly in the so-called "shoulder" season, before the crowds get into camping. In the U.S., the great majority of the facilities are clean, although you certainly do run into some not-so-appetizing buildings. In Belgium, they are not only spotlessly clean but also nice smelling. However, you won't find toilet paper in the toilet stalls or soap in the sinks. In Paris, the facilities are clean but not nice-smelling. They do not smell bad, just not nice. They have toilet paper but no soap.

In the rest of France, facilities vary. We've had showers with every kind of controls, though mostly they have had one control, with a red dot in the middle indicating that the water is *chaud,* or hot (actually mostly lukewarm). We've been in places where the hot water is turned on only during certain hours. We've even had mixed-gender *toilettes* (yuckie), though most are marked for men or women. We've had commodes with and without seats. In southern France, most don't have seats. You have to sit on the porcelain. On cold mornings! (Why don't they have seats? A guess: better for not accumulating germs?). They're also found with and without toilet paper. And we have been in places with "Turkish" toilets. That is what they are called. Anyway, these have a porcelain base, with places to put your feet and squat, and no commode. All of this is behind full doors on each stall, which is why we didn't realize that WCs with seats were for the handicapped. Fortunately, all the toilets have been pretty clean and several have been spotless. Some of the buildings are open under the eaves and under the doors, which may be okay in the summer but makes them pretty cold in some of the northern areas.

In the U.S. and in Belgium, we found that everyone greeted us when we went out with some version of "Good morning." Since we all spoke different languages in Belgium, the greeting could have been anything. But in Paris, no one even made eye contact! Let me amend that. We met two American men camping there. The first we met when we saw him looking at the map in a subway station, trying to figure out where to leave the metro station for the bus for the campsite. The second stopped by to say hello the next night—prompted by our license plate. However, we find that people in motor homes whom we see on the road often wave to us. And the people in the campgrounds in France (but not Paris) are somewhat friendlier. We got more than an occasional *"Bonjour"* when we were out of Paris.

There seem to be a lot of children in the campgrounds. Sometimes they seem to be children living in the mobile homes at the sites, but not always. Don't these children ever go to school? We can't figure it out. We're pretty sure that a lot of the campers we see live in these *"campings"* all the time. They have trailers with all kinds of stuff outside—like tables and chairs, satellite dishes, and tented enclosures on the side, adding a kind of Florida room.

In Belgium and Holland, most of the other campers were in "caravans," i.e., little trailers. There are very few fifth-wheel trailers (though we saw one the other day) and very few pickup trucks. We do see pickups and SUVs on the road now and again, but nothing like at home. In France, we saw an equal number of little motor homes...mostly smaller than us, but only by a foot or two. However, we seem to have the oldest motor home in Europe. All of the others are much newer and much fancier than ours. Many of them have diesel engines, for obvious reasons.

There are some ways in which camping in Europe is harder than camping in the U.S. For example, in the U.S., most campsites give you 30 amps of electricity, but many give you 50 amps. In France, we get between 3 and 10 amps. We can't run two things at once, and our appliances are under a terrible strain. They are definitely hungry for electricity. Our microwave works—but slowly—and it groans! When we are given 6 amps, all is well.

When we wash clothes in the campsite laundromat, they don't dry properly. So far, the campgrounds have all had American-made machines. At first I thought the not-so-dry clothes were my fault, because I put in too many clothes. But that's not the case. These are American machines. They need more electricity than is available. The dryers just never get hot enough! This explains why we saw campers in Paris who had clotheslines with towels on them. The towels can't possibly dry totally in dryers under these conditions. And the price of one load of laundry varies from $6.00 (wash and dry) to $9.50 (in Paris). We should also mention that the *laveries* always have washing machines, but not always dryers. We bought clothespins.

The lack of electricity also impacts doing the dishes. We can't use our water heater, so we often do dishes in cold water. Since we use as few pans as possible, serve from the stove, and use paper plates, there are very few dishes. In fact, Ron will often take all the dishes to the sinks with hot water provided in most campgrounds for doing dishes. We never noticed such sinks in American campgrounds, but that is because we always were able to use our hot water heater. We don't remember if such kinds of facilities are offered in the U.S., but they're certainly not as convenient as using your own sink.

In the U.S., most places have concrete slabs so that you are always level and don't track in a lot of mud. Here you are on either grass or mud— the space is not too level and your shoes are always dirty when you come in.

Some European campgrounds have really nice things that are missing in the U.S. They often have little cafés, for example. Some bring in fresh baguettes in the morning. The campground in Ghent was wonderful; it had a good restaurant, a cafeteria, a store, and a snack shop.

Costs are modest. They have ranged between €9 and €12 a night, including electricity. In Arles, one charged €20. R&A

LETTER #19—THE FOOD LETTER

Our biggest mistake was making this trip now, when we know about fat and health and can't eat much salt. Had we come here when we were 20, we could have eaten anything at all that we wanted. Of course, when we were 20 we didn't really know what good is. Life is not fair.

But one of the reasons we thought coming in a camper was a good idea was that we often wanted to try things that we saw being sold in markets. Usually you can't buy much because you're in a hotel. But we can buy almost anything because we have a refrigerator and a way to cook. As a result, this trip has been quite different from our previous trips. Here we go grocery shopping together and we go often. We buy all kinds of stuff just to try it. Most of the things we've tried have been wonderful. However, there have been bummers. For example, we bought a lot of veggies at the huge street market in Toulouse. When we cooked the white asparagus, we discovered they were bitter, so we ended up throwing them out. Still, nearly everything we've had has been delicious. We even had a can of cassoulet (in this case, beans, duck, and sausage) for dinner the other night! We were in the land of cassoulet, after all, and we certainly weren't going to start from scratch!

The best markets in France, so far, were in Périgueux and Dijon. Shopping was a lot of fun and everything except one little regional cake was delicious. But I expect that by the time we go home, we'll have had a lot of things that looked better than they tasted. Most mornings Ron goes out to buy a baguette. This is great bread—although it is a cleaning lady's nightmare. Crumbs all over. Often lunch is something on the rest of the baguette. For dessert, we've had Belgian chocolate with our fruit as well as spectacular French pastries. Tonight we're having raspberries and chocolate mousse. Mmmmmm! And the raspberries are so much sweeter than those we buy at home!

Ron wants everyone to know that he has decided the wine he's been buying at $3 or so per bottle isn't as good as even the boxed wine he often drinks at home. So he's going to start buying wine that is a little more expensive. And he wants to make it clear that he has standards. He will not buy a liter of wine that sells for less than Stop & Shop's sale price of soda. We saw a sign today advertising the local wine for 71 cents, and he declined. Gotta keep up his standards.

There are all kinds of prepared foods and mixes available, but I don't think I'll have enough time to try them all. Stay tuned, though. There are a lot more meals coming. R&A

LETTER #20—THINGS ARE DIFFERENT IN FRANCE

Things really are different in France. First of all, we have a very hard time admitting that these little kids really do know how to speak French …they can conjugate verbs and use masculine and feminine nouns! James Thurber wrote that he was sure no one could really speak French. He was convinced that it was all a huge conspiracy against him because he never could master it. We totally agree!

We're getting along fine. But we've had to learn some tricks. For example, we've learned a lot and have formulated a number of unsubstantiated generalizations about France.

Generalization #1
It is easy to find people who know less English than we know French.

Generalization #2
Never look for a highway number. The signs are few and far between

and they are rarely obvious when you need to make a decision about where to go. Instead, look for signs to towns that are along your route. Eventually you'll see signs that verify your choice.

Generalization #3

There are some conventions. For example, roads indicated in blue on French road signs are always toll roads. In our travels we've opted for the roads indicated in green because these are the national routes, two-lane highways that go through every small town.

Generalization #4

Learn to be humble as you go into the rotary. The signs are clear that traffic already in the rotary has the right of way and you must yield to it. This is a lesson to be taken seriously. Also, you have to master your emotions, because the total lack of authority you have before entering the rotary is immediately followed by total authority once you're in it. Huge trucks coming along and trying to enter the rotary must come to a halt while you are inside it. Their turn comes only after you pass their point of entry. So you go from total powerlessness to total power to total power-lessness again seconds later when you leave the rotary. There is almost always a rotary before a town and at least one after it. In larger towns there can be a series of eight to ten rotaries before you find the road to your next destination. These rotaries are a way of handling crossroads, and we must admit they have their advantages. The main advantage is that, unlike in the U.S., you can go through small towns without ever having to stop at traffic lights. Rotaries therefore speed up the flow of traffic and save some gasoline because you don't have to get into and out of first gear.

Generalization #5

There are a lot of towns in France that do not rate mention on a map. Many consist of only a few houses and none are pretty. There are no front yards, although there may be back yards. But even the lack of some green in the front would not be a problem if all the houses, except in a few areas, were not very old stucco or cement, built ages ago, and never painted. As a result, the colors are beige and brown, both equally dirty. In Provence, some of the houses are painted and look almost pretty. But elsewhere, whitewash or pink paint (as is common in Italy) would be a big improvement.

Generalization #6

The French are more trusting than we are. We'll frequently follow signs slavishly—only to find that signs for the place we're going suddenly stop. There may have been a sign pretty far back saying we should stay on this road, and we're supposed to trust that we'll be told if we need to turn. It's hard for us (but obviously not for the French) to have that kind of trust.

Generalization #7

All Frenchmen are frustrated LeMans drivers. They're always in a tearing hurry—probably rushing to get home for their two-hour lunch break. Even supermarkets, gas stations, and big "Home Depot" type stores are closed from 12 or 1 to 2 or 3!

Generalization #8

French roads experience strong emotions. For example, at least two road signs today said *"Route est perturbée!"* We didn't see any big reason for this upset, but what do we know? (The sign actually means that the road surface is broken up, but the resemblance to our "perturbed" made it funny for us.)

Generalization #9

The French are very blunt about warning you to be careful at certain dangerous spots in the road. The French authorities are also much more moralistic than U.S. authorities. Occasionally there will be a huge sign saying "Five people died on this road since January. This must stop!" Or the message may have a more political tone, e.g., "Stop the massacre." Or it may be more threatening, e.g., "Slow down or die!" None of this seems to slow down any of the French drivers, though.

Generalization #10

If you don't understand the French language very well, you will lose touch with the rest of the world very quickly. If you're in a place that gets the BBC, you may be somewhat better informed, but you also may get nauseated. They go over and over the same stories until you want to kill them. I believe the expression is "They natter on"—especially when the big story of the day is that ITV has declared bankruptcy and can't fulfill its contract with the football teams.

Generalization #11

French radio is unbelievably in love with the sound of talking. Even on music programs, they talk incessantly. Music enters the program only as a short break for the host. The use of correspondents on news programs is minimal. Mostly it's just the host going on and on and on! Of course, we only can understand one word out of ten, maybe. Often these words are *"Coh-leen Pow-elle,"* or *"Boosh."*

Generalization #12

Even on French classical music stations there is almost as much talk as there is music. The music is also way too eclectic. There are some lovely classical orchestral pieces. But they play a lot more vocal music (not opera) than we're used to, usually French, and they do a lot of explaining. While they do play some old American jazz, there's also a great deal of "new" music, the kind played by the Kronos Quartet, for example.

And there's often some guy with a dripping faucet, a slateboard that he scratches with his fingernails, and a microphone.

Generalization #13
Not hearing the news every day is not as serious a problem as you might imagine. Every so often when we are in a large town or city, we can get the *International Herald Tribune* and or one of several English newspapers for a couple of euros. So far the world seems to have changed very little. The Israelis are still killing Palestinians and the Palestinian suicide bombers are still killing Israelis. *"Pow-elle"* is still being tough on both sides, but tougher on Arafat than on Sharon. So what is new?

Generalization #14
It is usually pretty easy to get into a French city. However, it is often very hard to get out of it. The signs for "Centre Ville" are usually very clear, but your departure clearly means less to them than your arrival. Signs are small, meaning you have to get close to them in order to read them. The result is that you'll discover—too late to do anything about it—that you're going in the wrong direction. When available, street names are high up on buildings and have one-inch letters. Try reading that from a vehicle.

There are a few other things we might mention. For example: (1) There are no senior discounts in France. (2) Manufactured things seem very expensive to us. That is easy to say on this trip, because the euro is so close to the dollar that converting prices doesn't require any math. (3) Buses stay on schedule. (4) French traffic lights have a wonderful feature: on the lower part of the pole is a small set of lights showing the changes if for any reason you can't see the high main light. (5) In all this time, we've seen very little that we like in the windows of the clothing stores. People are less formally dressed than in the U.S., but there are always suits evident, and working women seem to wear suits and pant suits. Still, a lot of the clothing seems to be aimed at the teenage/20-something market. Kicky clothes without too much interest. We've seen lovely clothes for very small children, one or two gorgeous (and wildly expensive) gowns, and lots of middle of the road, so-so clothes. But, at least for us commoners, there seems to be very little evidence of France as a world center for fashion. The oddest thing is the cost of an old fashioned "house dress," brand new but in a circa 1950 style. A plain shirtwaist in cotton or a cotton mix is sold on the street or at a *marché* for 55 or 65 euros!

Tha-a-a-t's all, folks. R&A

APPENDIX B

Letters from the Road: The United Kingdom

Note: Because these letters were written during our 2003 trip, certain things, such as prices, have changed since then. Also, our method was generally for Adelle to write the letter and then for Ron to put in his two-cents' worth. This means that you may or may not be able to figure out which one is "I" in any particular reference, but most of the time it will be obvious.

Letter #1—Amsterdam, Thursday, July 26, 2003

Here we are in the Amsterdam Bos Campground, about 3 kilometers from where the RV was stored. Ron has just finished the nasty job of removing the roof air conditioner, which was not working and caused the roof to leak. He replaced it with a 2 x 4 sheet of plywood. We just hope that it is exterior plywood. We are now free to start for the UK.

You know, when you store a motor home for more than a year in a foreign country, anything can happen. Our motor home happened to have been put up for storage immediately after a whole day of very heavy rain last year. A lot of the interior had been soaked because of the damaged roof. As a result, we were concerned about what we'd find when we returned a year later. Would the brakes be rusted so that the front calipers would freeze up and cause the brakes to hold tight when moving? Would there be mold all over the walls and carpet? These were some of the thoughts that went through our minds on our way here. But . . . not to worry! The interior smelled nice, everything was dry inside, there was no mold at all. And the brakes are fine. The motor started up immediately and has made several runs between stores, campgrounds, and the *stalling* (storage) place.

We are parked in the campground next to a couple from San Diego who had just bought a VW camper. They have been buying and reselling every year for a number of years and have camped all over. They've been to Norway, Finland, and Sweden and this year they plan to go to Germany and then to Croatia, Bosnia, and maybe even Bulgaria. They've promised to keep us informed about the camping conditions in those countries. We would not plan such a trip ourselves.

They had never thought about storing over here, but we told them about what we did and they will look into it. See, many people do what we do, and love it.

Tomorrow we will attend the wholesale flower auction in Amstelveen. Then we'll probably change campgrounds because we prefer to be on a metro line! It's more convenient for Amsterdam's daily outdoor market named for Albert Cuypstraat, the artist. After the weekend we will head for the Hoek (Hook) of Holland to wait for a ferry to Harwich, England. After disembarking we'll be part way up the east coast of England and then we'll head north, stopping at all kinds of places. R&A

LETTER #2—AMSTERDAM, JULY 27, 2003

We visited the flower auction this morning, and it was mind-blowing, to put it mildly. The building is huge—apparently about the size of 140 football fields (!)—but only a couple of stories high. On the ground floor are literally hundreds of workers on all kinds of motorized bikes, carts, tractors, etc., each going a different way at different speeds. Some are pulling trolleys loaded with the most beautiful flowers of every description. Others seem to be on their way to pick up stuff. It can only be described as organized mayhem. Tourists are on a catwalk overlooking the flower floor. You literally cannot see the end of the catwalk from its beginning because the other end is so far away.

Today I did the requisite walking at the Albert Cuypstraat market. Gotta have two kinds of cheese in the camper when in Holland. Otherwise the cheese (and flower) police will get us!

Even after all of Ron's work, we had a little leak. But we found the cause, and Ron says he's definitely gaining on it.

Tomorrow we are off to the Hoek of Holland to book our crossing on a ferry to merrie old England. There may not be room on the Sunday crossing, but we can get a campsite and wait until Monday. R&A

LETTER #3—CAMBRIDGE, ENGLAND, JULY 29, 2003

Two days ago we drove to the Stena Line office in the Hoek, walked in, and asked about passage to England. "When would you like to go?" we were asked. "As soon as we can," we replied. "This afternoon at 2:30 all right?" the young lady said. We had no trouble at all getting on the afternoon ferry, and were in England by 8 PM. While we were on line for the ferry we met an English couple with a small caravan and they assured us that the campground we had already picked out in Colchester stayed open late so that campers coming off the ferry could get there. And, miracle of miracles, the navigator (i.e., Adelle) didn't make any errors. We followed the rather complicated directions and found the campground about 20 miles away. Since the ferry had served sandwiches at 5 PM, we didn't even have to cook! But we were invited by our new acquaintances to have a beer in their small but very well appointed new caravan—which we did.

Spent Monday in Colchester, visiting the castle (a Norman structure begun shortly after the battle of Hastings—1066 and all that—on the remains of a Roman temple). But we had nearly as much fun just sitting on a bench in the park outside the castle, looking at beautiful flowers and listening to the English speak as they passed by. We enjoyed the young woman who called her husband a "grouchy sod" (I concurred); and another lady who said that she was "a bit peckish" (hungry). We must give equal time to the opposite point of view, however. Sitting on the bus this afternoon, a gentleman who heard us talking asked if we came from New York. We wondered why he would think such a thing, just because we talked of having a cup of "cawfee," walking our "dawg," and looking at the "skoi"!

We left Colchester this morning and took the local roads instead of the dual carriageway to get to a campground in a town called Cherry Hinton just southeast of Cambridge. Managed that trip very well. Ron has had no trouble staying on the "wrong" side of the road and even going left around the many roundabouts. His big problem while driving a rental car on our last trip to the British Isles was expecting the car to end at his left elbow, as vehicles in the U.S. do. Our RV does indeed end at his elbow, and therefore we're doing well on the roads.

We went to several stores and then we set off to find a "Park & Ride" to get into Cambridge. The first one we tried had hanging barriers that were too low for us. The man in charge of that facility helped us turn around in a very small space and gave us directions to get to a lot that our RV could use. As we drove out, a man who obviously had been standing on the sidewalk and had observed the incident walked over to us. He asked where we were going, and then said he'd take us there. We weren't at all sure where he was taking us, since we couldn't exactly remember what he'd said. Our Good Samaritan, however, led us directly to a Park & Ride lot that was very convenient and in a place that allowed us to get back to the campground easily. He signaled as he drove to make sure Ron knew what his directional intentions were, slowed down to make sure we could follow, and actually drove into the car park to make sure we got in. Is that wonderful or what?! The British are really friendly and extremely easy to talk to.

We are having a wonderful trip so far. There is something to be said for the ability to talk to everyone without the stress of having to communicate in a different language. And I stand by that statement, even though there are certainly big differences in language! We are trying to get used to saying "different to" rather than "different from." There are "boot sales" (flea markets) on Sundays, "marrows" (squash) for sale in the supermarket, and other wonders, but it's all intelligible.

The weather has been cloudy more often than sunny and also rainy and cool. Ron has been sleeping in a zipped up sleeping bag. He swears that yesterday in the Colchester campground there was a bit of frost on the grass in the early morning. And this is July! The campgrounds here are nicer than those on the Continent. There's hot water in the sinks for shaving and washing dishes. No extra charge. And clean. Wow. R&A

LETTER #4—CAMBRIDGE, ENGLAND, JULY 31, 2003

We are really on our way now. Our two days in Cambridge included three rainstorms—one of them really bad. But we saw as much as we were interested in before making our way about 10 miles south to the Imperial War Museum at Duxford.

At Cambridge, we visited the Fitzwilliam Museum at the university. The Fitzwilliam has an impressive collection of Egyptian and other archaeological artifacts taken from the countries under British control when England ruled the seas. The very people who uncovered all the tombs in the Valley of the Kings donated many of the items on display. There was also a nice collection of paintings. Very impressive, and small enough to see without having to kill oneself. That's not exactly fair. It should read "without killing Adelle," since my walking abilities still leave a great deal to be desired. But I visited the museum and then Kings College Chapel, which is stunning. The stone fan-shaped ceilings were spectacular, and the painted and colored glass windows beautiful.

A highlight of the visit was a long conversation with an English gentleman who had been a structural engineer in his youth. He explained a lot of the construction details to us. He also was interested in knowing that we were American. He had never been to our country, but he had good memories of his 1941 trip in an American owned and operated troop ship. It may have been part of Lend Lease. The British troops were on their way to "the desert" somewhere, but their orders were changed on December 8, 1941, and instead his entire unit was diverted to Singapore as the Japanese began a serious push through Malaysia. Most of "the chaps" died on the Burma Road. He himself was transferred to India, where he spent the remainder of the war. It was a very interesting conversation.

We could not remain an additional evening in the campground because there was no pitch available, so I picked up my cell phone, telephoned another campground, and booked one night in a new place. We pulled out this morning, drove to Duxford, and when we left, simply drove to a new campground about twenty miles from the first one. I love the Caravan Club. Their directions are so clear that even a direction-impaired person like me (Adelle) can follow them.

Duxford had been a U.S. Eighth Air Force Base in World War II. Now it features a very large museum (The Royal Air Museum) in one building and an equally interesting second museum that concentrates on (and is run by) the U.S. Air Force. It has lots of airplanes and a big display about the land war, as well as a long paneled glass wall etched to represent the 6,300+ American aircraft and 30,000 airmen lost.

Among the most interesting displays were the two caravans that Montgomery used as a bedroom and his office. He stayed close to his troops, apparently annoying his fellow officers by his absence in their precincts. A short time later we happened to be on the premises when a couple of Russian officers started tooling around in old Russian tanks. The noise and the smell of diesel fuel were just overpowering. I can't even imagine how terrible it would be to see, hear, and smell a whole group of tanks bearing down!

England is beautiful. All the towns seem to have huge flower tubs hanging everywhere and everything we've seen is like a picture postcard. Tomorrow we begin our northward journey. We'll be on our way to Nottingham. Maybe we'll get to meet Robin Hood! R&A

LETTER #5—NOTTINGHAM, AUGUST 2, 2003

We had planned on visiting a number of cathedrals and other sights between Cambridge and here, but it rained—no, teemed—all day, and we decided we might as well just drive all day and skip the rest. Our idea of "all day" is about three hours of driving. On the road from Comberton (where our last campground was) to Nottingham, we passed the towns of Diddington, Stirtloe, Maddingly, Godmanchester, Eaton Socon, Little Paxton (no larger ones were evident), Brampton, Coppingford, Great Stukelay, Steeple Bidding, Stilton (of cheese fame), Little Stukelay, Wood Walton, Sutton Stubbington, and Tichencote. Then there were Fotheringhay, Uffington, Warmington, Richworth, Colly Weston, Woodsthorpe by Thistleton, Richworth, Burton Coggles, Tinwell, Bottesford, Cropwell Butler, Cropwell Bishop, Goadly Marwood, and Barrowly. Say these aloud for today's poetry fix. We love the names of English towns, compared to which U.S. town names lack imagination.

All the guidebooks say that if you go into an English pub, you'll meet lots of new friends. I'm sure that's true, although we haven't gone into one. But it misses the point. People in and out of pubs are extraordinarily polite, helpful, and glad to meet you. They ask where you come from and where are you going. They recommend other places you might enjoy. The lady on the bench in a park recommended a couple of places. The bus driver in Nottingham recommended many more. People really go out of their way for us. We told you about the man who drove us to a new Park & Ride. When we left the supermarket at Cherry Hinton to go to Duxford, we were not sure how to get to the main road—the M11. So Ron took a map over to a parked tour bus and asked the driver. He gave him directions on how to go through town to get to the highway—and then hurried over to say that he had to start now, and he'd go the way we needed to go so we could find the M11. He said that when we came to a dead end he would go right and we should go left, and that it was marked by a signpost to the M11. We followed him all through Cambridge and when we came to the dead end he did not turn right but turned left and took us all the way to the entrance ramp to the highway. Think that would happen in America?

Another example. My bad knee really began to bother me as we traveled and I walked more and more. While I was limping around next to the remains of Nottingham Castle, I met a man who worked in the shop. He gave me the usual tourist information (which Ron had gone off to get from the Tourist Office). Then he suggested that the next day I stop first near a department store and look for a storefront called ShopMobility where they would supply me with a motorized wheelchair for the day—at no charge. He said, "This isn't America. We take care of our people!" I had to agree. I didn't do it, because today I started out feeling so much better, but it was wonderful just to know that it was available. I should also say that I probably should have obtained a chair, because walking around quickly took its toll. I was soon back in pain and limping.

Our first stop this morning was the library. It had Internet service (free, of course), and was by far the best, most comprehensive library we've seen. Nottingham has a population of 300,000. It's not a big metropolis. But it has a huge library, with probably fifty computers for public use and extensive collections of books in all European languages as well as in Chinese, Urdu, Hindi, Vietnamese, and a whole lot more.

Our plans now are to go to Lincoln and York and to visit a number of interesting places on the way: Sherwood Forest, of course, and Edinstowe Church (where the mythical Robin Hood and Maid Marion were supposed to have been married).

On our way out of Nottingham we *had* to stop at Sherwood Forest. The biggest attraction besides the Robin Hood Fair (a medieval-but-not-

Renaissance fair) was the eight-hundred-year-old oak tree. We've seen only one other tree purported to be that old—in Korea—and that one has no leaves on it that I can recall. This one is still alive—although it certainly needs help. It is, of course, enormous. It is also a one-mile walk to get there. I'd never have made it, except for the tent in the parking lot with a sign reading "Fair Mobility." Just for the hell of it we went in and discovered that they will lend you a motorized scooter for the day—for nothing. You do have to put down a refundable deposit, but there's no charge. It was just like what the man in Nottingham had told me about. This time I decided to do it, and it was wonderful. This made it possible for me to get to the old oak and return without a problem. And Ron didn't have to walk very, very slowly!

We asked about this service and discovered that there's one in almost every city. I'm going to ask about it in York! It's a charity, not a government service, and it's just wonderful.

After leaving Sherwood Forest we drove through the next town, which has Edinstowe Church. Beautiful town, beautiful church, horrible traffic. And no place for us to park. We just drove on to our next destination, York. R&A

LETTER #6—THIRSK, YORKSHIRE, AUGUST 6, 2003

York is one of our favorite places. Why? Who knows. But we've been here twice before and decided to come again, even if coming back here means we won't have time for new places we've never been before.

Getting to our Caravan Club campsite turned out to be a nightmare. The instructions were written for folks coming into York from the north, and we happened to be coming in from the south. However, I just didn't realize this until long after we were obviously lost. The instructions said that we should get off the main highway at a sign that read "Thirsk, A1237." We came to such a sign—but it was many miles south of York, not north of York, which is where the campground was. (Had we continued on the local road we probably would have eventually gotten to the right place.)

The instructions then said that there would be a sign for the campsite—and there was a sign, but it was for a campground too far out into the country to be useful for going into the city. We followed that sign for a while, until it became obvious that it was the wrong campground. Eventually, of course, I realized that the map showed the campground to be north of the city, and a cell phone call confirmed that. That's when we got back onto the main road, and we did manage to get off the road at the correct exit and find the double roundabouts indicated on the map. Then I couldn't figure out which of the exits to take off the first roundabout in order to get to the second one! We ended up spending some time on the "scenic route." Finally we did get to the campground. Incidentally, it is a beautiful campground with a great neighbor—a farm that raises thoroughbred horses. But we did do a lot of useless riding about before we figured the directions out

When we eventually got to York, we found it as nice as ever. We didn't redo the things we've already done. Our first stop was to Level 3 of Marks & Spencer in the car park. That's where we signed up for Shop-Mobility and were given a motorized scooter for use during the day. As a result, we were able to get to the market, to the library to send out a letter, to an archeological dig, and to an archeological museum. Because I had the scooter for long distances, I was able to do some walking around in the smaller spaces.

In the afternoon, we left to head for Thirsk—about 20 miles away. This was an easy trip and it was a snap to find the campground. Thirsk is the town in which Alf Wight was the veterinarian. Think you've never heard of him? Wrong. Think James Herriot! Think *All Creatures Great and Small.* He wasn't allowed to use his real name because the law prevented vets from advertising, so he adopted a pen name. The house that he actually lived in has been turned into a terrific little museum, telling the story of his career and the television series about it that aired on British and American TV some years ago. It included the show's indoor set and had a lot of exhibits designed to give children plenty of opportunity to learn about farm animals in a wonderful and informative way.

That was our morning stop. In the afternoon, we drove around the Yorkshire Dales in 85+ degree heat. The heat wasn't a problem. The air conditioner powered by the engine still works, so we were comfy in the cab (the living quarters that the roof air conditioner used to cool are something else again). But the roads were another story. They are narrow, curvy, and often quite steep. Still, we saw the Dales, which are truly beautiful. In some ways they're like the best parts of Vermont, but the houses are uniformly aged stone buildings, and there is often a castle or an ancient church in the middle of the towns.

Ron says he'll never get the whole story about Alf Wight straight, but I found the entire little museum charming and enjoyed the ride through the Dales. Of course, I didn't have to drive! This morning, even Ron didn't have to drive. We took a bus trip through the Yorkshire Moors, which are stunning, wild, and full of heather. We had a wonderful day, going to places where we would never have dared to drive. In fact, we could hardly believe that the bus driver could drive on some of those roads.

Our next letter will be from Northumberland. Then onward to Scotland, as the adventure continues. R&A

LETTER #7—CONSET, NORTHUMBERLAND, AUGUST 10, 2003

We've come from spending three days with some American friends and

their youngest daughter. They now live in a rural area in northern England. Among the villages neighboring theirs are two of our favorites: Pity Me and Unthank.

Their house is a seventeenth-century stone farmhouse that has recently been fixed up. It is surrounded by lush green fields crisscrossed by high stone walls, hayfields, and huge pastures and meadows on which sheep graze as far as the eye can see. Little white and beige cottonballs with black faces dot the green grasslands everywhere.

Ever since we started traveling in Europe, I (Adelle) have been dying to knock on the doors of these very old homes we see everywhere—and ask the people to let me see inside. Now I don't have to do that. I've not only seen one of these homes but stayed in one! I can report that the house is beautiful. It has two-foot-thick walls, wonderful exposed beams, a slate roof. and lots of rooms. Despite the fact that it was built centuries ago, it is modern and comfortable.

We could not have had better hosts. They wanted us to sleep in their guest room, but we prefer sleeping in our RV, where we are quite comfortable. We were entertained royally and were treated to a guided tour of as many local attractions as we could fit in. We saw a great deal of Northumberland—the Hexham Abbey, Durham Cathedral, a beautiful botanical garden, and a lot of Hadrian's wall.

The Hexham Abbey is our friends' home church. It is very old and very beautiful, and includes a basement crypt dating from the sixth century. We saw used stones salvaged from Roman ruins.

Durham Cathedral is famed for having begun its life as a Romanesque structure—heavy and ponderous with round arches. Before it was finished, though, it became one of the first Gothic cathedrals because of the add-ons—light, airy with pointed arches. It is home to the remains of both Saint Cuthbert and Venerable Bede, besides being, as they say, "drop dead gorgeous." Our first president's family was from nearby and the cathedral has the Washington coat of arms displayed as well as a plaque mentioning that the family has won fame in distant lands.

The ruins at Hadrian's wall were spectacular. They included barracks for the soldiers, the house and office of the commandant, and a bath house complete with communal latrine. When we arrived at the site, a "Roman soldier" was giving a talk. He was very entertaining and informative as he described the life of a legionnaire and also explained quite clearly their superiority in contemporary techniques of warfare. We enjoyed it as much as the kids who were his natural audience.

We learned a bit more about the lingo. For example, the British do not pass a car, they "overtake" it; you put your vehicle into a car park, not a parking lot. In a high rise building, you take a "lift," not an elevator.

The only bad thing about our visit was that we had to leave. It is on to Edinburgh in Scotland. R&A

LETTER #8—EDINBURGH, SCOTLAND, AUGUST 15, 2003

We left England on Monday in the late morning, getting to Edinburgh in the late afternoon. We were lucky to find a campsite. It is festival time in Edinburgh, and it is unbelievably crowded. But we got a site on the outskirts of the city and have been able to use the parking lot of the local TESCO supermarket while getting a bus into the city. We stayed three nights, spending two days in the city.

After we had settled in at the campground on Monday, Ron painted the top of the RV with a sealer. Tuesday we went into the city—first to the Information Center and then to the National Gallery art museums, one holds only portraits and the other, a world-class collection. On the walk we passed a most beautiful display of begonias next to a huge floral clock that kept time.

Next morning, we returned and visited Edinburgh Castle, which sits on a "tor" (rocky hill), and is a huge, brooding presence even on a bright, sunny day. There is a bus up to the top of the Royal Mile, and an unbelievable number of people were visiting. The queue (line) for tickets was at least twenty minutes. In fact, a steward told us later that there had been 7,200 visitors that day. We walked for hours through the grounds, several museums devoted to Scotland's military, the royal apartments, etc. We also listened to a military bagpipe and drum band belonging to the army of the Sultan of Oman. Obviously the Royal Scots had trained his army. There was also a group of musicians and dancers performing traditional music from the coast of India. Standing there in this setting, which had once represented the best in military defense in a quite earlier age, we certainly enjoyed the concert with the men in long white robes and their tartan-clad drum majors.

The castle museums explained a lot about Scotland. Over the centuries, being soldiers was apparently a typical way of making a living for the Scots. The regiments of Scots lost 145,000 men in World War I alone! That's a great many to lose for a country that even now has only about five million people. The most amazing thing is to realize that unarmed pipers can and do lead forces into battle against machine guns and tanks!

After some hours, we decided to leave. Ron saw a van and got us a ride down the hill with the Castle Courtesy Vehicle. Is this a great country or what? From there, we walked down the Royal Mile to the library, where we made an appointment to e-mail a letter. Then we visited the Royal Museum, where we saw a number of exhibits about science and industry, including an exhibit of the first locomotive ever made. At 4:45, we heard the chimes of the museum's millennium clock, which was created by a number of artists and consists of a huge collection of gears and bells and fantastic figures that begin to move at different times. It is very much a Rube Goldberg installation, and a lot of fun to see.

That's all from Edinburgh. Next stop, Aberdeen. R&A

LETTER #9—ABERDEEN, SCOTLAND, AUGUST 18, 2003

On Thursday morning, we left for Aberdeen. But we have to start much farther back than that.

First, let us say that we have had an astonishing run of luck recently. The leak seems to be fixed. The weather has been dry for quite a while. In fact, it has been too dry and fields in Scotland actually are parched. And it has been cool in the northern parts where we have been, so we have not suffered at all from the heat wave that has been affecting many parts of Europe and the UK.

But the first lucky thing actually occurred in June 2002, when we were in the Bos Campground in Amsterdam. We had been parked just across from this huge, beautiful Winnebago. Yes, an American made Winnebago. We could not help liking the Scot who owned it, and we exchanged addresses with him at the time. He asked if we would put him on our mailing list for e-mails, which we did. We have been corresponding with him ever since. Our trip to Aberdeen was to visit this new friend.

In Holland, before we had really met, we kept thinking that the language we were hearing this man and his friends speak was English. That turned out to be true, but it was English as spoken by Scots. Our friend later told a story about being in France and meeting an elderly French gentleman who was very friendly and spoke to him in English. At the end of the conversation, he congratulated the Frenchman. "Sir, your English is very good." And the French gentleman replied, "So is yours."

So, now that we were in Scotland, we were on our way to see our friend. We met him in a lay-by (an off-road parking area) as directed, and we followed him as he drove home to a tiny rural Scottish village.

The scenery as far as we could see was so lovely that we agreed, sitting in our RV, that it was too beautiful to leave to go anywhere else! We drove by field after field with huge rolls of straw and saw crops of green and tan. We found out afterwards that the green that we didn't recognize was mostly "neeps" (turnips) used to feed cattle in the winter, and that the short tan crop was what the Scots call corn—but is really oats. What we call corn is referred to as maize. We were able to recognize the fields of "tatties" (potatoes) without any outside help!

After a 15-mile drive through a beautiful countryside, we stopped at a lovely old granite-block farmhouse. The greeting committee consisted of our hostess and Sam, the black Labrador gun dog who lives outside in a kennel.

First, let us tell you that our friends live in one of the houses on an enormous estate. The house is in a beautiful valley, surrounded by pasture. It is an enchanting place. The pasture is part of one of the farms, and when we arrived we saw a herd of cattle grazing in the far corner. We discovered that if you call to them, they all come running up to the electric fence line to see what is up. Somehow, we never expected that they would be curious, but as our hostess pointed out, the British expression "nosy cow" has a basis in fact.

The estate has a mansion, which, like many of the buildings in the area, is built of gray granite quarried on the estate. This manor house dates from the 1800s. There are thousands of acres of farmland, many tenants, a golf course, a pheasant raising (and shooting) operation, and a number of other enterprises aimed at making enough money to support the estate. The entire thing is like being in the setting of a Dorothy B. Sayers mystery or a BBC costume drama.

The following morning, our host took us around to see the sights—the towns nearby and a Bronze Age burial site! That afternoon we toured the mansion house—an unusual and interesting experience. Then we spent a day on a mountain covered with heather and full of grouse (small game birds). We even went to a house party in Aberdeen. Needless to say, we were the only non-Scots in the group! Actually, we were the only non-pipers (or drum majors) in the group!

I'm not going to say too much about our day on the moors, except to note that it was an experience to be treasured. There is only a narrow track, very rough, through wilderness and you must have a four-wheel drive car to get through it. Our host has a Range Rover, the first we had ever been in. What an animal. It has two sets of controls for the gearbox, both of which have extra-low gears for pulling up a grade and going down. I think that one of these is for four-wheel drive. Equipped with these, this beast can go anywhere.

We drove on the track for hours, going for long stretches without seeing a soul. Instead we saw many coveys of grouse walking along and then jumping straight up into the air and very quickly veering off right or left. We also saw a few raptors, lots of mountain sheep, so-called blue hares, and both red and roe deer. The latter are much smaller than the white-tailed deer we have in Connecticut and are similar in size to the Key deer in the Florida Keys.

We had a picnic in a hut where shooters have their lunch. Our host and hostess had worked together for at least an hour in the morning preparing our lunch. And what a lunch! Smoked pheasant, sliced beef, smoked salmon, and salads. There was a fruit salad with Amaretto for dessert. It was all served from a real picnic hamper with wine in crystal glasses and china dishes as well as a cloth tablecloth and napkins. And me without my morning frock and Ron without his Ascot!

As we left the area, we stopped to tell the head gamekeeper that we were off the land—and met yet another friendly couple whom we liked immediately. I had the feeling that I could live happily in a small Scottish village because the people are so nice. Whatever happened to the image of the dour Scots? We hope that the Scottish people we met during this wonderful weekend will come to the U.S. to visit. We may not be able to duplicate the great experiences, but we can sure try. R&A

LETTER #10—BRAEMAR & OBAN, SCOTLAND, AUGUST 20, 2003

We left our friends on Monday morning. It was a beautiful, sunny day and our original intention was to drive only about 50 miles to a town in the Scottish Highlands called Braemar, close to Balmoral Castle where the Royal Family spends their time when in Scotland. Braemar is a beautiful little town, and we spent a couple of hours wandering around, going shopping, and seeing a film that told of the history of the town and the region. We learned that the local residents owe a great deal of their prosperity to Queen Victoria and Prince Albert. The Royals decided it was a great place to visit and came here on occasion to hunt, fish, and enjoy other leisure pursuits. We walked along the streets and went into a number of the stores. Because it was still very early, we decided to continue on rather than going to the local campground. We could still drive to the western shore town of Oban if we started right away. So we bought food for lunch from the Braemar butcher shop and left town.

Good thing we did. Our trip through the Highlands was perfect—the sun was shining and the high hills looked crisp and beautiful. We had asked our Scottish friend what the difference was between the moors near where he lives and these Highlands. He had answered that the moors were "softer." Now we saw what he meant. The moors have slopes of perhaps 35 or 40 degrees, and are covered in green or lavender. These hills have much steeper slopes—perhaps 65, even 70 degrees—and are much more rocky and craggy. They are certainly "harder." Even though we held up traffic as we slowly climbed from the valleys between those hills, it was a great trip. When we got to Loch Earn on the western edge of the hills, it suddenly got misty and then it started to rain. And it continued to rain the rest of the day and for the two days we were in Oban! If we'd waited to begin our journey, our trip through the desolate Highlands would have been in heavy rain. As it was, we never took off our raincoats from the time we got to Oban until we left.

Got to put in an aside. Ron and I have begun a list of rules. Rule 1 is from last year's stay in the Netherlands. Don't bother to pack suntan lotion when traveling to a country where there are stores that sell only umbrellas. Rule 2 is: Don't go into the lawn sprinkler business in Scotland.

We got to the campground with no trouble. This may be the biggest one we've ever been in. According to our book, it has 30 acres on the bay. The Isle of Mull is visible in the distance. The camp is full to the brim with campers and motor homes despite the definitely inclement weather. Ron loves the water view, but I am much more enamored of the wavy hill on the other side of the road, especially in the evening when all those little white dots scattered on the hillside start baa-ing to each other!

We took the bus into Oban the next morning, found ShopMobility, and "borrowed" a scooter. Then we wandered all over—looking at the stores and buying some stuff. We tried to find an Internet outlet that would take a Microsoft Word document (there were none and the librarian had the day off). We were hoping to find a reasonably priced place for lunch (there seemed to be none). In Oban, an order of fish and chips to take away was 7.95 pounds which translated to more than $11—for one serving that you had to eat on the street! We finally did stop for lunch at a Chinese restaurant and then ended our day by doing grocery shopping.

The next morning we took the ferry to the Isle of Mull. Once again we found our fellow travelers very friendly. When we got off the ferry, we got on what is called a "service bus," which takes the ferry passengers to a little town called Tobermory about 20 miles away. The bus was crowded but we still managed to get a seat.

Tourism seems to be the main source of income for the people in Tobermory. And there are are a lot of tourists. First are people who come just to be on an island. Then there are families whose very young children are big fans of a program called *Balamory* that is filmed in this town. The characters live in the houses that are each painted a different color. Then there are the people who come to sample the single-malt Scotch called Ledaig made here by the Tobermory Distillery.

We walked along the street, checked all the shops, and visited the Mull Museum where there is a good exhibit detailing life on the island from pre-history through recorded history. The displays include information about geology and some relics of a ship from the Spanish Armada that broke up near the island. By 2 in the afternoon we were anxious to make it onto the 3 o'clock ferry and get back to Oban. Fortunately, so were a great many others, and although the service bus didn't run at that hour, people with return tickets were allowed to get onto a tour bus that was returning to the ferry!

It had rained off and on all day, but at night it really started to pour. And we are nice and snug in our leakless vehicle! Tomorrow we're off to Glasgow and Saturday we'll be in Blackpool. Is this wonderful or what?! R&A

Letter #11—Kirkby Lonsdale, England, August 24, 2003

The weather in England, as the BBC "presenter" said this morning, is "resolutely cloudy"—no rain is in sight. I'd like to add that the people we have met in England are "resolutely friendly." The British really do talk—and complain—about the weather all the time, but they certainly do not live up to their stereotype as cold and unfriendly.

Let me back up to Glasgow. There were no campgrounds listed near Glasgow, so we decided to try something new. In the book of campgrounds that is published by the Caravan Club, there is a long list of "Certified Locations," each of which can take up to five campers. We called one in a suburb of Glasgow called Milton of Campsie. (The Campsie is a low mountain range or area.) A very British-sounding lady said she had room, and so we arranged our stay.

We had no trouble finding the campsite, although I had a lot of trouble figuring out where the T-junction was (since I had no idea *what* it was), but we found our way to the right street. Couldn't find the farm road, though, and drove into a residential area that was difficult to get out of. Ron had to turn around. There was a gentleman with a beautiful standard poodle watching us, and sure enough, (a) he noted our plight, (b) he knew where we should go, and (c) he said he'd meet us at the junction to be sure we got there! The farm road turned out to end in the parking lot of the church hall. Without his help, we'd never have found it.

We pulled in and the expected "little old lady" met us. She was very friendly, and she asked where in the U.S. we were from. It turned out that she herself had a Connecticut connection. In 1760 or so, her great, great, great grandfather was traveling in the Colonies when he became ill. The family of a blacksmith in Stratford, Connecticut, cared for him, and he married the blacksmith's daughter Glorianna. He brought her home to Scotland when his father pointed out that he was the next baronet and should be in Scotland, and eventually they had either 17 or 19 children. Our landlady, who is now 83, was the youngest of the children of what I believe she said was the 12th baronet. None of her siblings had had children, so her eldest son now lives in the big house on the estate we were on and she lives in a cottage at the bottom of the hill and across a meadow. The land was not entailed, so they still own it, but an American descendant of one of the other lines of the family is the baronet. He lives in Indiana! She told us that the family followed William the Conqueror over in 1068. They have lived on this land since 1508! So she is certainly Scottish, not English at all. What about her decidedly English accent? "Well," she explained, "we are landed gentry and none of us speak like the Scots do, even though we are Scots."

We loved Glasgow. It is totally different from Edinburgh, and very much like an American city, shabby in some sections, elegant in others. Quite dirty with high-rise apartment buildings, which we did not see in Edinburgh. But we covered more of Glasgow riding buses than we did Edinburgh. We spent only one day in Glasgow, but it was a busy one. One of the first things we did was get a scooter. Then we walked to one of the two attractions we wanted to see. It was a terrible walk, up long hills and then down—and when we finally got there we discovered it wasn't going to open for hours! We often seem to forget to check the schedule before we go to an attraction!

So we went to the McClellen Art Museum (scooter and all) and then returned the scooter and got on the bus to go see the Burrell Collection, another museum devoted to the idiosyncratic—and very discerning—collection of a very rich man. Lots of Degas paintings, three Rodin sculptures, incredible numbers of ancient relics from Greece, Rome, Egypt, and China, a large number of the most beautiful medieval tapestries, old stained glass—and more. We missed the museum devoted to the hometown favorite, Charles Rennie Macintosh, an artist and architect whose Art Deco work you would recognize if you saw it. But we did see one of his buildings and some of his art at the McClellan Museum.

We found Glaswegans' speech more difficult to understand than that spoken by Scots from other parts of the country. While we were on the bus, a young man got on and talked to the bus driver for quite a long time. We understood not a word. And the very nice young man at Shop-Mobility who was trying to find out if I understood how to drive the scooter kept asking me to show him various maneuvers with the scooter. He probably thought I was an idiot, because I didn't seem to be able to follow his instructions. The problem was that I couldn't understand a word he was saying! Fortunately, Ron managed to make just enough sense of his words to tell me what to do! Otherwise, I'm not sure I would have been trusted with a scooter.

After we left our Glasgow site, we stopped just for the night to break up the journey in Kirby Lonsdale. On Sunday, there was a "boot sale" (flea market) in that little town. Great—especially for Ron, who had been suffering from flea market withdrawal pains. This was our first one since we landed. R&A

LETTER #12—BLACKPOOL, ENGLAND, AUGUST 25, 2003

From Glasgow we headed for Blackpool, England's combination of Coney Island and Las Vegas, the largest, tackiest amusement park—not a theme park, an amusement park—in Europe. It is on the Irish Sea below Morecombe Bay. Like Las Vegas, Blackpool has a strip, a three-mile street from south to north bordered by a tramway. This is just west of the boardwalk, the beach, and the sea. Located near the center of the strip is Blackpool Tower. This construction of Victorian ironwork is over 500 feet high and contains a ballroom in which there is a mighty Wurlitzer organ. There is also an auditorium (we didn't go inside) where a circus can be seen. Admission to the circus is included in the price of admission to the tower. There are three amusement-laden piers jutting out into the ocean along the strip, one at the south end, one in the center, and one at the north end. I (Ron) walked out on the center one, which has a very large ferris wheel, some large pubs, food stalls, children's amusement rides, and ironwork benches filled with mostly elderly folks sitting and surveying all the hubbub. From the end you can see all the way up and down the strip. The south end of the strip has a huge roller coaster, and the south pier has swings that can seat several people and swing them over the water in a huge arc, and bungy cars—which get dropped from great heights and bounce way down and then way up. The north pier is so long that it has a tram to take you out to the end.

In between these piers, and on the side of the street opposite the beach, are yet other large amusement parks, a "SeaWorld" kind of place, horror houses, and small hotels and B & Bs, as well as eateries, most of which sell fish and chips. We took a tour bus and learned that there are 2,500 hotels with 9,100 beds along the strip or on the street that parallels it. Obviously these are small three- and four-room residential hotels for the most part. And the days we were there all these were occupied because it was Bank Holiday, which is the equivalent of our Labor Day weekend. The crowds were huge.

One of the amusements for children is to take a donkey ride on the beach, which at low tide is about 600 yards wide. A major amusement for all ages is simply to sit on a bench overlooking the beach and the water, either on the west side of the tramway or on one of the piers. There were virtually no people in the water. We were told by a person who goes there often that the reason no one goes into the water is because it is filthy.

We are inexplicably fond of tacky beach places, so we *quite* enjoyed our stay. We had a *wizard* day. (Did you catch the Britishisms? If so, *brilliant!*)

We are on our way to Liverpool and south to the parts of England that are even more interesting historically to those of us who remember World War II. R&A

LETTER #13—LIVERPOOL, ENGLAND, AUGUST 27, 2003

We found a campsite outside Liverpool in a town called Bebington. The site is actually a Certified Location called Grange Farm on Little Storeton Road. It is a working farm, with an area set aside for caravanners. Our closest neighbor was an absolutely beautiful Welsh Cob—an enormous dappled brown-black horse who, we were told, did show jumping in the summer and went on the hunts in the winter. Also close by were the chickens. They were hoping there was something nice to eat near our

RV. We had picked this place because when we called, we were told that we could get to Liverpool by taking a bus to Birkenhead. Even better, this bus stopped near the farm. Then we could go across the river Mersey by bus, train, or ferry to Liverpool. And indeed the bus did stop outside the door. More impressive, however, was when we came back from the city on the first night. We couldn't remember the name of the farm. As we stuttered on about the farm and Little Storeton, the bus driver said, "Alan's place? Grange Farm?" He knew. He left us off across the street from the entrance to this same farm! Is this service, or what? (Just as an aside, the farmer was not a taciturn type. Instead, he was friendly, had a good sense of humor, etc. No stereotypical Englishman here either.)

We spent two days in Liverpool. The city is famous in modern times, of course, as the place where the Beatles got their start, in a downstairs nightclub called the Cavern. But they weren't what drew us to the city. As you all know, Ron and I are very interested in World War II, and there's a lot of WWII history here.

Liverpool is one of the biggest ports on the western coast of England and it unloaded a large number of the convoy ships that kept Britain alive during WWII. In addition, it was the heart of the ship construction that kept going throughout the war. Consequently, it was bombed a lot. We could certainly see that as we walked from the Walker (art) Museum to the wonderful Maritime Museum on the Albert Dock. Our walk took us along Lord Street and right past a monument to Queen Victoria, a huge marble construction with the Queen (all black) sitting on a high throne under a circular cupola surrounded by other figures.

The Maritime Museum had a temporary exhibition about Britain in the Blitz. There were aerial photos of the area from the Albert Dock to Lord Street taken after one of the most devastating bombing raids. There was virtually nothing left standing, with the exception of the Victoria monument we had passed on our walk to the museum. It was untouched and looked exactly as it did when we passed it. The exhibit included a talk by "Albert, an ARP (Air Raid Patrol) warden." He was giving a lecture on how to behave during the Blitz—things like observing the blackout rules and what to do on hearing the air-raid siren. Although almost none of this was new to us, it was very interesting to see how it was presented to a much younger generation.

The museum also had a big display about the war in the Atlantic. Again, we were familiar with most of the information, but one thing was quite surprising to Adelle. There was a huge map with pins showing where merchant ships had been sunk by U-boats. Most were very close to America! The area from New York Harbor to the Caribbean was referred to as the Turkey Shoot at the beginning of the war. And I'm not sure that I (Adelle) knew that the British Navy had rammed a U-boat and captured an "Enigma" machine—a device that coded (and decoded) Nazi radio transmissions. It was many years after the war before this was public knowledge, of course.

We saw only the smallest part of the Maritime Museum, but that's all I (Adelle) can handle in an afternoon, even though I had the wonderful scooter, again from ShopMobility. Albert Dock is also home to a branch of the Tate. We skipped it because we're not enthusiastic about modern art.

We've been all over England and seen very few outdoor markets, although we've been in several that are indoors. They are never as wonderful as those on the Continent—especially in France—but then no one comes to England for the food! Still, it is exciting to be in the places we've read about all our lives.

From our campsite in Bebington, we could see the marine laboratory where they plotted the tides for the D-Day invasion and we could also see the mountains of Wales, our next stop. R&A

LETTER #14—CONWY, WALES, AUGUST 29, 2003

Once when we were driving along a beautiful road in Scotland with our friends, Adelle said "Look, there's a castle." And Mike said, "Oh, castles are like bums. Everyone has one." That may be true, but not everyone has a castle like Conwy (pronounced Conway).

Actually, that's not quite true. There are four such castles in Wales, all built by Edward I to maintain control over a land not his own at the time. The castle in Conwy had fallen into great disrepair 300 years ago when the then Lord Conwy (who owned the castle then) needed money. He raised it by selling the lead covering that protected the wooden roof. This misdeed was explained to us by our guide, an elderly man who can only be described as "a hoot." It is no wonder that the cable TV program *Modern Marvels* featured his tour of the castle!

But that is moving ahead of the story. First stop after Liverpool was Chester, right on the Wales border. This small city (it has a cathedral and that makes it a city) has a center that was built in 1300 and repaired in Victorian times. As a result, it is the best Tudor city remaining in England. The half-timbered houses were built with covered balconies on the second floor that allow you to go from one building to another without going down to the street. They are known as "the Rows" and they date back to the thirteenth century. No one knows why the idea took so long to take hold in other places.

Chester even has an outer medieval wall remaining. Ron walked (I scootered) along that wall for a while, right along a racetrack where races were to be held a little later that day, but we ran into a place that had steps and had to stop. As we stood there looking for a place for me to get across the street without having to go down a high curb, a man said "Here, luv. I'll carry it down for you." And he and a friend did just that. Would this happen in America?

Back to the castle. Conwy is in Wales. Don't even think about Welsh names. A couple of my favorites: Rhosllanerchrugog and Penrhydeu-draeth, which may or may not be names. My all-time favorite, though, is Llanfair-Pyllgwyngyu. It has many letters but almost no vowels, and I can't find it on the map. I saw it on a road sign. Ron is particularly partial to Stiwdio, which he thinks means Studio. (By the way, some signs in Scotland are in Gaelic, which is pronounced "Gallic," I think. For example, "Post Office" seems to be "Oifice a Phuist.") In Wales, road signs are in Welsh first and English second. I (Ron) quickly got used to seeing "ARAF," followed by "SLOW."

One of the most interesting things we learned was that the entire castle had been white—inside and outside—like a Mediterranean house today. Lots of the lime that originally covered the stone walls of the castle is still left. And not only on the castle. There was lime on the Elizabethan town house (circa 1500) that we also visited. Somehow, we didn't expect all white.

After walking an hour through the castle ruins and then through Plas Mawr (which means "Big House"), including lots and lots of stairs, Adelle had had it. We moved on to Caernarfon. R&A

LETTER #15—CAERNARFON & DUBLIN, AUGUST 30, 2003

Caernarfon has a matching castle (another one built by Edward I), but we didn't intend to visit that one. We picked the town because it had campsites and we wanted to stay the night. While we were there, we planned our next two days' activities. We reserved space on the Snowdonia Mountain Railway for Saturday and arranged a trip on the ferry from Holyhead in Wales to Dublin, Ireland, for Sunday. There is a big push on to get people to take a day trip to Dublin. Sounded good to us—18 pounds, about $28, for two, round-trip.

The mountain train ride was on a cog-and-pinion railway line. In the middle of the tracks is an additional track that has a series of cogs laid out in a straight line. It looks a lot like the inside of a huge watch. The train moves up and down the mountain—very slowly. Of course, every time a tooth is engaged there is a slight hesitation, so you almost bump along. The scenery was spectacular—very wild with nothing but a few little huts near the track for the trains and a lot of sheep who are spending their summer eating on the mountain, not even realizing that some farmer is planning to eat some of them soon! The summit is only 3,500 feet high, and we were told that from there you can see four kingdoms— England, Wales, Ireland, and Heaven. We can't argue with that, nor can we verify it, because there were no signs on the summit showing you either the direction in which you were gazing or what was there in the distance. Would have been a boon for all the tourists. There are lots and lots of people hiking up the mountain, as well as a train full of people every half-hour.

After our day on the railroad, we moved on to a campsite on the island of Anglesey. It was in a town called Bodedern near Holyhead. That put us in a good position for the next morning. We had to be at the ferry dock in time to walk onto an Irish ferry that sailed at 9:20 AM. We opted to take the "swift"—a ship called the Jonathan Swift—that gets across the

One of the spectacular views from the Snowdonia Mountain Railway trip.

Irish Sea in only 1 hour and 49 minutes, going through the water at 50 miles an hour. Since we were only taking a day trip, we wanted to minimize the time spent on the ferry.

Fortunately, there was another camper at our campsite who had taken the trip recently. She told us that we would have to park in a particular place and needed to be there about an hour early because we would have to get a bus from the parking lot to the terminal and another bus from the terminal to the dock. She also suggested buying tickets for a sightseeing bus in Ireland before we left Wales. The price was better. We followed her advice and did all that.

The ship itself was a nice, reasonably new ship, although the upholstery on many of the chairs was torn and shabby. It had been named for the author of *Gulliver's Travels,* but not because of his writings. He had been the dean of one of Dublin's largest Church of Ireland cathedrals and was very influential in the city's development.

We only had about six hours to spend in Dublin, so taking a a tour bus was a good choice. The bus driver said that the most popular stop was the Guinness Brewery, where the tour includes a free pint of Guinness. We didn't stop, so we can't tell you anything else about it.

The most interesting place for us was Trinity College, the only place we got off the bus to visit. The Old Library contains the Book of Kells. Many consider this to be the most beautifully illustrated medieval text in the world. The book dates from the 800s and contains the four gospels. The Trinity Library displays four pages of the original at a time. They change the pages shown frequently because, even in a glass case that is climate controlled, there can be damage to the book. The beauty of this work is not exaggerated.

Perhaps as beautiful in a different way is the "Long Room" in the library—which also is very high, with an arched ceiling stretching the whole long length of the room, the walls of which are covered with bookshelves and old books from ceiling to floor.

We enjoyed our trip to Dublin. Before setting out, we had gotten a price for taking the RV to Ireland and discovered that it would be horribly expensive, so that is why we decided to leave the RV in Wales and make it a day trip. R&A

LETTER #16—SHREWSBURY & IRONBRIDGE, SEPTEMBER 2, 2003

The morning after we returned from Dublin, we drove east through

Wales to get to a place called Ironbridge, a remarkable collection of museums that had been recommended to us by English friends. The museums are located between Shrewsbury and Telford, west of Birmingham.

The trip itself through northern Wales can only be described as a "Wow." Wales is really beautiful. Different landscapes—but always wild and mountainous. Sometimes lots of trees, sometimes heather, and frequently a sprinkling of sheep. The road goes through the mountains. There's an occasional tunnel, usually just on the edge of one mountain with another one seeming to loom directly ahead of you and no evidence of a road on it. Of course, there is always a road, but you can't always see it before getting to it. Wales is definitely wild and wooly!

Eventually, the road signs that were in two languages disappeared and the scenery became more "civilized." The towns again became "picture-postcard-perfect-rural-cum-church" and we were back in England. We headed for a rendezvous with Brother Caedfael, which is to say we stopped at Shrewsbury. The abbey is long gone. The town, the birthplace of Charles Darwin, is full of half-timbered houses, some plain and some with fancy designs. There is a beautiful church and a castle and there are lots of shops. Par for an English town. We stayed only for the day.

In the morning we set out for Ironbridge Gorge in Shropshire. It took us most of the day to get there. Ironbridge can be viewed as the place where the Industrial Revolution began. We didn't have a campground picked out for that city and, for a change, we decided to try our luck at finding one that wasn't listed in our book. Sometimes you really do get lucky! We found a very nice and very convenient campground and registered for two nights. The next morning we set off to visit at least some of the 10 museums that make up the complex.

The museums themselves were among the most interesting ones we'd seen, but the local signs leading to them left a lot to be desired. We didn't get lost, but that was really just luck. This is an enormously important tourist site—a UNESCO World Heritage site. You'd think the local government would pay more attention to the signs. The first museum we came to was the Bliss Victorian Village. We were a little bit hesitant about this one, because we've been to so many re-creations before, but we were very glad that we decided to go in. There were things here we'd never seen or thought about!

For example? How about the steam-driven winding engine that pulls the men and coal out of the mines. It really worked. And Sampson and David, the huge engines that supplied the air to the blast furnaces, the remains of which are still there. All kinds of industrial enterprises, including the remains of the first blast furnace to use coke instead of charcoal, dating from 1709 and now housed under a roof to preserve it.

It was the development in the early eighteenth century of a way to utilize coke to make iron that made the process of making iron efficient enough to make possible the mass-production of the iron machines that powered the Industrial Revolution. That's why this particular town can be viewed as the birthplace of the Industrial Revolution.

Before the time of Abraham Darby, who invented the new process, iron making was extremely inefficient. Charcoal was used to reduce the impurities in iron. Charcoal is made by smoldering wood. This quickly depleted forests, thereby driving up the price of wood. Darby developed a way of making coke out of coal, which, along with water and lime, was plentiful in this area. And coke turned out to be as good as charcoal in the process of smelting ore into iron.

After a while, others heard about Darby's process and came to the area to learned his method. And that was the beginning. The foundries that Darby established were run as a family business for a number of generations. As time went on, the foundries developed other processes (such as a way of casting iron pots, many of which were used by New England whalers) and a method of casting cylinders for steam engines (which were used to power industrial tools as well as trains and boats).

The place gets its name from an iron bridge—the first ever built—that spans the Severn. The bridge was designed and built by Abraham Darby III, a member of the third generation of the family. The rest is our history. All this, as I said, began right here, in Ironbridge.

We've always just assumed that the iron was available for James Watt to invent the steam engine, but of course, it wasn't. After viewing all the exhibits, all we can say is that there is not a person in the so-called "civilized world" who is not personally indebted to Abraham Darby, because there would be no modern world without his iron-making process and blast furnaces. He changed the world.

We stayed a couple of days and visited all the museums. The Coalport China Museum was notable for its displays of old bone china. We almost missed this one, and then it occurred to us that we'd seen antique china made by this company in museums, and we were interested in learning about the process of making bone china. The displays of china were beautiful. The workers who made the china in the old days probably didn't think so, because the conditions were deplorable, but that's an another story.

After the China Museum, we left the area to drive down to Bristol. We didn't stop at Gloucester, Welles, Worchester, or Tewkesbury. The thing is that there is something to see in nearly every town of any size. We can't stay *that* long! On to Cornwall. R&A

LETTER #17—TINTAGEL IN CORNWALL TO PLYMOUTH IN DEVON, SEPTEMBER 4, 2003

After Ironbridge, we headed for the area around Bath and Bristol but we could not find a campground that would give us good access into either, so we decided to go on to Cornwall. (Note, however, that on our second try, a week and a half later, we found two excellent campgrounds, one in each city!)

Cornwall is in the extreme southwest of England, the part that juts out into the sea almost in the direction of the U.S. Penzance, the Lizard, and Land's End are all here. The drive to Cornwall from the M5 was across long rolling hills and through only a few towns. The day was sunny and the trip was a pleasure—until we had to get from the motorway to our campground near Tintagel on the coast. This town is a tiny, quaint village on the edge of a precipice and it is full of tourists. It is supposed to have been one of the homes of King Arthur and Queen Guinevere.

The roads to the campground were—to put it mildly—very narrow and exceptionally twisty and curvy, since they all led through a mountainous area to the rocky coast of Cornwall. Our campground was perched high on a cliff with a view of the beautiful shore. The Cornish coast is justly renowned, though I think you have to see it in a storm to get the full effect. We stayed overnight and walked through town before leaving the following day.

Towns on Cape Cod are named after towns on this peninsula—Falmouth, Barnstaple, and Truro, which was to be our next stop. It wasn't too long a drive. We got there without a problem and followed the signs for parking, which turned into a nightmare. The traffic was just awful. There certainly was parking, but all the lots were jammed, and they were barricaded so as not to allow trucks, campers, or caravans into them. The streets were narrow and filled with wall-to-wall cars. We followed a bus through town because we knew that if he could pass through the street, so could we. Finally we found ourselves outside of town, and we decided that under no circumstances would we chance going back in! We headed instead to Devonshire and to that famous city, Plymouth.

Plymouth is not much today. It is a nice city, to be sure, but most of it is not too pretty, and not much in the city itself is worth singling out for special attention. That is because the Nazis bombed it severely during the war, destroying most of the dock area and the whole central part of the city. Rebuilding after the war was for efficiency, not for beauty. Nevertheless, this city has at least two great things going for it. One of those things is its harbor. The other is its history, which this harbor made possible.

The harbor is large and very beautiful, with great bights on either side. The bight on the port side is straighter than the one starboard side, so that you see a great sweep of land on the port side as you look out to sea. And on the starboard side, the bight is very irregular with small promontories. Behind them are several snug anchorages sheltered from south, southeasterly, and southwesterly winds. The landward shore of the harbor provides shelter from all points north. Two rivers empty into the harbor. The smaller one is the Plym. It provides the city with its name (Plym-mouth) and, in turn, also provided Plymouth, Massachusetts— 3,358 miles away, according to the sign in the museum—with its name. The other, larger river is the Tamar, which on the map looks like a whole fleet could anchor in its mouth.

The history of this sheltered harbor is such as to inspire awe and reverence in anyone who visits. The local history museum claims that three expeditions launched from this place changed the world. I think they undercounted. The first was Sir Francis Drake's voyage in the Golden Hind in the sixteenth century. He ended up circumnavigating the globe thanks to stolen charts and log books supplied by a Portuguese pilot. The expedition returned with great loads of material riches stolen from the Spanish colonies in America. On this trip Drake charted the west coast of what is now the United States. There is no doubt that this expedition helped create the idea of the British Empire.

The second was the Pilgrims' voyage in 1620 to settle in what was to become the United States. This ultimately led, for better or worse, to the creation of the most powerful economic, military, and cultural power on earth. It is worth noting that an earlier expedition, sent by Sir Walter Raleigh in 1584 to set up the Virginia colony, also sailed from here. That colony failed.

The third of the world-changing set of expeditions were the three voyages by Captain Cook in the eighteenth century, which charted much of South America and the Pacific, including Australia and New Zealand, and brought back a great deal of scientific information about those Pacific areas. This certainly facilitated the actual creation of the British Empire.

Now consider further that the HMS *Beagle* also sailed from here. One could certainly argue that that voyage changed the world significantly— perhaps even more than the other three—because it was on that voyage that Charles Darwin began formulating the theory of evolution.

Also consider that the British fleet that defeated the Spanish Armada sailed from Plymouth harbor and engaged and scattered their enemy in sight of citizens of Plymouth who were watching from the shore. Indeed, most of the great captains of the British fleets, including Lord Nelson, led their usually victorious fleets from this place. In more recent times, immigrants to both Australia and New Zealand began their journeys here. Last, and perhaps least, the first transatlantic seaplane voyage by the American seaplane, the N.C. 4, landed here in 1919.

Some places are worth a visit not because they are beautiful or contain fascinating artifacts of culture. They are interesting because of what happened there. These are events that will never happen again. After all, future world changes probably won't result from maritime expeditions. Those days are over forever. Nevertheless, it is inspiring to be in a place that played such an important role in forming the world that we have today. R&A

LETTER #18—CAMPING DETAILS FOR NON-CAMPERS, SEPTEMBER 5, 2003

A very few of the people with whom we correspond are also campers. The rest of you may have questions about how we live which we will attempt to answer here. If there are any inquiries we haven't anticipated, please e-mail us. We'll be glad to answer.

First of all, those of you who have seen our little RV know that we have a little bathroom of our own. We don't use it much, because we don't relish the idea of having to dump all the time.

In the U.S., motor homes use their own facilities. Most don't take showers in the unit because the showers are so small, but they do their dishes, wash up, etc.

In Europe there are lots and lots of tents in every campground, so every campground has an area where everyone goes to wash dishes. You'll be interested to know that most of the dishwashers are men—including Ron! After dinner, we pile the dirty dishes into a dishpan, add a sponge and detergent, and he goes off to do the dishes. It's quite a social affair. He's met a lot of fellow campers while doing the dishes.

We are accustomed to the parsimonious use of dishes and pots, because we spent 20 summers camping on our boats, the 1938 and 1939 ELCO cruisers.

We take our showers in the "sanitary block" provided by the camp-grounds. There are showers with privacy cubicles, as well as sinks for shaving, in individual compartments. In all the time we've been here, I've rarely had to wait to take a shower, and then the wait was about two minutes. Privacy is not really an issue, because each cubicle is very private, although you certainly have to go to a central location.

Which reminds me. Our tour guide in Conwy pointed out that the British are often a bit behind the times. He said that thirty years ago there were still communal bathrooms in hotels all over Britain—except in London. You had to queue up in front of the toilets and, in fact, when you checked into a hotel, you chose the evening that you wanted to use the bathtub. We're talking about the 1970s, not the 1920s. Then the idea of "en suite" took hold. People simply cut off part of the area of the room and put in a bathroom, and "now," our tour guide said, "we wouldn't think of anything but en suite." I said later that he must be mixing up the dates with the 1930s and 1940s. I was wrong. We met a very elegant lady in a museum afterwards, and she remembered privies in the 1950s. Furthermore, she said that her job in the 1960s was to arrange hotel accommodations for American pilots who were coming to train British pilots to fly Boeing's planes. She said that in the 1960s she had a hard time finding rooms with private bathrooms, and the Americans would accept nothing less.

We wash one load of laundry a week. There is usually a machine available in UK campgrounds—although there are often places without one on the Continent. We pick enough things to fill the very small tubs of the British machines and leave anything that doesn't fit until the next time. Everything is washed together. It's not ideal, but it is not too difficult, although it tends to be pretty expensive.

There is a minimum amount of housework that needs to be done. While Ron is doing the morning dishes, I clean the sinks, etc., and I use pre-moistened "wipes" to clean up the other surfaces as necessary. There is nothing fancy that needs to be polished or cleaned. The rug is kept vaguely clean because it is swept. We do have a broom, but the result is better if I use a whisk broom.

Once the bedding (i.e., sleeping bags) has been stowed, the cabinet doors checked to be sure they are secure, and various other things battened down, we are ready to roll. We rarely spend more than two days at one campsite, but we arrive in the evening, stay the night, take a bus into the city in the morning, return for dinner, and leave the next morning.

Those are all the housekeeping subjects I can think of. If there is something I didn't cover, let me know.

On to another subject. Ron does all the driving and I'm supposed to navigate. This is a good example of a job that doesn't fit the person. I'm really bad with a map, although I guess I am finally getting better. The main problems arise when the signpost says something I'm not expecting and Ron has to make an instant decision on which way to go, based on no information. It takes me too long to figure things out. And there is no room at the side of the road to pull over. There are rarely shoulders, frequently curbs, and all too often three- or four-foot-high stone walls!

England is better than the Continent in one way, however. Road signs are larger. They tell you which way you are going when you enter a limited access highway (e.g., south). In places where you will need to make turns, there are huge painted signs on the roadway showing you which lane will be leading to which highway. We have, however, run into problems when the last sign leading you to a particular destination is missing, and that has happened several times.

Food is not as good as in France, but it's not bad. We usually shop every other day. Here we almost always shop in supermarkets. In France, Belgium, and Holland we often bought things in open-air markets. There are very few open-air markets in England. They do have market buildings here, but that's not quite the same.

Breakfast is simple. A roll with butter and coffee (although Ron eats smoked fish too). Lunches are either sandwiches made before we leave or light lunches in the city. Dinner always has three components: protein, starch, and vegetable. Often the vegetable is salad. Dessert is usually fruit, but we do buy various kinds of sweets.

We often take our sandwiches with us because the prices are so high. Think of a sandwich costing three pounds ninety-five pence in the cheapest restaurants. Looks like about the price of a sandwich at home. But, since every pound is approximately $1.60, that translates to $6.32! In a more standard restaurant, a sandwich will cost the equivalent of $10! A pot of tea looks inexpensive at one pound ten. That is $1.76. So, a lunch out is a minimum of $20 even if you go to the cheapest places. Burger King is quite expensive. We haven't eaten there, but we priced a Whopper. It's 2 pounds 69 pence, or a little more than $4 minimum. If we are tired in the afternoon and want two cups of coffee, we have to be willing to pay $4–$6 for it.

Strangers have been absolutely wonderful to us. We've mentioned some Good Samaritans, but there have been many more than that. We would never have made it through this trip without the ShopMobility scooters. We've managed to get into many campgrounds that we hadn't even known existed thanks to previous campground wardens who gave us a name.

Looking confused while standing with a map always brings someone to ask if they can help. We've been told that it is because once we open our mouths it is obvious that we are Americans. Apparently the English are not so helpful to each other. But the man who told us that also told us that people in America were wonderful to him when he was there. Perhaps a different accent has its effect on both sides of the Atlantic. We didn't find such friendliness when we drove across the U.S.

I've had a bit of a problem with the new telephone service here, which is expensive and difficult to use, despite lots of billboards advertising this new service. But, on the other hand, British Telecom has pay phones everywhere. If there are six houses in a village in the middle of nowhere, there is a red box. Even better, these public phones allow me to use the pay phone to make 800 calls without requiring that I put in a card or money. That makes staying in touch with home easier. Adelle

LETTER #19—CROWCOMBE, SOMERSET, SEPTEMBER 10, 2003

On our trek through Great Britain, we have been privileged in a way that very few people have been. Because we visited friends whose lives are very different from ours, we have been allowed to see, and at least partially experience, very different ways of living.

We visited friends in Northumberland—and had our first taste of the *real* Britain—not the usual monuments and art museums, but the way people live. In their case, they lived in a farming community on what used to be a farm, more or less isolated from a village community. They had neighbors, good neighbors, but there was no village in that immediate vicinity. The nearest town was Hexham, perhaps eight or nine miles away. Then we visited folks in Scotland. They live nearer to a village but still not in one, and we were enthralled with all the aspects of another way of life among the Scots—living on a gaming estate, pipe bands, raising pheasants, gamekeepers, managing heather to sustain and encourage the breeding and feeding of grouse, and other things. It was hard to believe that we could experience anything that would equal that. But we did.

We found ourselves a personal "Guide to the English Village." Our visit to old friends who live right in a village in Somerset gave us the experience of what English village life is like. In some respects it is similar to village life as described by Agatha Christie in her mystery stories, and also similar to the village of Dibley (the BBC program called *The Vicar of Dibley*). But it was actually much more than that. Despite the fact that I (Adelle) consistently made the mistake of calling this location a "town," it really is a "village."

We got directions from our friends on how to find them. As directed, we drove on the main highway until we were very close to the village. We took the correct cut-off from the main road and turned into a lane. If we were really careful, there was just enough space for a car coming toward us to pass. The lane was edged with seven- or eight-foot-hedges on both sides. For people in a wide vehicle, it was a nail-biting experience. Fortunately, the road wasn't more than a couple of miles long!

We finally began to see the lovely stone houses, some with thatched roofs, and a remarkably old-looking church. We stopped and asked a young man where to find our friends, and found that in a village of 400 people, everyone knows everyone else.

We spent the next couple of days in the village. With our host, we visited the ancient church. The tower is the older part but the church building itself is from the 1500s. We met other residents of this little village and had sherry and Scotch in a fifteenth-century house owned by a couple whose son is now teaching in the U.S. We toured several houses in the village, including one dating from the 1400s that had both Elizabethan and Victorian additions. We could not help but be impressed by the people of this village and by the pride they took in their local antiquities.

One day we drove around the area. We looked at other equally beautiful and ancient villages as well as other equally old churches which are part of the local "benefice," a grouping of communities with one vicar who makes the rounds, providing services in each of the churches over a span of several weeks. A parish council supervises each church, but the vicar runs the benefice. It is the only affordable way of staffing so many small village churches. We also saw the 20-mile-long track of a steam train and waited for the locomotive to pull the train into the station. We shivered in the autumn chill of the waterfront in the town where Samuel Taylor Coleridge began writing "The Rime of the Ancient Mariner."

Our host took us for an hour-and-a-half hike through Exmoor. Let me amend that. He and Ron hiked around the mountainside and enjoyed the spectacular views of the coast on the Bristol channel and Wales on the other side of it, while Adelle rode a four-wheeled motor scooter on loan from a 90-year-old lady in the village. The three of us began the circuit after riding for an hour through some of the most spectacular scenery you could ever see. The road was narrow and twisty, as usual, but it also went up and down in a very spectacular way. The road sign warned of hills that were 1:4, i.e., a grade of 25 percent, both up and down! A white knuckle experience. The hike, incidentally, went literally around the mountain on an old roadbed once used by a narrow-gauge rail train to haul minerals out of the area. It ended with lunch in a pub. We said good-bye very sadly, but we had many more places to visit. R&A

LETTER #20—STONEHENGE & SALISBURY, SEPTEMBER 11, 2003

We decided we would go back to Bristol. We had been there before, on our way to Tintagel, but left without seeing anything because the only campground we were able to find was not convenient for getting into the city. This time we were able to "book into" the Caravan Club site on the Bristol waterfront. They could let us stay just one night because they were fully booked the next day. We left in the morning to visit the SS *Great Britain,* the first steam passenger liner, and the *Matthew,* a replica of the ship in which John Cabot sailed to Newfoundland. Pulled into the parking lot and "paid and displayed." (Most parking lots in the UK require you to put money into a central meter and then put the receipt on the front dashboard.) But in the end, we decided that we'd pass up these ships in favor of other things.

When the warden at the Bristol Caravan Park told us that he couldn't let us stay another day, he recommended we try the Bath Marina campground. Finding the telephone number for this facility was an interesting experience. For some reason—and apparently with some controversy—telephone information has recently been privatized in Britain. Now instead of British Telecom's old 192 for all phone numbers, you dial 118 and then a set of three-digit numbers for one of the new information services.

I did this—but kept getting disconnected. So I tried another tack—calling Tourist Information. All this got me was a loss of money and another number—and that number also resulted in a loss of money but no other number.

I (Adelle) was steaming by then, and I said that I didn't even want to see Bath! A cooler head prevailed and we decided to visit the town by park .ing at the Park & Ride facility we had seen on the map.

Getting there by highway was quite an experience. We followed the signs faithfully, and found ourselves spending 30 minutes driving around Bristol before we finally hit the highway. The two cities are very close together once you get out of town! We parked at the Park & Ride, went into town, stopped at the Tourist Office, and found the number for the campground. They had plenty of room, so we arranged to spend the night there.

Then we borrowed a scooter from ShopMobility. Ron walked and I rode miles to see various architectural marvels in this most beautiful city—the Assembly Rooms mentioned in Jane Austen's novels and the Circus and the famous Royal Crescent featured in many period BBC productions, as well as the wonderful plantings of flowers at the park. Then we found the new campsite—which turned out to be only a short block from where we had been parked.

The next morning we headed for Stonehenge and Salisbury. Getting out of Bath proved as difficult as getting out of Bristol. We were not even lost. They really routed us through the scenic route. There must have been 20 roundabouts before we finally got onto a highway!

Having found there was a campground near Stonehenge, we headed there first. Then we visited the monument. Everyone knows what it looks like, and we have nothing to add except to agree that it is spectacular and extraordinary, even larger than we had expected and, of course, mysterious. Its mystery was not at all cleared up by the recorded lecture we were provided upon entry to the site. Most of this seemed made up just to have something to say. But not a lot is really known about Stonehenge. It certainly boggles the imagination to think of people moving those huge stones such long distances. We were surprised to find that the road goes right by it. It is on the Salisbury Plain, which is empty of houses but has miles of fields and grazing sheep. We approached from the west and got to the parking lot before seeing the stones. But later, after we had driven on to the east and were returning, we could see Stonehenge off in the distance, alone in an otherwise empty and huge space. That was spectacular.

We walked around the stones, took pictures, and then had to make a decision. Should we go to Salisbury for the afternoon? We discussed it, but I (Adelle) was exhausted, so we decided to go back to the campground and just "chill out." First thing in the morning would be time enough for Salisbury.

There was no bus service into Salisbury, but the campground owner told us that there was a parking lot we could use if we got in early. It was market day in Salisbury. As we headed for the parking lot, we found that our RV was too tall for an overpass. Not knowing how else to go anywhere, we parked in the car park of a local supermarket. There were signs all over warning that you were not allowed to park for more than three hours on any one day—and that there was a patrol.

We were planning to go to the cathedral, but we got sidetracked because we found our favorite thing—an outdoor market. This was the only market we saw in all the time we spent in England. We bought a lot of stuff and then found ourselves with a dilemma. If we walked back to the RV, we'd be within the three-hour limit, which was fine. If we went on to the cathedral, which was far away, we'd be in trouble. We opted to go back to the supermarket and then take the RV to one of the many car parks shown on the map.

This sounds like a rational solution, until you drive a motor home in Salisbury. We won't bore you with all the details—but it was a nightmare. All the car parks had barriers to keep out any vehicle higher than two meters. (We need a clearance of nearly three meters.) And the streets are narrow, with lots of curves, and crowded. The result was that we simply left. We would have liked to visit the cathedral—especially since it holds an original copy of the Magna Carta—but there was no way to do it. Sad. It is true, however, that on our trips we have seen a large number of cathedrals. We will just have to do without Salisbury's.

After finally getting out of there, we drove to Portsmouth. R&A

LETTER #21—PORTSMOUTH, SEPTEMBER 18, 2003

When we left Stonehenge to visit Salisbury, we had very few leads about campsites in the Portsmouth area. Lucky for us, we had gone into the Salisbury library to use the computers, and there in front of us were telephone books for all English cities. So we copied the page of campgrounds listed in Portsmouth. While we had never tried this before, we realized that it was an additional resource that we might want to use again in the future.

I was able to call a listed campground with my cell phone. It was way down near the water in Portsmouth, off the road that runs along the large harbor. Of course, it was many miles from the sights we wanted to see. But it was still convenient, so that's where we went.

We started out with the RV to see the sights the following morning, hoping that the museums would have parking lots. We were within sight of the D-Day Museum when we saw a "boot sale." Well, we know what's important. So we parked and went to the boot sale and then just walked half a block to the D-Day Museum. Our favorite exhibit was a copy of the map used by the invasion planners to show the details of routes the ships would take and to plot the progress of the fleet. The original map is still on display in the manor house that served as headquarters for Eisenhower, et al.

When we left, we found the Naval Museum. This is in a different part of the harbor and it houses several museums as well as three historic ships. We visited the *Victory* (1796), the ship on which Admiral Nelson died during the Napoleonic Wars. In addition, there was the *Warrior*, an enormous iron warship that was built in 1860 and had both sails and a steam engine. The remnants of the *Mary Rose*—a man-o'-war built by Henry VIII—were in a special room. Our first thought was just to go into the museum and skip the ships, but the price of the whole package was only two pounds more than museum entrance alone, so we bought a ticket to see everything, and the fee even included a cruise around the harbor.

To see the comparatively small and not very sophisticated (but pretty) *Victory*, we had to take a tour. Our guide told us a lot of facts, some of them new. We already knew that the British Navy in the eighteenth century couldn't allow sailors shore leave. Most of them had been kidnapped and impressed into the Navy and would have simply disappeared instead of returning to their ships. So, when the ships were in a home port, they allowed the sailors' families to live aboard. Must have been quite a scene on the gun deck, which is where they all lived. Very intimate, indeed.

Babies were often born on the gundeck, under the guns—hence the expression "son of a gun." And there were other nautical arrangements that spawned sayings. For example, meals on board were served on squares of wood with moldings around the edges to keep the food from falling off, hence "three square meals a day." The food was placed in the middle, but you might be able to bribe the cook to give you more food. This would be placed on the edge of the plate, called the fiddle—hence the British expression denoting something somewhat illegal, "on the fiddle." Discipline was harsh, and when a tar broke a rule, he was confined to an area on the weather deck where there were leg irons. He then had to braid the kind of whip that is known as a "cat-o'-nine-tails." This would be for his own flogging! If it was done to his officer's satisfaction, the officer put it into a red bag, to be taken out when punishment was officially meted, hence "letting the cat out of the bag."

Anyway, we toured the *Victory* with the guide, who told us all these interesting facts. Then we walked around the *Warrior* and ended up exhibit-viewing with a tour of the huge room constructed to preserve the remains of the *Mary Rose*. These are not extensive, mostly just a part of the ship's skeleton. The structure is continuously sprayed with water to prevent drying and consequent rotting.

Our campground was on the outside edge of the city, and from there we could see evidence of the several attempts made by Henry VIII to fortify the harbor—three round forts at the entrance—as well as more modern installations. Plymouth may have been more influential than Portsmouth in terms of big events beginning there, but Portsmouth certainly has been important in British (and American) history. Most recently, of course, because the D-Day invasion was coordinated here. We then moved on to Brighton, about 40 miles to the east. Another seaside town (like Blackpool) but not so tacky. There was a campground there, but it wasn't suitable for us at all. Getting to public transportation would have required too long a walk. The campground warden directed us to a campground farther away but with good train service into the city. So all's well that ends well.

Walked around quite a bit, going into antique stores and through the street markets. In fact, we had a very nice day and didn't realize until we were on the train that we hadn't seen the beach or the amusement section at Brighton. It was an oversight that may never be rectified, but only one among many.

Our next scheduled stop was Chartwell, which had been Winston Churchill's home. We drove along the country lanes (read narrow, curved, single-lane tracks with obstructions on both sides) that lead to the estate and found the parking lot, only to find that the house is open only from Wednesday to Saturday. This was Tuesday. So we added Chartwell to places we missed. There are so many places we've been unable to see that we could make up a trip of missed sights! Since we wanted to spend two weeks in London at the end of the trip, and it was now two weeks before we planned to leave, we figured that we'd done a pretty good job of managing our time. R&A

LETTER #22—LONDON, SEPTEMBER 22, 2003

Let us open with two observations.

1. Riding on a London city bus is not for the fainthearted. Even the camp warden here at the Crystal Palace campground, who used to be a bus driver, concedes that riding a bus is like being on a fairground ride. Apparently all bus drivers have pilots' licenses for low altitude flying! Rides are fast, with quick accelerations and lots of slamming on the brakes.

2. We have never stayed in a campground with such an odd warning attached to the information about the site. We reprint it in its entirety.

BE AWARE
FOXES ARE ON SITE
PLEASE KEEP ALL SHOES ETC
INSIDE YOUR VAN OR VEHICLE
AS THEY WILL REMOVE OR
CHEW THEM

And this is in southeast London! Moreover, we have since discovered that foxes are a big nuisance all over London. Our friends in Kensington have a fox den in their back yard—which is probably not a good thing!

Getting into London could not be considered a pleasure. The amount of traffic made it more like torture. But we followed instructions and had no trouble finding the site. The trip convinced us, however, that we are better off if we stay in the campground until we are ready to make a few other stops and don't try taking the RV out for any side trips.

The bus service is good and the stop is not too far away, even for those of us who are sissies. It does take 45 minutes to arrive at Oxford Circus, which is one stop past Piccadilly Circus and two past Trafalgar Square, but it is doubtful that we could ever find a hotel in London for 14 pounds (about $22 a night)!

While I was resting in the RV and Ron was at the supermarket, I heard someone approaching. Thinking it was Ron returning with groceries, I opened the door and found a stranger there. He had come to leave a note inviting us to visit him and his wife in their Toyota Dolphin camper, a duplicate of our RV. His RV has a six-cylinder engine, is newer, and has been repainted. He said he had pulled in this afternoon and had seen us. He'd never seen a Toyota Dolphin here in all the time he's been camping in England—and he's been doing it for six months a year over the past four or five years.

He is the fourth person we've met who owns the same RV. He also used to do his camping in boats. And he lives in North Reddington in Florida, not 20 miles from our own place in Florida! All four of the people we've met who own similar rigs have been boaters, and they all live either in Connecticut or Florida. This is getting a bit creepy!

We started this letter days ago. During this time we've been back to the British Museum, visited the Victoria & Albert Museum (art and design) and have gone through the Wallace Collection (art) for the second time.

One day was a housekeeping day: Internet access at the Brixton Library and then through the open-air market. We came home early so that one of us could get off her feet—which had been much better up until the British Museum! The feet were good enough to allow a trip to Greenwich to visit the Royal Maritime Museum and the Royal Observatory. Since Ron is a big fan of John Harrison, the Yorkshire carpenter/clockmaker who invented the chronograph, this is prime Ron-Milavsky-territory.

The chronograph has had a number of practical consequences, ranging from considerably safer travel at sea to timetables that are accurate across time zones. This is the reason we can know what time it is anywhere on earth at any point in time and, in turn, why it is possible to have accurate (on paper at least) railroad and plane schedules.

London is filled with people. In that regard it resembles a Chinese city more than it does most Western capitals. There are crowds of people everywhere. Wherever the buses stop, you'll see large numbers of people waiting. And if you look on the streets, there is a never-ending line of buses—bumper to bumper. The streets are certainly not as clean as those in the less congested areas of England.

We have to agree with some politician who recently called London "the modern Tower of Babel." No matter where you go, you hear all kinds of "foreign" languages, not all of which we are able to recognize. The streets are filled with people from all over the world. R&A

LETTER #23—LONDON AND BEYOND, SEPTEMBER 29, 2003

We did indeed manage to spend two full weeks in London—and we still didn't do everything we wanted to do. We never saw the Globe Theater, for example, and were unable to visit Hampton Court Palace.

We did manage to tour the Houses of Parliament, see a lot of museums, and visit Westminster Abbey, the Royal War Museum, the wonderful Museum of the City of London, and more. Ron walked by a house with a blue plaque that proclaims for all to see that this was the residence of Captain Bligh.

That is one of the wonders of visiting London. You suddenly feel close to so many people of historic or literary significance. R&A

LETTER #24—DOVER, ENGLAND, SEPTEMBER 30, 2003

Are you thankful that the stream of letters will end soon? In a way, I (Adelle) am. We are nearing the end of our sojourn. We have traveled just a little more than 3,000 miles from the end of July till now. You have been with us the whole time, so you know many of the things we have done and seen and learned and also, in a sense, gotten to meet some of the interesting people we have encountered. It's been a wonderful trip, but at least half of this team (the one of the female persuasion) is anxious to get home.

But first, we wanted to visit Kew Gardens (the Royal Botanical Gardens) in London. It had turned out to be too hard to get there by public transit, so we planned to drive. We figured there had to be parking at such a facility and we decided to go there on our way out of London.

The wardens at the Crystal Palace campground gave us a map showing the route to Kew Gardens. You take the ring road. Now, for those of you who are unfamiliar with this term, a "ring road" is a circular highway around a city. All we had to do was stay on the ring road (Route 205) until we got to Kew Gardens.

Apparently, however, by the time it occurred to the authorities that London should have a ring road to alleviate traffic, it was too late. There was nowhere to build such a road. They settled instead for designating certain city streets as part of such a road, stringing them together in such a way that you drive on city streets all around London! It took us an hour and forty minutes to get to Kew Gardens, although it's only a distance of about 10 miles as the crow flies! We went from the southeast side of London to the southwest! Despite the highway designation number, there was not one inch of highway involved!

It was autumn and had been a very dry year, so the gardens were not as beautiful as they might have been. But they were lovely and we saw some spectacular flowers.

After leaving London we went to visit family friends who live near Oxford. Their three daughters were great fun. Young English girls speak with a delightful (to us) British accent, but their giggles and their morally outraged disagreements sound the same as those of American young girls.

The first evening we were in Oxfordshire, our hosts gave a dinner party, inviting friends from the village who also have a camping van and travel all over Europe on their vacations. We all had a great time telling funny stories about traveling.

The next day we planned a visit to a place that has always fascinated us since its existence became known and has been on our "must see" list from day one. If you're not familiar with Bletchley Park near Oxford where the British had an enormous decoding operation during World War II, you should be. It is yet another place where things occurred that changed the world. The Nazis had invented a machine called the Enigma. This encoded all operational orders to their military in an extremely complicated way. The mysteries of the Enigma were solved in this place. We weren't able to see everything, but what we saw was fascinating. There was lots of information and there were even real machines.

Between 9,000 and 10,000 people worked at Bletchley Park during the war, but the secret of the existence of the unit was kept until 1969, I think. No one talked about it for years. The funniest story was that one of the guides was making just this point to a group of tourists recently when one of the older women in the tour group said, "I used to work here." At this point, her husband said, "So did I." Neither one had ever told the other! If that isn't amazing, I don't know what is. Bletchley Park was one of the most interesting places we've been in.

We had one more day before we had to head out, and we decided to visit Stratford-upon-Avon. It's the right thing to do if you are a tourist.

We left our friends on Monday and had a booking on the ferry on Wednesday morning. We had just time enough to visit Canterbury before we got to Dover. Canterbury had that wonderful British institution—a Park & Ride. You park the van in the lot and a bus comes every 10 minutes to take you into the center of town. It's a wonderful idea everywhere, but especially in this part of England because this shire (county) of Kent has the worst roads we experienced in England. They are barely wide enough for our RV and a very small car with a very cautious driver coming the other way. A white line down the middle of the road was a source of great excitement for us. Most of the roads are country lanes (single track), with no shoulders and many curves.

We were disappointed to find that there were no pilgrims in Canterbury. They must be with Robin Hood somewhere! But there is a truly beautiful cathedral, with a shrine that has a long history of pilgrimages made to the scene of Thomas Becket's murder.

After a long drive down a country lane, we got to a farm-cum-campsite where our RV and the sheep were the only inhabitants (other than the farmer and his family). Getting out of there required a long ride down country roads whose narrowness created a lot of tension in our RV, but there was no real problem. The next day we drove on to Dover.

We thought we should find a campground before doing anything else, so we found ourselves on another country lane that no self-respecting town of 100 people would allow in the U.S. We managed pretty well until we came upon a dump truck on the side of the road. The truck driver was busy doing something, and there was a very long wait, since it was quite clear that we could not both fit on the road. When the truck driver finally finished his job, he moved the truck forward enough to let the RV—and the tail of cars stuck behind us—go ahead.

We were quite shaken by the time we got to the campground—especially since we'd have to get back to Dover for the day, return after we'd seen the town, and then go back to the docks in the morning. We were then directed to an easier route (though it was still narrow), and eventually even found a more convenient campground. We may have been nervous about the roads, but the people in Kent seem to be perversely proud of their country lanes.

After finding out details about the next morning's ferry ride, we decided to visit Dover Castle. We could see it up on a hill, but it took a while to find it, since the city streets snaked around and got nowhere and we couldn't find a good sign! Perseverance paid off, however, and we enjoyed the rest of our visit. R&A

LETTER #25—AMSTERDAM, HOLLAND, OCTOBER 6, 2003

We begin this letter back in our old haunt—Gaasparplas Camping in Amsterdam. They greet us here like old friends—which we are.

On Wednesday, October 1, we took the ferry from Dover to Dunkirk. We had hoped to do some grocery shopping in France, but that didn't work out. We simply drove to the campground in Ghent, Belgium.

In the morning, we started off to find the Ganda Gas LPG Bottling Plant. We know that it is at the edge of the city. They had filled our propane tank before we left last year, and that filling had lasted us this whole trip. Sad to say, the navigator on this trip had the courage of her convictions—which were wrong. We had to make a right hand turn off a highway onto what looked to me like a bike path—so I told Ron to pass on by. That mistake cost us. There are a great many places on the ring road that circles Ghent where there is an entrance on one side of the highway but not the other. As a result, we were unable to turn around and we ended up making an enormous circle! Second time around, though, we did make the turn, and in half an hour we were at the plant.

The people at Ganda Gas remembered us, filled our propane tank, gave us a new regulator with a fitting that will go on French and other European tanks, and charged us only 7 euros. This is very little (apparently they remembered us fondly), and we continued on our way.

We were still able to stick with our plan, and on Thursday we found a campground near Tilburg in the Netherlands, so we could say hello and goodbye to our friends from that city.

Next stop was Amsterdam. Holland isn't very large, so after we left Tilburg, we followed the signs for s'Hertogenbosch, Utrecht, and then Amsterdam. We got here Friday afternoon. Ron hurried off to the Albert Cuypstraat open market immediately, while I took a nap. I know how to live!

We are both "museumed out," so we opted to just walk around yesterday to look once again at the canalside with the Dutch buildings leaning against each other for support. We stopped to get *Vlaamse frites* (Belgian fries) at a place that Ron had noticed the day before. They were wonderful. No one in Europe ever calls them anything but Belgian fries—since they never were a French specialty.

Before last year's trip, a Connecticut friend had recommended a number of places we should see. We got to most of them, but never managed to visit the seaside town of Volendam. So we took a bus there today, and loved it. The harbor is lovely, the town not at all tacky although full of souvenir shops and restaurants, and the most interesting boats come in and out.

It was a lovely afternoon. We stopped for coffee and an applecake in a waterside café. Ron was able to buy a huge smoked mackerel for his dinner for only €2 and, from a waterside *vishandler,* a *stuk* of *nieuwe haring* with onions to eat on the spot for €1.25. Is this living, or what?

This letter marks the end of our latest grand trip. Looking forward to home. See you all soon. R&A

APPENDIX C
Useful Things to Know About...

(See Appendix F for the URLs of sites that display standard European road signs.)

AUSTRIA

I. PRIOR TO THE TRIP

Tourist Information Prior to Trip
Austrian National Tourist Office
P.O. Box 1142
New York, NY 10108-1142
212 944-6880

Useful Web Sites
www.tourist-net.co.at
www.info.wien.at

II. NOW THAT YOU'RE IN AUSTRIA

Useful Organizations
Öesterreichischer Camping Club
Schubertring 1-3
1010 Wien (Vienna)
Tel: 01 7136151
E-mail: office@campingclub.at
Internet: www.campingclub.at

Österreichischer Automobil-Motorrad-Und
  Touring Club (ÖAMTC)
Schubertring 1-3,
1010 Wien (Vienna)
Tel: 01 71190
Fax: 01 7131807
E-mail: oeamtc@apanet.at
Internet: www.oeamtc.at

Emergency Telephone Numbers
Police 133
Fire Brigade 122
Ambulance 144

Tourist Information
Usually found in "Stadt Mitte," the center of
  the city.
Offices will use "Tourist" and "Information"
  in their name.
A green "i" will indicate tourist information.

III. HIGHWAY INFORMATION

Austria has a very good road system. It
  includes *autobahns* (federal highways)
  and *"länder"* (provincial roads).
In built-up areas, the speed limit is only 25
  miles per hour.
In less built-up areas, the speed limit is 44
  to 52 miles per hour.
The *autobahn* speed limit is approximately
  80 miles per hour.
No vehicle is allowed on the *autobahn*
  unless it can go 60 kilometers (37 miles)
  per hour.
Vehicles weighing more than 3,500 kg
  (1,590 pounds) have lower speed limits:
  70 kilometers (43 miles) per hour on the
  autobahns and 60 kilometers (37 miles)
  per hour on other roads.

IV. ESSENTIAL EQUIPMENT

All vehicle occupants must wear seat belts.

All imported vehicles must be equipped with a red warning triangle. In case of breakdown, it must be placed on the road 20 to 25 feet behind the vehicle.

All vehicles must have a license plate in the front and the rear of the vehicle. (See page 63 for what to do if your state issues only one plate.)

An international driver's license is required for all.

You must have a *vignette* (tax sticker) in order to use many of the roads and tunnels. These stickers are available at any gas station along the border, from the ÖAMTC (see II, above), or even at the border crossings. You are responsible for purchasing the *vignette;* drive without it and you may have to pay a hefty fine.

Some tunnels and roads have additional tolls.

V. BREAKDOWN INFORMATION

AAA has a reciprocal agreement with Austria's Automobile Club, but there is still a charge.

VI. RULES OF THE ROAD

There is no right turn on red in Austria.

On roads of more than one lane going in one direction, stay to the right except to pass.

Road signs will indicate who has the right of way where roads intersect. In the absence of such signs, traffic from the right has the right of way.

Do not enter an intersection unless you can clear it.

VII. ROAD SIGNS & TRAFFIC LIGHTS

Most road signs conform to regulation European standard signs.

In addition, these signs are used:
    One way street = white arrow, red border on sign saying *einbahn*
    Detour = yellow rectangle with a point, black writing saying *umleitung*
    Parking lights required at night = red rectangular-shaped sign with stripes at the top and bottom
    Dead end = blue square sign with inverted T
    Light about to change = flashing green or red light

Non-standard Road Signs Include:
Änhanger—No trailers allowed
Ausweiche—Detour
Beschrankung für halten oder parken—No stopping or standing
Lawinen gefahr—Watch for falling rocks
Ortsanfang—Congestion ahead. Speed limit reduced.
Ortsende—Congestion ends. Return to speed limit.
Strasse Gesperrt—Road closed

VIII. FUEL

Unleaded gasoline is found in pumps marked *Benzin*. Unleaded fuel is *Bleifrei*.

IX. PROBLEMS, POLICE & FINES

Fines for violations are high, and may be payable to police officers on the spot. Usually only euros are accepted in payment, although travelers checks may be acceptable.

X. CAMPING AND SECURITY

There are over 150 campgrounds in Austria.

Dry camping is not encouraged and may be prohibited by signs.

Roadside camping is prohibited.

The International Camping Card is not required but frequently gives the bearer a discount on various services.

Be sure to ask for a *Gaste Karte,* which may may entitle you to discounts on certain facilities such as cable cars.

XI. TELEPHONE SERVICE

The international direct dialing code for Austria is 43.

Most public telephones require a prepaid card even if you are dialing a toll-free 800 number.

BELGIUM

I. PRIOR TO THE TRIP

Tourist Information Prior to Trip
Belgian Government Tourist Office
780 Third Avenue, Suite 1501
New York, NY 10017
212 758-8130

Useful Web Sites
www.visitflanders.com
www.belgiuminfo.com
www.brusselsdiscovery.com
www.visitbelgium.com

II. NOW THAT YOU'RE IN BELGIUM

There are two languages in Belgium:
French and Flemish (similar to Dutch)

Useful Organizations
Federation Francophone des Clubs de
Camping de Belgique
Rue des Chats 104
B-1082 Bruxelles
Tel: 02 4659880

Touring Club Royal de Belgique (TCB)
Rue de la Loi 44
B-1040 Bruxelles
Tel: 02 2332211
E-mail: webmaster@touring.be
Internet: www.touring.be

Emergency Telephone Numbers
Police 101
Fire 100
Ambulance 100

Tourist Information
Usually found in the center of the city.
In those areas where French is spoken, look
for Office du Tourisme.
In those areas where Flemish is spoken,
look for Touriste Kantorr.
Often signs will include an "i" for
information.

III. HIGHWAY INFORMATION

Motorways in Belgium are free and have a
speed limit of 90 kilometers (56 miles)
per hour.
Speed limit in built-up areas is 50 kilometers (31 miles) per hour.

IV. ESSENTIAL EQUIPMENT

Seat belts must be worn by all occupants of
vehicle.
All vehicles must be equipped with a warning triangle. In case of breakdown, it
must be placed on the road 20 to 25 feet
behind the vehicle.

V. BREAKDOWN INFORMATION

The telephone number for assistance in an
emergency anywhere in the country is
070 344777. There is a charge for this
service.
On motorways, motorists can use the telephones located every 2 kilometers.
In the Flemish-speaking part of the country, ask for Touring Wegenhulp.
In the French speaking part of the country,
ask for Touring Secours.

VI.   RULES OF THE ROAD

Even if you are driving on a main road, traffic approaching you from the right has the right of way.

The only exception is that a driver on the main road has the right of way if there is a diamond-shaped orange sign on the main road.

Where trams are in use for public transit, the trams have the right of way.

VII.   ROAD SIGNS & TRAFFIC LIGHTS

Standard European road signs are used.

Frequently both the Flemish name and the French name of a city will appear on the sign. Examples of cases in which the two names are not similar include: Kortrijk (Courtai), Rijsel (Lille), Antwerpen (Anvers), Ieper (Ypres).

Signs will change abruptly from one language to another as you move into a new province.

VIII.   FUEL

Motorways usually have stations selling fuel open 24 hours a day for those using credit cards.

Most Belgian stations are open from 8 AM to 8 PM. Some are able to dispense fuel later at night to those using credit cards.

Unleaded 95 or 98 octane gasoline is called *Sans plomb* or *Loodvrije*.

IX.   PROBLEMS, POLICE & FINES

Police may impose fines payable in euros on the spot for traffic offenses such as speeding, running a red light, etc.

X.   CAMPING AND SECURITY

There are over 800 campgrounds in Belgium.

Casual camping is prohibited in Flanders.

Holders of an International Camping Card often are given discounts on site charges.

XI.   TELEPHONE SERVICE

The international direct dialing code for Belgium is 32.

Most public telephone booths require a telephone card even for toll-free 800 numbers.

DENMARK

I. PRIOR TO THE TRIP

Tourist Information Prior to Trip
The Scandinavian Tourist Board
P.O. Box 4649
Grand Central Station
New York, NY 10163
212 885-9700

Useful Web Sites
www.visitcopenhagen.dk
www.tivoligardens.com
www.kulturdanmark.dk
www.legoland.dk

II. NOW THAT YOU'RE IN DENMARK

Useful Organizations
Dansk Caravan Club
Sankelmarksvej 42
DK-8600 Silkeborg
Tel: 86 82 62 88
E-mail: landscormande@dek.dk

Forenede Danske Motorejere (FDM)
DK-2800 Lyngby
P.O. Box 500
Tel: 45 27 07 07
E-mail: fdm@fdm.dk
Internet: www.fdm.dk

Emergency Telephone Numbers
Police 112
Fire Brigade 112
Ambulance 112

Tourist Information
Available in most cities.

III. HIGHWAY INFORMATION

Highways are free, but tolls on bridges and tunnels are common.
There are frequent rest areas and service areas on the highways.
Vehicles over 3,500 kilograms (about 1,600 pounds) are restricted to 70 kilometers (45 miles) per hour
Frequent use of "shark's teeth" instead of stop signs.

IV. ESSENTIAL EQUIPMENT

All occupants of vehicle must wear seat belts.
Use of a warning triangle required if vehicle breaks down.

V. BREAKDOWN INFORMATION

Assistance is available from Dansk Autohjaelp, an organization with more than 120 service stations. To reach them, call 70 10 80 90. (This organization is separate from FDM, the Danish equivalent of AAA.)
Charge for vehicles over 5,000 pounds is 470 DKK or about $75.

VI. RULES OF THE ROAD

Traffic on the right has the right of way.
Parking may require a disc or a ticket that proves that you have paid for parking. These are available from banks, post offices, gas stations, and other vendors.

At stop signs, "shark's teeth or other traffic controls, cyclists and buses signaling their intention to turn have the right of way.

VII. ROAD SIGNS & TRAFFIC LIGHTS

Standard European road signs are used. Cars must park on the right side of all but one-way streets.

Non-standard Road Signs Include:
Ensrettet korsel—One-way street
Fare—Danger
Farlight swing—Dangerous bend
Gennemkorsel forbudt—No through road
Omkorsel—Detour
Vejen er spaerret—Road closed

VIII. FUEL

Unleaded gasoline pumps are marked *Blyfri Benzine.*

IX. PROBLEMS, POLICE & FINES

Police are empowered to collect fines on the spot in euros.

X. CAMPING AND SECURITY

There are over 500 organized campsites in Denmark.
The government rates them on a scale of 1 to 5 stars.
An International Camping Card is required in many places.
There is a system of "Quick Stop" facilities if you arrive after 9 PM. and leave before 9 AM. The price is about 2/3 of the regular charge and includes the use of sanitary facilities.
There are very few security problems in Denmark.

XI. TELEPHONE SERVICE

The international direct dialing code for Denmark is 45.

FINLAND

I. PRIOR TO THE TRIP

Tourist Information Prior to the Trip
Finnish Tourist Board
P.O. Box 4649
Grand Central Station
New York, New York 10163-4649
212 885-9700

Useful web sites
www.finland-tourism.com
www.hel.fi

II. NOW THAT YOU'RE IN FINLAND

Useful Organizations
S.F. Caravan R.Y.
Viipurinte 58
Fin-13210 Hameenlinna
Tel: 03 615311
E-mail: sf-caravan@karavaanarit.fi
Internet: www.karavaanarit.fi

Autoliitto-Automobile & Touring Club of
Finland (AL)
Hämeentie 105A
P.O. Box 35
FIN-0551 Helsinki
Tel: 09 77476400
E-mail: autoliitto@autoliitto.fi
Internet: www.autoliitto.fi

Emergency Telephone Numbers
Police   10022
Fire   112
Ambulance 112

III. HIGHWAY INFORMATION

All highways are free.
Headlights must be on at all times.
International Driver's Permit suggested.
Speed limits vary:
    Limited Access Hwy 120 kilometers per
    hour (74 mph)
    Divided Hwy 100 kph (62 mph)
    Main Roads 80 kph (49 mph)
    Built up Areas 40-60 kph (24-37 mph)
Keep a lookout for elk crossing the road.

IV. ESSENTIAL EQUIPMENT

All vehicle occupants must wear seat belts.
Warning triangle required.

V. BREAKDOWN INFORMATION

All accidents must be reported to the police
    and to:
    Finnish Motor Insurance Center
    Bulevardi 28
    FIN-00120 Helsinki
    Tel: 09 680401
Any car experiencing a breakdown or acci-
    dent must use a warning triangle.
For Breakdown Only: Tel: 02008080

VI. RULES OF THE ROAD

Traffic rules conform to European standard.

VII. ROAD SIGNS & TRAFFIC LIGHTS

Speed limit signs are in two languages:
Finnish has the word Perusnopeus and
kilometers per hour limit.
Swedish has the word Grundhastighet
and the kilometers per hour limit.
On some roads, speed limits are indicated
on square or rectangular signs with
white figures on a blue background.
Finland uses standard European road signs.

VIII. FUEL

No leaded fuel is available but 99-octane
gasoline has an additive to compensate
for lack of lead.
No LPG available.
Many stations accept credit cards.
Some stations open 24 hours.

IX. PROBLEMS, POLICE & FINES

Fines start at €130 euros but can go much
higher; they are based on your income.

X. CAMPING AND SECURITY

There are about 350 campgrounds in
Finland, but only 70 are open year-round.
Summer visitors should carry mosquito
repellent.
Finland is one of the safest countries in
Europe.

XI. TELEPHONE SERVICE

Public phones generally require a telephone
card.
The international direct dialing code for
Finland is 358.

FRANCE

I. PRIOR TO THE TRIP

Tourist Information Prior to Trip
French Government Tourist Office
444 Madison Avenue, 16th floor
New York, NY 10022-6903
212 838-7800

Useful Web Sites
www.franceguide.com
www.tourisme.fr
www.paris-touristoffice.com
www.intermusees.com

II. NOW THAT YOU'RE IN FRANCE

Useful Organizations
Camping Club de France
5 bis, Rue Rouvier
F-75014 Paris
Tel: 01 58 14 01 23
E-mail: secretariat@campingclub.asso.fr
Internet: www.campingclub.asso.fr

Automobile Club National (ACN)
8 Place de la Concord
F-75008 Paris
Tel: 01 53 30 89 30
E-mail: info@automobileclub.org
Internet: www.automobileclub.org

Emergency Telephone Numbers
Police 17
Fire Brigade 18
Ambulance 15

Tourist Information
Usually found in "Centre Ville," the center of the city.

Offices may be called Syndicat d'Initiative or Office du Tourisme.
Small cities may offer tourist services only in the Bureau de le Mairie (Office of the Mayor).
An "I" or "i" may be used to indicate a Tourist Office but it may also be used to indicate only the presence of a large-scale city map. In transportation hubs, the sign may refer only to information about travel on the railroad or bus.

III. HIGHWAY INFORMATION

"A" roads or *autoroutes* are 4- to 6-lane highways. They are always *péage*
(toll roads). General charges are the equivalent of 10 to 13 cents per kilometer (0.6 miles). These roads are indicated by wide blue lines on Michelin maps.
"N" roads are national roads, usually one lane in each direction. These roads are free and go through every town.
Indicated in red on Michelin maps.
"D" and "C" roads are departmental (state) and local roads. Also free, they are yellow on Michelin maps.
On normal roads, speed limit is 90 kilometers (56 miles) per hour.
On dual carriageways (two lanes in each direction), the limit is 110 kilometers (68 miles) per hour.
On *péage autoroutes*, the limit is 130 kilometers (81 miles) per hour.
If your vehicle weighs more than 3,500 kilograms (1,590 pounds), however, it is classified differently and the limits are: normal roads, 50 miles per hour; dual carriageways, 50 to 62 miles per hour; *autoroutes,* 68 miles per hour.

Vehicles of more than 7 meters (a little over 23 feet) in length must leave 50 meters (about 165 feet) between themselves and the vehicle in front of them.

On two-lane highways, a motorist who wishes to pass you or believes he has the right of way, will flash his lights.

IV. ESSENTIAL EQUIPMENT

Seat belts must be worn by all occupants of the vehicle.

All imported vehicles must be equipped with a warning triangle. In case of breakdown, it must be placed on the road 20 to 25 feet behind the vehicle.

All vehicles must have a license plate in the front and the rear of the vehicle. (See page 63 for what to do if your state issues only one plate.)

V. BREAKDOWN INFORMATION

The charge for "motorway assistance" is set by the government. It is fixed at the equivalent of $62 for the first 30 minutes. Fees for towing motor homes may be even higher.

AAA has a reciprocal agreement with the Automobile Club National, but there is still a charge.

The phone number to call is 800 08 92 22.

VI. RULES OF THE ROAD

On roads of more than one lane going in one direction, stay to the right except to pass.

Rules governing right of way are different from those in America, and they are also changing. The old rule was that the driver on the right always had right of way and this is still the case in some places.

At roundabouts, drivers must give way to traffic already in the circle except when there is a sign saying *"Vous n'avez pas la priorité"* or *"Cédez le passage."*

VII. ROAD SIGNS & TRAFFIC LIGHTS

Be careful about highway signs pointing 90 degrees to the left. If the sign pointing left is on the far side of the intersection, it probably means that the main road is straight ahead. If it is on your side of the intersection, it probably means that the main highway takes a turn at this point.

The police are trying to slow traffic down. Be particularly careful if you see a sign that says *"Ralentissez"* (slow down) because it is a warning that there are "rumble strips" ahead.

Most signs conform to the international symbols.

Non-standard Road Signs Include:
Chausée Deformée—Uneven Road
Creneau de depassement—Both lanes on two-lane road can be used for passing
Déviation—Detour
Fin d'interdiction de stationner—End of prohibited parking
Gravillons—Loose matter on roadway
Nids de poules—Potholes
Péage—Toll road
Ralentissez—Slow down
Rappel—Continued restrictions
Route barrée—Road closed
Route perturbée—Road surface problems ahead
Sortie d'usine—Factory exit
Tout droit—Straight on
Travaux—Road construction
Virages—Dangerous curves ahead

VIII. FUEL

Unleaded gasoline is found in pumps marked *Benzine* and *Essence sans plomb* (which means "without lead")

Diesel pumps are called *Gas Oil* or *Gazole.*

IX. PROBLEMS, POLICE & FINES

Toll booths on motorways have computers that can tell whether you have been speeding!

Fines for violations are high, and may be payable to police officers on the spot. Usually only euros are accepted in payment, although travelers checks may be acceptable.

X. CAMPING AND SECURITY

There are over 10,000 campgrounds in France.

Dry camping allowed in very remote areas, not in forests or parks.

Roadside camping is prohibited.

Stopping overnight is allowed in some *aires* (rest areas at the side of the road or motorway). Since motorways are *péage* (toll) roads, you should be sure that your ticket is good for 24 hours! A guide to such *aires* can be obtained from Federation Française de Camping et de Caravaning. The *Guide Officiel des Étapes de Camping-Cars* lists sites where there are facilities for campers.

XI. TELEPHONE & INTERNET SERVICE

The international direct dialing code for France is 33.

Most public telephones require a prepaid card even if you are using a toll-free 800 number.

Internet service is widely available in cafés and other facilities marked with the sign "@."

GERMANY

I. PRIOR TO THE TRIP

Tourist Information Prior to Trip
German National Tourist Office
122 East 42nd Street, 52nd Floor
New York, NY 10168-0072
212 661-7200

Useful Web Sites
www.deutschland-tourismus.de
www.bavaria.com
www.berlin-tourism.de

II. NOW THAT YOU'RE IN GERMANY

Useful Organizations
Deutscher Camping Club
Mandlestrasse 28
D-80802 München (Munich)
Tel: (089) 3801420
E-mail: info@camping-club.de
Internet: www.camping-club.de

Allgemeiner Deutscher Automobil-Club
   (ADAC)
AM Westpark 8
D-81373 München (Munich)
Tel: (089) 76760
Internet: www.adac.de

Emergency Telephone Numbers
Police 112
Fire Brigade 112
Ambulance 112

Tourist Information
Usually found in "Stadt Mitte" or
   "Zentrum," the center of the city.
Offices will use "Tourist" and "Information"
   in their name.

III. HIGHWAY INFORMATION

Over 5,000 miles of highways without tolls.
One of the most modern systems in Europe.
Roads in western Germany still better than
   those in the east.
Frequent service stops on highways.

IV. ESSENTIAL EQUIPMENT

All vehicle occupants must wear seat belts.

V. BREAKDOWN INFORMATION

Assistance can be obtained by using call
   boxes on highway.
ADAC can be reached by calling
   01802 22 22 22.

VI. RULES OF THE ROAD

Traffic on the right has right of way.
Traffic in the roundabout has right of way
   over incoming traffic.

VII. ROAD SIGNS & TRAFFIC LIGHTS

Most signs conform to European standard
   road signs.

Non-standard Road Signs Include:
Fahrbahnwechel—Change lanes ahead
Freie Fahrt—All previous restrictions on
   driving removed, including speed limits
Radweg Kreuzt—Bicycle path crossing
Rollsplitt—Loose road surface
Strassenchaden—Road damage ahead

VIII. FUEL

Unleaded gasoline is found in pumps marked *Benzin*. Unleaded fuel is *Bleifrei*.

IX. PROBLEMS, POLICE & FINES

Fines for violations are high, and may be payable to police officers on the spot. Usually only euros are accepted in payment, although travelers checks may be acceptable.

X. CAMPING AND SECURITY

There are more than 3,500 campgrounds in Germany.

Dry camping is not encouraged and may be prohibited by signs.

Roadside camping is allowed if there are no signs against parking.

Camping allowed in parking lots, but outside tables or chairs prohibited.

International Camping Card recommended.

XI. TELEPHONE SERVICE

The international direct dialing code for Germany is 49.

Telephone booths accept both coins and cards.

GREECE

I. PRIOR TO THE TRIP

Tourist Information Prior to the Trip
Greek National Tourism Organization
Olympic Tower
645 Fifth Avenue, 9th Floor
New York, NY 10022
212 421-5777

Useful web sites
www.greektourism.com
www.culture.gr
www.greek-islands.net
www.athensguide.com

II. NOW THAT YOU'RE IN GREECE

Useful Organizations
Campers Association of Northern Greece
16 Tsimiski Street
GR-54624 Thessaloniki
Tel: 031 286697

The Automobile & Touring Club of Greece
   (ELPA)
395 Messogion Street, Agia Paraskevi
GR-15343 Athena
Tel: 01 6068800
E-mail: elpa@techlink.gr

Emergency Telephone Numbers
Police 100
Fire 199
Ambulance 166 (Athens)

III. HIGHWAY INFORMATION

Most roads reportedly in good condition.
Mountain roads in less good condition and
   exceptionally narrow.
Greece has highest rate of road fatalities in
   Europe.
Many places accessible only by ferry.
Some ferries allow you to "camp on board"
   and offer sanitary facilities & electricity.

IV. ESSENTIAL EQUIPMENT

International Driver's Permit required.
Vehicle occupants must wear seat belts.
Warning triangle required.

V. BREAKDOWN INFORMATION

ELPA provides assistance 24 hours a day.
Towing charges €100 minimum.
In some areas, motorists can dial 104.

VI. RULES OF THE ROAD

Rules conform to European standards.

VII. ROAD SIGNS & TRAFFIC LIGHTS

Signs conform to European standards.
Road signs are in Greek and English.
Experienced travelers suggest that you have
   duplicate maps, one in English and one in
   Greek to help you identify place names.

VIII. FUEL

Stations in rural areas open fewer hours than those in urban areas.

Only some stations accept credit cards.

Experienced motorists suggest keeping gasoline tank topped off.

No LPG available.

IX. PROBLEMS, POLICE & FINES

Foreign motorists advised to report all accidents to police.

All motorists must stop to assist injured people in case of accident.

Foreign motorists are advised to notify ELPA (see II, above) in case of accidents.

X. CAMPING AND SECURITY

Greece has 350 sites licensed by its tourist office (NTOG).

Large chains of campgrounds are run by:
Harmonie
Sunshine Camping Club

International camping card recommended.

XI. TELEPHONE SERVICE

Public phones generally require a telephone card, but street kiosks that let you pay after making local calls are also available.

The international direct dialing code for Greece is 30.

IRELAND

I. PRIOR TO THE TRIP

Tourist Information Prior to the Trip
Tourism Ireland
345 Park Avenue
New York, NY 10154
800 223-6470
Internet: www.irelandvacations.com

Useful Web Site
www.camping-ireland.ie

II. NOW THAT YOU'RE IN IRELAND

Irish Tourist Board
Baggot Street Bridge
Dublin 2
Republic of Ireland
Tel: 1850 230 330
Internet: www.ireland.travel.ie

Northern Ireland Tourist Board
59 North Street
Belfast BT1 1NB
County Antrim, Northern Ireland
Tel: 028 9023 1221
Internet: www.discovernorthernireland.com

Emergency Telephone Numbers
Police 999
Ambulance 999
Fire 999

Tourist Information
Available in most cities.

III. HIGHWAY INFORMATION

Roads in both the Republic of Ireland and Northern Ireland tend to be narrow, but at least in areas of the Republic that are heavily traveled by tourists, in good repair.

IV. ESSENTIAL EQUIPMENT

All vehicle occupants must wear seat belts.
Warning triangle required for use in accident or breakdown.
All vehicles must have a "Nationality Plate" on rear bumper.

V. BREAKDOWN INFORMATION

AAA has a reciprocal agreement with AA in both parts of Ireland.
Dublin-based AA rescue service number is 1-800-66-77-88. There may be a charge associated with towing.

VI. RULES OF THE ROAD

You must drive on the left in Ireland. This means that the slower traffic is on the left, and the passing land is on the right.
Entering a roundabout, you drive to the left.

VII. ROAD SIGNS & TRAFFIC LIGHTS

Most road signs conform to international standards.

VIII. FUEL

Unleaded gasoline is found in pumps marked "petrol."
Diesel is called diesel.

IX. PROBLEMS, POLICE & FINES

Fines for violations are high (€80 for speeding as we go to press) and must be payed to the local court in cash or by credit card.

X. CAMPING AND SECURITY

There are few organized campgrounds in Ireland. It is possible however to arrange with farmers to camp in their fields.
Both the caravan clubs in England will give you a listing of Irish campgrounds.
There are no security problems reported.

XI. TELEPHONE SERVICE

The international direct dialing code for Ireland is 353.
Phone booths take either cash or phone cards.

ITALY

I. PRIOR TO THE TRIP

Tourist Information Prior to Trip
The Italian Government Tourist Board
630 Fifth Avenue, Suite 1565
New York, NY 10111
212 245-4822

Useful Web Sites
www.enit.it
www.italiantourism.com
www.museionline.it

II. NOW THAT YOU'RE IN ITALY

Useful Organizations
Federazione Italiana Campeggiatori
Via Vittorio Emanuele 11
1-50041 Calenzano
Tel: 055 882391
E-mail: federcampeggio@tin.it
Internet: www.federcampeggio.it

Automobile Club d'Italia (ACI)
Via Marsala 8
1-00185 Roma
Tel: 06 49981
E-mail: p.diamante@aci.it
Internet: www.aci.it

Emergency Telephone Numbers
Police 112 or 113
Fire Brigade 115
Ambulance 118

Tourist Information
Available in most cities.

III. HIGHWAY INFORMATION

There are about 5,000 miles of highways and many tunnels.
Highways *(autostrade)* are mostly toll roads, and tolls are high.

IV. ESSENTIAL EQUIPMENT

All occupants of vehicles must wear seat belts.
Use of a warning triangle required if vehicle breaks down.
Triangle also necessary if parked on a bend in the road.

V. BREAKDOWN INFORMATION

Assistance is available from ACI (see II, above). Staff answering telephone at 800-116800 or highway phones speak English.
Vehicles over 5,500 pounds charged $150, but charges for smaller vehicles are lower.

VI. RULES OF THE ROAD

Traffic on the right has the right of way.
Motorscooters are notorious for ignoring traffic laws.
Italian drivers in general are very aggressive.

VII. ROAD SIGNS & TRAFFIC LIGHTS

Standard European road signs are used.
White lettering on green indicates an *autostrada*.
White lettering on blue indicates state/local roads.

Non-standard Road Signs Include:
Senso unico—One-way street
Destra—Right
Incrocio—Crossroads
Lavori in corso—Road repairs ahead
Rallentare—Slow down
Senso vietato—No entry
Sinistra—Left
Svolta—Bend in road
Uscita—Exit

VIII. FUEL

Unleaded gasoline pumps are marked *Super Senso Piombo*.
Some pumps are self-service with use of regular currency.
Extended lunch hours are common.

IX. PROBLEMS, POLICE & FINES

Police are empowered to collect fines on the spot, especially from foreign drivers.
Driver's license should have picture on it or else use International Driver's Permit
Italy has a number of security problems that travelers should be aware of in advance of any trip there (see Caravan Club publications and U.S. Dept. of State information).

X. CAMPING AND SECURITY

There are well over 2,000 campsites in Italy.
Government classifies them as 1 to 4 stars.
Electricity likely to be low amperage.
International Camping Card often necessary.

XI. TELEPHONE SERVICE

The international direct dialing code for Italy is 39.

LUXEMBOURG

I. PRIOR TO THE TRIP

Tourist Information Prior to Trip
Luxembourg National Tourist Office
17 Beekman Place
New York, NY 10022
212 935-8888

Useful Web Sites
www.visitluxembourg.com
www.luxembourg-city.lu
www.alltravelluxembourg.com

II. NOW THAT YOU'RE IN LUXEMBOURG

Useful Organizations
Federation Luxembourgeoise de Camping
    et de Caravaning
c/o Corinne de Braeckeleer
18 Rue de la Gare
L-4571 Obercorn
Tel/Fax: 58 35 34

Automobile Club de Grand-Duche de
    Luxembourg (ACL)
54 Route de Longwy
L-8007 Bertrange
Tel: 45 00 45-1
Fax: 58 35 34
E-mail: acl@acl.lu
Internet: www.acl.lu

Emergency Numbers
Police   113
Fire   112
Ambulance   112

III. HIGHWAY INFORMATION

The Grand Duchy measures only 51 miles
    north to south and 32 miles east to west.
There are 115 kilometers of highway in the
    Grand Duchy (about 70 miles).
All highways are free.

IV. ESSENTIAL EQUIPMENT

All vehicle occupants must wear seat belts.

V. BREAKDOWN INFORMATION

Call ACL Service Routier, 45 00 45 1.
    Operators speak English.

VI. RULES OF THE ROAD

Speed limit is 90 kilometers (56 miles) per
    hour on motorways.

VII. ROAD SIGNS & TRAFFIC LIGHTS

All signs conform to European standard.

VIII. FUEL

Signs on pumps will be in French..
Gasoline is *essence.*

IX. PROBLEMS, POLICE & FINES

Police can levy fines in euros and collect
    fines on the spot.

X. CAMPING AND SECURITY

There are 120 campsites in the Grand
   Duchy.
There are no reported security problems.

XI. TELEPHONE SERVICE

The international direct dialing code for
   Luxembourg is 352.
Luxembourg does not use area codes.

THE NETHERLANDS

I. PRIOR TO THE TRIP

Tourist Information Prior to Trip
Netherlands Board of Tourism
355 Lexington Avenue, 19th floor
New York, New York 10017
212 370-7360

Useful Web Sites
www.goholland.com
www.keukenhof.nl (spring tulip gardens)
www.simplyamsterdam.nl
www.amsterdam.nl

II. NOW THAT YOU'RE IN HOLLAND

Useful Organizations
Koninklijke Nederlandse Toeristenbond
   (ANWB)
Wassenaarseweg 220
NL-2596 EC
Den Haag
Tel: 070 3147147
E-mail: info@anwb.nl
Internet: www.anwb.nl

Nederlandse Caravan Club
Nieuwe Stationsstraat 36A
NL-6711 AG
Ede
Tel: 031 318 619 124
E-mail: info@ncc.nl
Internet: www.caravanclub.nl

Emergency Telephone Numbers
Police 112
Fire 112
Ambulance 112

Tourist Information
Tourist offices in all large cities. In
   Amsterdam across from main railroad
   station. In other locations always indicated by three inverted "V"s grouped as a
   pyramid in a circle.

III. HIGHWAY INFORMATION

Roads are good and well-maintained.
Highways are free.
Many highways lead to other countries.

IV. ESSENTIAL EQUIPMENT

Vehicle occupants must wear seat bealts.
Triangle required for use if stopped.
Two license plates required. (See page 63
   for what to do if your state issues only
   one plate.)

V. BREAKDOWN INFORMATION

Call the Wegenwacht (WW) at 0800-0888.
Some roads patrolled by ANWB.
There are emergency telephones every 2
   kilometers on highways.

VI. RULES OF THE ROAD

Use of zebra crossings on wide roads: an
   area for pedestrians to stand while waiting for light to change.
Traffic on right has right of way, especially
   at roundabouts.
At intersections, traffic going straight has
   right of way.
"Shark's teeth" are equivalent to a stop sign.

Speed limits are variable; frequent use of overhead signs.

VII. ROAD SIGNS & TRAFFIC LIGHTS

Road signs are the universal European signs.
Frequent use of road narrowing barriers to slow city traffic.

Non-standard Road Signs Include:
Doorgaand verkeer gestremd—
  No throughway
*Langzaam rijden—*Drive slowly
*Pas op!—*Attention
*Stop-verbod—*No parking
*Uit—*Exit
*Wegomlegging—*Detour
*Werk in uitvoering—*Construction zone
*Woonerven—*Densely populated

VIII. FUEL

Unleaded sold from green pumps marked *Loodvrije Benzine.*

IX. PROBLEMS, POLICE & FINES

All accidents must be reported to police. Police can collect fine for infraction. Ask for a receipt.

X. CAMPING AND SECURITY

The country has about 2,500 campgrounds.
International Camping Card necessary in many places.
Some CL-type sites available on farms. For a list, call:
  VeKaBo
  Havenstraat 14
  9591 AK Onstwedde
  Tel: 0599 333355

XI. TELEPHONE SERVICE

The international direct dialing code for The Netherlands is 31.

NORWAY

I. PRIOR TO THE TRIP

Tourist Information Prior to Trip
The Scandinavian Tourist Board
P.O. Box 4649
Grand Central Station
New York, NY 10163
212 885-9700

Useful Web Sites
www.visitnorway.com
www.fjordnorway.no
www.virtualoslo.com
www.bergen-guide.com

II. NOW THAT YOU'RE IN NORWAY

Useful Organizations
Norsk Caravan Club
P.O. Box 104
N-1920 Sorumsand
Tel: 63 82 99 90
Internet: www.camping.no

Norges Automobil-Forbund (NAF)
Storgaten 2
N-01555 Oslo
Tel: 22 34 14 00
E-mail: telefonservice@naf.no
Internet: www.naf.no

Emergency Telephone Numbers
Police 112
Fire Brigade 110
Ambulance 113

Tourist Information
Available in most cities.

III. HIGHWAY INFORMATION

There are very few four-lane roads in Norway. Most of them are around the biggest cities.

Other roads range from good to very narrow, with lots of hairpin turns; some roads may be difficult to maneuver in a large rig.

There are over 500 tunnels in Norway. All require payment of a toll.

There are long distances between stops in many areas.

IV. ESSENTIAL EQUIPMENT

All occupants of vehicle must wear seat belts.

Use of a warning triangle is required if vehicle breaks down.

Use of headlights in daytime is required.

V. BREAKDOWN INFORMATION

Call NAF Emergency Centre at 81 00 05 05.

VI. RULES OF THE ROAD

Traffic on the right has the right of way except where otherwise indicated by signs.

Towing may result if you park in a no-parking zone.

VII. ROAD SIGNS & TRAFFIC LIGHTS

Signs are the standard European signs.

Non-standard Road Signs Include:
All stans forbudt—No stopping allowed
Arbeide pa vegen—Road repair ahead
Enveiskjoring—One way
Ikke mote—No passing
Kjor sakte—Slow
Los grus—Loose stones
Moteplass—Passing allowed
Rasteplass—Turn-out

VIII. FUEL

Unleaded gasoline pumps are marked
Blyfri.

IX. PROBLEMS, POLICE & FINES

Police are empowered to collect fines on
the spot.

X. CAMPING AND SECURITY

There are more than 1,200 organized campsites in Norway.
The government rates them on a scale of 1
to 5 stars.
An International Camping Card is required
in many places.
Campgrounds often have a kind of electric
hookup that is different from that used
in other countries. You may have to borrow or buy an entirely different plug.
The Caravan Club warns of problems with
reversed polarity and suggests that
campers check the polarity as they
pull in.
There are very few security problems in
Norway.

XI. TELEPHONE SERVICE

The international direct dialing code for
Norway is 45.

PORTUGAL

I. PRIOR TO THE TRIP

Tourist Information Prior to the Trip
Portuguese Trade Commission
590 Fifth Avenue, 3rd Floor
New York, NY 10036-4702
212 354-4610

Useful Web Sites
www.portugal.org
www.portugalvirtual.pt
www.atl-turismolisboa.pt

II. NOW THAT YOU'RE IN PORTUGAL

Useful Organizations
Roteiro Campista
Rua do Giestal 5, 1st Floor
1300-274 Lisboa
Tel: 21 3642370
E-mail: info@roteiro-campista.pt
Internet: www.roteiro-campista.pt

Automovel Club de Portugal (ACP)
Rua Rosa Araujo 24
P-1250 Lisboa
Postal Address: Apartado 2594
P-1114-804 Lisboa
Tel: 21 3180100
E-mail: cm.acp@mail.telepac.pt
Internet: www.acp.pt

Emergency Telephone Numbers
Police	112
Fire	112
Ambulance	112

III. HIGHWAY INFORMATION

There are more than 500 miles of divided
  highway in Portugal. Most are toll roads.
Other roads are reportedly narrow.
Roads in the south are reportedly better
  than those in northern regions.

IV. ESSENTIAL EQUIPMENT

International Driver's Permit required.
Seat belt use is mandatory.
Warning triangles must be used in case of a
  breakdown or accident both in front of
  the vehicle and in back.

V. BREAKDOWN INFORMATION

There are emergency telephones every mile
  on the highway.
To call ACP Breakdown Service:
  In Lisbon (and regions south of Pombal):
    21 9429103
  In Porto (and regions north of Pombal):
    22 8340001

VI. RULES OF THE ROAD

Speed limits vary:
  On auto-estradas (divided highways),
    120 kilometers (74 miles) per hour.
  On regular highways, 100 kmh (62 mph).
  On smaller roads, 90 kmh (55 mph).

VII. ROAD SIGNS & TRAFFIC LIGHTS

Portugal uses standard European signs.

VIII. FUEL

Available in "posto de gasolina" (gas stations).
Not all stations accept credit cards.

IX. PROBLEMS, POLICE & FINES

Portugal has a high rate of accidents.
Police can levy fines and demand payment
in euros on the spot.
Accidents where there is an injury can subject motorist to prison.

X. CAMPING AND SECURITY

There are 170 campgrounds in Portugal.
Most are on the coast.
An International Camping Card is often
required.
Do not plan to camp overnight on the
motorways, even though it is allowed.
Beware of gangs who target campers, espe-
cially motorhomes, using hypnogas and
other methods.
A chain of campgrounds is run by Orbitur.

XI. TELEPHONE SERVICE

The international direct dialing code for
Portugal is 351.
Most public phones can be operated with
either coins or cards.
International calls can be made from spe-
cial booths in post offices.

SPAIN

I. PRIOR TO THE TRIP

Tourist Information Prior to Trip
Spanish National Tourist Office
666 Fifth Avenue, 34th Floor
New York, NY 10103
212 265-8822

Useful Web Sites
www.tourspain.es
www.okspain.org
www.cyberspain.com
www.typicallyspanish.com

II. NOW THAT YOU'RE IN SPAIN

Useful Organizations
Federación Española de Empresarios de
    Campings y Caravaning (FEEC)
San Bernardo 97-99 (Edificio Colomina)
E-28015 Madrid
Tel: 914-48 12 34

Real Automobil Club de España (RACE)
P.O. Box 95
E-Madrid
Tel: 902 40 45 45
E-mail: inforace@race.es
Internet: www.race.es

Emergency Telephone Numbers
Police 112
Fire Brigade 112
Ambulance 112

Tourist Information
Available in most cities.

III. HIGHWAY INFORMATION

Highways with six or more lanes are called
    autopistas. Exits on these highways are
    numbered consecutively.
Two-lane highways are *autovias*. Exits are
    numbered by the distance from Madrid.
The Spanish government has a web site
    with highway information:
    www.autopistas.com

IV. ESSENTIAL EQUIPMENT

All vehicle occupants must wear seat belts.
Use of a warning triangle is required if
    vehicle breaks down.
English Caravan Club recommends bring-
    ing an additional pair of glasses, which is
    required by law of Spanish drivers who
    wear glasses.

V. BREAKDOWN INFORMATION

Motorists may call a Madrid telephone
    number (902-30 05 05) from anywhere
    in the country to get an English speaking
    operator. This is a 24-hour service.
On highways, help available from RACE.
    Look for blue and yellow vehicles
    marked "RACE Asistencia." Charges will
    vary; payment must be in euros.

VI. RULES OF THE ROAD

Traffic on the right has right of way at
    intersections.
Traffic in roundabout has right of way over
    traffic entering.

VII. ROAD SIGNS & TRAFFIC LIGHTS

Spain uses the standard European signs.
Continuous white line means no stopping.
Police enforce all traffic laws very strictly.

Non-standard Road Signs Include:
Carretera de peaje—Toll road
Ceda el paso—Yield
Cuidado—Be careful
Desviación—Detour
Gravilla—Loose material on surface
Obras—Road repairs
Peligro—Danger
Salida—Exit

VIII. FUEL

Unleaded gasoline is *gasolina sin plombo*.

IX. PROBLEMS, POLICE & FINES

Police have authority to impose fines in euros, payable on the spot.
Bail coverage is necessary, since police will detain foreign drivers and possibly impound the vehicle if they don't have it.

Be sure to have the name of an insurance agent in Spain in case of emergency.
You must have a driver's license with your picture on it.
Travel authorities suggest carrying an International Driver's Permit.

X. CAMPING AND SECURITY

Spain has over 1,200 campgrounds, mostly on seacoasts.
International Camping Card is recommended.
Spain has a number of security problems that travelers should be aware of in advance of any trip there (see Caravan Club publications; U.S. Dept. of State warnings).

XI. TELEPHONE SERVICE

The international direct dialing code for Spain is 34.

SWEDEN

I. PRIOR TO THE TRIP

Tourist Information Prior to Trip
The Scandinavian Tourist Board
P.O. Box 4649
Grand Central Station
New York, NY 10163
212 885-9700

Useful Web Sites
www.stockholmtown.com
www.turism.se

II. NOW THAT YOU'RE IN SWEDEN

Useful Organizations
Caravan Club of Sweden
Kyrkvagen 25,
S-70375 Orebro
Tel: 019 234610
E-mail: kansli@caravanclub.se
Internet: www.caravanclub.se

Motormannens Riksforbund
Sveavagen 159
S-10435 Stockholm
Tel: 08 6903800
E-mail: touring@motormannen.se
Internet: www.motormannen.se

Emergency Telephone Numbers
Police 112
Fire Brigade 112
Ambulance 112

III. HIGHWAY INFORMATION

Highways are free, but are all in the southern part of the country.
No service areas on highways.

IV. ESSENTIAL EQUIPMENT

Vehicle occupants must wear seat belts.
Use of a warning triangle is required if vehicle breaks down.

V. BREAKDOWN INFORMATION

Assistanskaren operates a 24-hour breakdown service all over the country. Call 020 912912

VI. RULES OF THE ROAD

Traffic on the right has the right of way.
Vehicles in roundabouts have the right of way.

VII. ROAD SIGNS & TRAFFIC LIGHTS

Sweden uses the standard European signs.

Non-standard Road Signs Include:
Enkelriktat—One way
Farlig kurva—Dangerous curve
Gusad vag—Bad road surface
Ingen infart—No entrance
Parkering forbjuden—No parking
Vanster—Left

VIII. FUEL

Unleaded 98 octane gasoline is not sold at all stations.
Lead substitute 96 octane called "Normal."
Lead substitute 98 octane called "Premium."

IX. PROBLEMS, POLICE & FINES

Police can assign fines but do not collect them.
There are customs units at the borders.

X. CAMPING AND SECURITY

There are more than 800 organized campsites in Sweden.
The government rates them on a scale of 1 to 5 stars.
An International Camping Card is required in many places.
Swedish campgrounds have European-style plugs.
There are very few security problems in Sweden.

XI. TELEPHONE SERVICE

The international direct dialing code for Sweden is 46.

SWITZERLAND

I. PRIOR TO THE TRIP

Tourist Information Prior to the Trip
Switzerland Tourism
Swiss Center
608 Fifth Avenue
New York, NY 10020
877 794-8037

Useful Web Sites
www.myswitzerland.com
www.berneroberland.com
www.lake-geneva-region.ch

II. NOW THAT YOU'RE IN SWITZERLAND

Useful Organizations
Touring Club Suisse (TCS)
Chemin de Blandonnet 4
CH-1214 Vernier/Geneva
Tel: 022 417 2727

Schweizerischer Camping und Caravanning
   Verband
Postfach 42
CH-4027 Basel
Tel: 061 3022626
E-mail: postmaster@tcs.ch
Internet: www.tcs.ch

Emergency Telephone Numbers
Police	117
Fire	118
Ambulance	144

III. HIGHWAY INFORMATION

Switzerland has 1,551 kilometers (930 miles) of multi-lane highways.

There are many tunnels and mountain passes going through the Alps.

As vehicles enter the country, they are required to buy a *vignette*, which allows them to drive on the major highways.

Even those who are not planning to travel on these roads should buy a *vignette*. The mountain passes are frequently closed and travelers are required to use other roads. If you do not have a *vignette*, there is a hefty fine.

Exception: if your vehicle weighs more than 3,500 kilograms (7,700 pounds), you must pay a "heavy good tax" instead. The cost of this tax will depend on the type of vehicle, its weight, and the duration of the planned visit.

Vignettes are sold at a wide range of places, such as gas stations, customs offices, tourist offices, and post offices.

You can buy a *vignette* before your trip from the Swiss Tourist Office.

IV. ESSENTIAL EQUIPMENT

Seat belts are required.
Warning triangles are required.
Vehicles should carry chocks to put behind wheels when parked on a slope.

V. BREAKDOWN INFORMATION

There are emergency telephones on the roads. Dial 140 or ask the operator for Patrouille TCS.

VI. RULES OF THE ROAD

Headlights must be on in all tunnels even if the tunnel is lit.

On mountain roads, slower vehicles are required by law to use frequent roadside turn-outs to allow faster vehicles to pass.

Yellow mail trucks have priority over other traffic.

Vehicles ascending mountain roads have priority.

Traffic in roundabouts has priority.

When parking on a slope, it is compulsory to turn front wheels in toward the curb.

Vehicles must have a chock behind their wheels when parked on a slope.

The law requires that you have either a steering lock or an anti-theft device.

VII. ROAD SIGNS & TRAFFIC LIGHTS

Signs conform to the European standard.

When a main road meets a secondary road, vehicles on the main road have priority.

The road sign colors identify which road is the main road, and which the secondary.

Signs on the main road identify the towns coming up with white lettering on a blue background.

Signs on secondary roads identify town names with black lettering on a white background.

VIII. FUEL

Since Switzerland has four official languages, signs on gas pumps may be in French, German, Italian, or Romansch.

IX. PROBLEMS, POLICE & FINES

Police can impose and collect fines (in Swiss francs) on the spot.

X. CAMPING AND SECURITY

Switzerland has 600 campgrounds, but most have only a few spots for transients. The remaining sites are for long-term camping.

The Swiss Tourist Office offers a map showing about 300 sites.

XI. TELEPHONE SERVICE

The international direct dial code for Switzerland is 41.

Public phones accept either Swiss francs or phone cards.

THE UNITED KINGDOM

I. PRIOR TO THE TRIP

Tourist Information Prior to Trip
British Tourist Authority
551 Fifth Avenue, Suite 701
New York, NY 10176-0799
800 462-2748

Useful Web Sites
www.visitbritain.com/usa

II. NOW THAT YOU'RE IN THE UK

Useful Organizations
Caravan Club
East Grinstead House
East Grinstead
West Sussex RH19 1UA
England
Tel: 01342 326944
Fax: 01342 410258
E-mail: caravanclub.co.uk
Internet: www.caravanclub.co.uk

The Camping and Caravanning Club
Greenfields House, Westwood Way
Coventry CV4 8JH
England
Tel: 024 7669 4995
Internet:
   www.campingandcaravanningclub.co.uk

Emergency Telephone Numbers
Police 999
Fire Brigade 999
Ambulance 999

Tourist Information
All cities have Tourist Information Centers.
   Look for the "i" sign.

III. HIGHWAY INFORMATION

Britain uses miles, not kilometers, for
   measuring distances on the highways.
England has excellent highways.
Major freeways are called motorways and
   are designated on maps as "M" roads.
Motorways are limited access highways and
   have speed limits of 70 mph.
These highways are free although there may
   be special toll bridges, etc.
"A" roads may be multi-lane or single lane
   in each direction. Multi-lane "A" roads
   are very similar to motorways, except
   that they have roundabouts at road
   junctions.
"A" roads have speed limits of 50 or 60
   m.p.h.
The more digits in the route number, the
   narrower the lanes; e.g., a road numbered A32 will be similar to a motorway.
   A road numbered A3202 will be a
   narrow lane.
Rotaries are called roundabouts. Before you
   get to a roundabout, there will be signs
   indicating what roads will be entering at
   the upcoming roundabout. Frequently
   there will also be names of cities and/or
   highway numbers painted on the roadway itself showing you which lane you
   should be in for that destination.

IV. ESSENTIAL EQUIPMENT

All vehicle occupants must wear seat belts.
All vehicles must have a license plate in the
   front and the rear of the vehicle. (See
   page 63 for what to do if your state issues
   only one plate.)

V. BREAKDOWN INFORMATION

AAA has a reciprocal agreement with The Automobile Association, Ltd. The charge for assistance is £60 per incident. Call 0800 028 9018.

VI. RULES OF THE ROAD

You must drive on the left in Britain. This means that slower traffic is on the left and the passing lane is on the right. Entering a roundabout, you drive to the left.

VII. ROAD SIGNS & TRAFFIC LIGHTS

Most road signs conform to regulation European standard signs.

VIII. FUEL

Unleaded gasoline is found in pumps marked "Petrol." Diesel fuel is marked "Diesel."

IX. PROBLEMS, POLICE & FINES

British drivers are polite. In a situation where an RV is having trouble maneuvering on a narrow road, drivers will stop and let the RV pass or even back up to give the larger vehicle room.

X. CAMPING AND SECURITY

There are over 2,800 campgrounds in the United Kingdom
Dry camping is not encouraged and may be prohibited by signs.
Roadside camping is prohibited in most places.
The International Camping Card is not required but frequently gives the bearer a discount on various services.

XI. TELEPHONE SERVICE

The international direct dialing code for Britain is 44.
Most public telephones will take either coins or a phone card.
There are red phone booths everywhere and they will allow you to dial an 800 number without putting in a coin.

APPENDIX D

Ports and Nearby Campgrounds

EMBARKATION PORTS IN THE U.S.

RO-RO (Roll On–Roll-Off) ships leave from a number of ports in the United States:

Newark, New Jersey

New York, New York

Baltimore, Maryland

Newport News, Virginia

Norfolk, Virginia

Portsmouth, Virginia

Charleston, South Carolina

Brunswick, Georgia

Savannah, Georgia

Jacksonville, Florida

Galveston, Texas

Those who wish to ship from further west should ask about service from the Pacific Coast. The cost of shipping will be considerably higher from the western U.S. and take longer. As always, the best source of information will be a freight forwarder.

Campgrounds Near Embarkation Ports in the U.S.

Since you will have to bring your RV to the port you have chosen, you will probably wish to stay overnight before dropping off your vehicle. You may have a telephone-book-size guide to campgrounds in the U.S. If so, consult it to find a convenient stopping place.

If you do not have such a guide but you have access to a computer, you can look on the Internet for campsites. There are many web sites with campground lisitngs. You might try starting with: www.tldirectory.com or www.campusa.com. The campgrounds that follow are among those that we have found. We have listed at least one campground for each Atlantic port in the U.S.

Newark, New Jersey
New York, New York
Our best information is that there is only one facility in the New York metropolitan area. It is Liberty Harbor RV Park in Jersey City, New Jersey. From this campground, both Newark and New York docks can be reached in less than an hour. For information and/or reservations, call: Liberty Harbor RV Park at 800-646-2066 or 201 386-7500.

Baltimore, Maryland
Rambling Pines in Woodbine, Maryland, is about 60 to 90 minutes from the docks in Baltimore. For information and/or reservations, call either 800 550-8733 or 410 795-5161.

Newport News, Virginia
Norfolk, Virginia
Portsmouth, Virginia
The Virginia Beach KOA is convenient to all three Virginia ports. For reservations, call 800 562-4150; for information, call 757 428-1444.

Charleston, South Carolina
There are at least three campgrounds in the Charleston area:
    Charleston KOA, 843 797-1045
    Fain's RV Park, 843 744-1005
    Lake Aire, 843 571-1271

Brunswick, Georgia
Savannah, Georgia
Golden Isles Vacation Park in Brunswick, Georgia, can be reached by calling 912 261-1025.

Jacksonville, Florida
There are two RV campgrounds near Jacksonville:
    Big Tree RV Park, 904 768-7270
    Flamingo Lake RV Resort, 904 766-0672

Galveston, Texas
Galveston Isle RV Park can be reached by calling 409 744-5464.
Gulfview Trailer Park takes transients; for information and reservations, call 409 744-3382.

ATLANTIC DISEMBARKATION PORTS IN EUROPE

Belgium: *Antwerp*
Zeebrugge

England: *Portsmouth*
Southhampton

France: *LeHavre*

Germany: *Bremerhaven*

Holland: *Amsterdam*
Rotterdam

Note: It is possible to ship to other ports by arranging to have the vehicle trans-shipped, but this is expensive. Not all ships call at all ports.

Campgrounds Near Atlantic Disembarkation Ports in Europe

Belgium:
Antwerp: Camping Vogelzang, Volgelzanglaan, 2020 Antwerpen
Camping De Molaen, Antwerpen-Strand, Thonetlaan, St. Annastrand, 2020 Antwerpen (Tel: 03 219-6090)
Zeebrugge: Camping Memling, Veltemweg 109, Sint Kruis, Brugge, (Tel: 050 355845)
Camping St. Michiels, Tillegemstrasse 55, 8200 St. Michiels, Brugge (Tel: 050 380819)

England
Portsmouth: Southsea Caravan Park, Melville Road, Southsea (Tel: 01705 735070)
Southampton: Ashurst Caravan & Camping Park, Lyndhurst Road, Ashurst, Southampton
Dibles Park Co. Ltd., Dibles Road, Warsash, Southampton

France
LeHavre: Camping du Domaine Catinière, Route d'Honfleur, 27210 Fiquefleur-Equainville (Tel: 02 32 57 63 51; www.camping-catiniere.com)
Camping La Briquerie, 14600 Equemauville (Tel: 02 31 89 28 32; www.regionnormande.com/labriquerie)

Germany
Bremerhaven: Camping Bad Bederkesa, Ankeloherstrasse 14, 27624 Bad Bederkesa (Tel: 04745 6487)

Holland
Amsterdam: Gaasper Camping, Loosdrechtdreef 7, 1108 AZ Amsterdam-Zuidoost (Tel: 020 6967326)
Het Amsterdamse Bos, Kleine Noorddijk 1, 1432 CC Aalsmeer (Tel: 020 6416868)

Rotterdam: Stadscamping Rotterdam, Kanaalweg 84, 3041 JE Rotterdam (Tel: 010 4153440)
Camping de Oude Maas, Achterzeedijk 1A, 2991 SB Barendrecht (Tel: 078 6772445)

MEDITERRANEAN DISEMBARKATION PORTS IN EUROPE

Italy: *Savona*   *Spain:* *Barcelona*
                                    Santander
Greece: *Piraeus*   *Vigo*

Campgrounds Near Mediterranean Disembarkation Ports in Europe

Italy
Savona: Camping Charly, Zinola, Via Nizza 96/R, 1740 Savona (Tel: 0198 62265)

               Camping Vittoria, Zinola, Via Nizza 111/113, 1740 Savona (Tel: 019881439)

Greece
Piraeus: Hotel & Camping Agiannis, 60066 Methoni Pierias (Tel: 0353 41386)

Spain
Barcelona: Camping Masnou, C/Camil Fabra 33, 08320 El Masnou, Badalona
                  (Tel: 935 55 15 03)
Santander: Camping Virgen del Mar, Ctra. Santander-Liencres, San Roman de Llanilla, 39000
                  Santander (Cantabria) (Tel: 942 34 24 25; www.ceoecant.es/aehc/virgenmar)

               Camping Cabo Mayor, Avda. Del Faro, 39012 Santander (Cantabria)
                  (Tel: 942 39 15 42)
Vigo: Camping Baiona Playa, Ladeira-Sabaris, 36393 Baiona (Pontevedra)
                  (Tel: 986 35 00 35)

               Camping Mougas, 36309 Mougas (Tel: 986 38 50 11;
                  campingmougas@vigonet.com)

(This is not an exhaustive list. There may be more sites available from tourist information organizations, the Internet, and guidebooks.)

APPENDIX E
Suppliers

AMERICAN FREIGHT FORWARDERS

There are thousands of forwarders listed on the Internet and in local phone books. Only some of them will accept one-time jobs and only some routinely ship cars via RO-RO ships. The following list includes forwarders whom we happened to find who were willing to accept such a job, as well as forwarders who were recommended to us by the shipping companies with RO-RO service. If you wish to find other forwarders, you will have more luck if you look for these criteria: "freight forwarding" and "overseas car shipping."

Note: We have not included their addresses because any of these companies can handle any shipment from any port. It is all done via fax!

AES	908 435-2150
American Cargoes	770 682-2887
ATI USA Inc.	908 351-3661
Auto Express Lines	407 773-223
Container Ocean Line	908 862-2262
E. H. Harms USA Inc.	800 647-3619
Horizon Auto Services	281 488-2604
John S. James	904 356-9646
Manaco International	954 463-6910
J. F. Moran	904 743-9742
Pride International	410 633-0033
Seabridge International	410 633-0550
Sea Riders International	954 764-0616
Sims, Waters & Associates, Inc.	904 356-4455
C. Martin Taylor	904 355-9742
E. A. Torms	410 631-1860
Trans Global	407 877-3223
World Wide Shipping	954 776-5611

EUROPEAN FREIGHT FORWARDER

Seabridge for Motorhomes
Tulpenweg 36
D-40231 Dusseldorf
Germany
www.seabridge@T-online.de

Handles details including marine insurance from Germany, mostly to Baltimore, Maryland.

INSURANCE PROVIDERS

For Your RV

American International Underwriters, North America
Personal Lines Division
505 Carr Road, R23-7A
Wilmington, Delaware 19809
800 343-5761

Michael I. Mandell, Inc.
6800 Jericho Turnpike, Suite 201 West
Syosset, New York 11791-4488
800 245-8726
info@motorcycleexpress.com

Thum Insurance Agency L.L.C.
International Insurance Coordinator
6119 28th Street South East
Grand Rapids, Michigan 49546
800 968-4636
info@thuminsurance.com
(Note: Thum also has contact with a freight forwarder, which allows it to be a a full-service agency; they can arrange for shipping as well as insure your vehicle.)

For Yourself: Medical Evacuation Insurance

Medjet Assistance
4900 69th Street North
Birmingham, AL 35206
800 963-3538
www.medjetassistance.com

SHIPPING COMPANIES WITH RO-RO SERVICE

HUAL (Hoegh Ugland Auto Liners)
Long Island, New York
516 935-1600
Baltimore, Maryland
410 354-8010
www.hual.com

K-Line
800 609-3221
www.kline.com

Wallenius Wilhelmsen Lines (USA) Inc.
Jacksonville, Florida
410 633-0880
Newark, New Jersey
201 307-1300
www.wina.com

BRITISH CAMPING CLUBS WITH CAMPGROUND GUIDES

These clubs offer Campground Guides for both the UK and the Continent.

Camping and Caravanning Club
Greenfields House, Westwood Way
Coventry CV4 8JH
Web address: www.campingandcaravanningclub.co.uk

Caravan Club
East Grimstead House
East Grimstead, West Sussex RH19 1UA
Web address: www.caravanclub.co.uk

BRITISH RV MAGAZINE & CLUB

ARVM (American Recreational Vehicle Magazine)
27 Nether End, Great Dalby
Leicestershire LE14 2EY
Tel: 08700 115111
E-mail: arvm200@aol.com
http://arvm.uk.com

ARVM is a technical magazine. ARVM subscribers get free membership in ARVE, American RV Enthusiasts, an informal organization of British owners (and would-be owners) of American RVs. The magazine and club are good sources of information, and you can get RV parts and accessories for your European travels by linking to ARVM's ABP Accessories affiliate through the ARVM web site. It offers everything from adapters to waste dump hoses.

STORAGE FACILITIES IN EUROPE

The following is not intended to be an inclusive list of European storage facilities. We offer it to get you started should you decide you want to store your rig in Europe for a future tour.

England (near London)

Bosham near Chichester
Sussex
Tel: 0124 357 2605

East Sussex
Tel: 0143 5813482

Holland

Near Amsterdam
Caravan Stalling De Wit
Legmeerdijk 220/222
1187 NK Amstelveen
Tel: 020 645 26 80
e-mail: wit2204@wxs.nl

Stalling De Shelter, BV
Legmeerdijk 226
Amstelveen
Tel: 020-647 62 64

Stalling De Groot
Legmeerdijk 239
1432 KB Aalsmeer
Tel: 020-645 26 41
www.stallingdegroot.nl

Stalling van der Zwaan
Hornweg 315
1432 GL Aalsmeer
Tel: 0297-320077
http://stalling.fol.nl

Near Rotterdam
Fa. Kaijen
Rijksstraatweg 134
2215 EJ Dordrecht
Tel: 078-6182294

ELECTRIC CONVERTERS

Minimax Electronics, Inc., 6 Michigan Avenue, Chicago, Illinois 60603,
1-800-856-8397
www.miniprice.com/SevenStar/PowerConverter/TCSeries

Stark Electronics
www.starkelectronics.com/st500

INTERNATIONAL CAMPING CARD

Family Campers & RVers Inc.
4804 Transit Road, Building 2
Depew, New York 14043
www.fcrv.org

INTERNATIONAL DRIVER'S PERMIT

Automobile Association of America
www.AAA.org

PROPANE BOTTLING PLANT

GandaGas Company
Singel 33, 9000
Ghent, Belgium
Tel: 09 255-5590

TELEPHONE SERVICES

Prepaid telephone card
Net2Phone
www.net2phone.com

English mobile phones
Orange PCS Limited
www.orange.co.uk

APPENDIX F
Useful Internet Sites

WEB LINKS

Guided RV Tours

General Information:
www.rvtoureurope.com

Campground Information

Campsites in France:
www.campingdefrance.com/ENG/default.htm

Campsites in Scandinavia:
www.camping.no/index_eng.html
www.solifer.dk/index3.htm

Campsites in the UK:
www.ukcampsite.co.uk/sites/index.asp

Campsites in Holland:
www.karmabum.com/belgium.htm

Campsites in Italy:
www.camping-italy.net/en/
www.trav.com/countries/campsites/italy.html

Campsites in Spain:
www.eurocamp.co.uk/camping_holidays/campsites_in_spain.htm
www.trav.com/countries/campsites/spain.html

Hotels (in Europe)

www.tobook.com/
www.euro-hotels.com/euro-default.asp
www.hotels-europe.ws/

Conversion Tables

Convert just about anything to anything else. Over 5,000 units and 50,000 conversions:
www.onlineconversion.com/

Currency converter on the Internet:
www.xe.com/ucc/

Current Fuel Prices

www.theaa.com/allaboutcars/index.html (Type "fuel" into the seach box.)
www.see-search.com/business/fuelandpetrolpriceseurope

Driving Directions

www.mapquest.com/directions/europe.adp
(MapQuest offers the same handy driving directions for Europe as it does for the U.S.)

Propane (LPG) Dealers

www.iwemalpg.com/LPGstations.htm
(This site also has pictures of the adapters used in various European countries.)

Road Signs and General Information about Driving

European road signs:
www.travlang.com/signs/index.html

General information about driving in Europe:
www.ideamerge.com/motoeuropa/links.html

RV Parts & Accessories

www.abp-accessoriesco.uk
(To adapt American fittings, etc. to work with European hoses,tanks, etc.)

General Travel Sites

Search site for National Tourist Boards in all countries:
www.culturaltravels.com/Services/Central_Search/Tourist_Boards.asp

The Karmabum Café, Camping and Budget Travel Europe:
www.karmabum.com/index.htm

General Information for RV Travelers

See the country fact sheets in Appendix C for URLs offering travel, motoring, and general camping information on 17 Western European countries.

APPENDIX G
Dealers Who Rent & Sell RVs in Europe

CANADA (RENTS IN EUROPE)

Owasco Camper Rentals, 2000 Champlain Avenue, Whitby, Ontario L1N 6A7, Canada
Tel: 1-866-579-2267; www.owascorv.com

ENGLAND / SCOTLAND

Bilbo's Trading Company, Eastbourne Road, South Godstone, Surrey RH9 8JQ, England
Tel: 44 1342 89 24 99; www.bilbos.com

Bowers Motorcaravans, Greenlawns Kinsbourne Green, Harpenden AL5 3FN, England
Tel: 44 158 271 3094

Cabervans, Caberfeith, Cloch Road, Gourock, Lanarkshire PA18 1BS, Scotland
Tel: 44 01-475 638 775
www.caravanmart.co.uk/cm_content/fs/9925901.5.htm

Motor Home Rentals, Ltd., 37-39 Upper Halliford Road, Shepperton, Middlesex TW17 8RX,
    England
Tel: 44 193 770 076

Roadgetaways
Sunseeker Rentals Ltd., 27 Stable Way, London W10 6QX, England
Tel: 44 181 960 5747

Turners Motorcaravan Hire, 11a Barry Road, East Dulwich, London SE22 0HX, England
Tel: 44 181 693 1132

UK Dealers Who Sell American-Made RVs

Note: If you have an unexpected problem, you may want to make a telephone call to any of these
dealers. They are not only familiar with American rigs but also carry or can get parts for them.

American Motorhome Center, Wall Hill Road, Allesley, Coventry CV5 9EL
Tel: 024-7633-641; www.american-motorhomes.co.uk

Cheshire American Motorhomes
Tel: 01606 884010 (sales) or 0161 427 6868 (rental); www.AmericanMotorhomes.co.uk

Dudleys of Oxfordshire, A 415, Abbingdon Road, Ducklington, Witney Oxon OX29 7XA
Tel: 01993 703774; Email: sales @dudleysrv.com; www.dudleysrv.com

UK Dealers Who Rent American-Made RVs

Midland Motorhomes
Tel: 08701 601 401; Email: Motorhomehire@hotmail.com

Elite Motorhomes
Tel: 01295 711157; www.elite-motorhomes.co.uk

Cheshire American Motorhomes
Tel: 0161 427 6868; www.Hire-Motorhomes.co.uk

THE NETHERLANDS

A-Point B. V. Volkswagen, Kollenbergweb 11, NL-1101 AR Amsterdam Zuidoost
Tel: 31 20 4301600

Braitman & Woudenberg, Droogbak 4A, NL-1013, Amsterdam
Tel: 31 20 6221168; www.bwcampers.com

Campanje Campervans and Campers, P.O. Box 9332, NL-3506 GH Utrecht
Tel: 31 30 2447070; www.campanje.nl

Volkswagen Campercentrum, Basicweg 5 a-c, 3821 Amersfoort
Tel: 31 33 4949 944; www.volkswagencampers.nl

GERMANY

Reise-Profi Service GmbH, Offenbachstrasse 6, D-Westoverledingen,
Tel: 49 4955-920905

Rutenkolk Caravaning GmbH, Friedberger Landstrasse 434, D-60389 Frankfurt am Main
Tel: 49 69 94 74 09-0; www.rutenkolk.de

Barbara Lohmer camper rentals, Boffertsweg 31, 53489 Sinzig
www.intercamper.de

TRV Trading Corp., Am. Hohenstein 3-5, D-65779 Kelkheim
Tel: 49 6195-960507; www.trvtrading.com

GLOSSARY

"@"	on a store sign, indicates that Internet service is available
Aires	rest areas at the side of the road in France
Benzine (or *Benzin*)	gasoline
Bleifrei (*Blyfri*)	unleaded (fuel) in German (Danish and Norwegian)
Boot sale	flea market (UK)
Bunker charge	fuel charge for shipping
Caravan	trailer
Certified Locations	sites equipped to handle five or six campers with a varying mix of facilities; also called CLs
Charcuteries	shops specializing in dressed meats and meat dishes
CLs	abbreviation for Certified Locations, sites equipped to handle five or six campers with a varying mix of facilities
Continental toilets	porcelain fittings on the floor with places to put your feet as you squat; also known as "Turkish" toilets
Essence	gasoline in French
Freight forwarder	a travel agent for freight
Gas-oil	diesel fuel in French
"Green card"	a piece of green paper certifying that you have liability insurance for your RV
Hardstanding sites	storage sites that are not grass
"i"	on a sign, indicates that tourist information is available
Lay-by	an off-road parking area
Le Camping	French word for campground
Loodvrije	unleaded fuel in Dutch and Flemish
"Mv waste"	abbreviation used in British guidebooks for campgrounds with in-ground dumps
Péage roads	toll roads (in France)
Petrol	gasoline (in the UK)
Pitch	an individual campsite in a campground; the equivalent of a "site" in the U.S.
Ring road	road or series of roads that circle around a city

RO-RO	"Roll On–Roll Off," a method of shipping vehicles
Roundabout	rotary
Sans plomb	unleaded fuel in French
"Shark's teeth"	a series of solid white triangles painted on the road; equivalent to a stop sign (See photo, page 101.)
Shoulder season	the travel season that falls between the most ("high season") and least ("low season") popular times to travel
Stalling	storage in Dutch
"Statics"	permanent residents in campgrounds
Third-party insurance	liability insurance
"Turkish" toilets	porcelain fittings on the floor with places to put your feet as you squat; also known as continental toilets
VAT	value added tax
Vignette	tax sticker
Vlaamse frites	French-fried potatoes in Flemish and Dutch
VoIP	Voice over Internet Protocol

BIBLIOGRAPHY

BOOKS

AA Caravan and Camping Europe
AA Lifestyles Guide
Automobile Developments Ltd.
Millstream, Maidenhead Road
Windsor, Berkshire S14 5GD
England

Put out by Britain's Automobile Association, this includes only campsites that happen to be in their database. It also has a lot of guidebook information.

AAA Europe TravelBook
AAA Publishing
1000 AAA Drive
Heathrow, Florida 32746

Designed for AAA members planning a driving trip through Europe, this book has no information about RVs in particular but is an excellent source of information about Europe. Available through local AAA offices.

Camping Europe
Carol Mickelsen
Carousel Press
P.O. Box 6038
Berkeley, CA 94706

This is written for tent campers, but it has good, though limited, campground information.

Europe by Van and Motorhome
Shore & Campbell
Odyssey Press
1842 Santa Margarita Drive
Fallbrook, CA 92028

Written for people who are planning to rent or buy in Europe.

Live Your Road Trip Dream
Phil and Carol White
RLI Press
P.O. Box 1115
Wilsonville, Or 97070

Offers excellent advice on planning and budgeting for a long road trip, as well as tips on disconnecting and re-connecting to your normal life.

Traveler's Guide to European Camping
Explore Europe with RV or Tent
Church & Church
Rolling Homes Press
161 Rainbow Drive #6157
Livingston, Texas 77399-1061

An excellent introduction to the concept of RVing in Europe, it offers good information about many different countries and a listing of campgrounds in a number of tourist cities, with good directions and information.

MONTHLY MAGAZINES

American Recreational Vehicle Magazine
27 Nether End, Great Dalby
Leicestershire LE14 2EY
England

This magazine is devoted to information about American-made RVs. Purchase of a year's subscription automatically enrolls you in ARVE, the American RV Enthusiasts club. (See also British RV Magazine & Club, page 297.)

Motorcaravan Motorhome Monthly (MMM)
P.O. Box 88
Tiverton, EX16 7ZN
England

An over-the-counter magazine. Many ads for dealers in American-made RVs.

Adelle and Ron Milavsky have been traveling together for 50 years. They met as students — she in high school and he in college — and married shortly after his college graduation in 1955. They raised two children and have two grandchildren.

The Milavskys began camping on the water in "a little boat" and gradually traded up to an antique cabin cruiser. Taking virtually all their vacations on the boat for many years, they developed the habit of going their own way—which is the essence of RV travel. Later, they took traditional trips in the U.S., Mexico, Canada, Europe, and the Far East, staying in hotels and renting cars. Buying their own RV a few years ago, freed them to go their own way once again, spending the time to explore in depth, whatever catches their interest along the way.

Adelle holds an Associate Degree from Hartford Junior College in Hartford, Connecticut. She has been a homemaker, jewelry designer, and active volunteer in her community, serving for seven years on the Executive Board of Windham Community Memorial Hospital in Willimantic, Connecticut.

Ron holds a B.A. from Wesleyan University in Middletown, Connecticut, and a Ph. D. from Columbia University in New York City. He was Vice President of News & Social Research for NBC for many years, and Professor of Mass Communications for the University of Connecticut from 1989 to 1996. While still with NBC, he co-wrote, *Television and Aggression: A Panel Study* (New York: Academic Press, 1982), which looks at the relationship between violence and TV content. He is a member and Past President of the American Association for Public Opinion Research.

Adelle and Ron toured the U.S. in their 21.5-foot RV in 2001 before touring continental Europe for 77 days in 2002 and the United Kingdom for 83 days in 2003. They kept their RV in storage in 2004 while they wrote this book, but will be back on the road come summer 2005 for another long sojourn in Europe.